Difficulties and Exultations

Acknowledgements

Thanks are due to the editors of the following publications in which some of these poems have appeared: *Ambit, Billy Liar, Blade, The Echo Room, The North, Oasis, PQR, RealPoetik, The Rialto, Scratch, Slope, Tears in the Fence, The Wide Skirt.*

Previous publications

Half Man Half Hammock Half Marlo Brandon (Syntaxophone 1979)
The Private Life of the Gauze Butterfly (Kawabata 1980)
The Lotte Poems (Torture Books 1981)
Baffled in Nacton (Greylag Press 1983)
The Flat of the Land (Wide Skirt Press 1987)
Something Cold and White (Bad Seed Press 1987)
The Gracing of Days: New & Selected Poems (Slow Dancer 1989)
Denying England (Wide Skirt Press 1989)
From A Recluse To A Roving I Will Go (collaboration with printmaker Dale Devereux Barker) (The Shed 1993)
Easter (Waldean Press 1994)
A Hundred Of Happiness and Other Poems (Smith/Doorstop 1995)
Two Sides of a One-Sided Conversation (interview by Tim Cumming) (Dog, 1996)
Conversations with Myself (Selected Reviews and Notes 1984-1998)(forthcoming from Stride, November 1999)
Poems On Various Subjects (Shoestring Press) 2000

Difficulties and Exultations

Martin Stannard

Smith/Doorstop Books

Published 2001 by
Smith/Doorstop Books
The Poetry Business
The Studio
Byram Arcade
Westgate
Huddersfield HD1 1ND

ISBN 1-902382-29-3

British Library Cataloguing-in-Publication Data. A catalogue record for this book is available from the British Library.

Typeset at The Poetry Business
Printed by Peepal Tree Press, Leeds

Cover picture: 'Jos's Cactus' by Dale Devereux Barker

Smith/Doorstop are represented by Signature Book Representation Ltd, 2 Little Peter Street, Manchester M15 4PS, and distributed by Littlehampton Book Services Ltd.

The Poetry Business gratefully acknowledges the help of Kirklees Metropolitan Council and Yorkshire Arts.

CONTENTS

The Happiness Business

Don't be complacent with relentless heaven, there's
eventually no rest there. It ends with balancing
a pile of crockery on the end of a stick
whilst riding a unicycle with a square wheel,
trying to say important things in your head
only to tumble down the cliff face with the stones.
This happiness business, it's full of holes.

Angels indistinguishable from ghosts sit at table,
picking over their food and grumbling at
the oncoming night. You say such terrible things
to yourself, as if hearing the truth is the same
as understanding it. Perhaps if you said
the same things to someone who wasn't interested
they'd be able to tell you exactly what
it all adds up to. It might not be much.
You are human after all, with all the failings
that entails. One truth is that here there is
a huge sky, full of stars and infinite possibilities,
but it can suddenly collapse around your head
like an old umbrella, shelter turning into storm
and the thunderbolt hits you, how stupid you are.

But you were a guest at the divine table, and
you can still taste the food on your tongue,
some of it is even now stuck between your teeth,
and as you walk home alone in the rain you don't know
whether to be happy for having been there or
distraught for knowing you'll not go there again.
This happiness business is, you know, full of holes.

The Overheard Speech of Portuguese Sailors

The desire to accumulate wealth
led to this. How much we don't know

turning into our eternal problem
The trouble with girls is all language
Our bodies are turning into the sea

but it's our living. We try and change
our dark hair, but it's all lies lies lies

When strangers come upon us in the night
the constant yelping of little dogs
is apt to drive us to distraction

They say we will sail over the edge of
don't care, and spend the rest of our days
Talking about home and thinking about home

The Man Who Went Into The Sky

Sometimes the rope you try and hang
yourself with turns out to be
miles too long. Night is heavier than an anvil.
You are not the brilliant centre of everything.
All the roads you drive down remind you
of what you are losing. Sometimes
the air here is too full of suffocation.

Sometimes you have to bite the bullet
and take off. The air is too thick
to lead a satisfying life. Crazy moves
don't convince a lot of people
you can be trusted, or you're a genius.
Sometimes what you believe in
turns out to be a bag of air with holes in.

Sometimes you have to be kicked out
of your life so the blindfold falls off
your eyes. Faith demands a certain degree
of effort and Easter doesn't always lead
to continued happiness. Sometimes you wake up
when you are asleep and someone is shouting
at your head and they've always been shouting
but you didn't hear them because
you weren't listening.

Sometimes a miracle insists on its place
in this world. A visit to the edge of the cliff
is all it takes. The bears there
reminded you, turning visible
from invisible. It was the move you had to make
though it was a move you didn't want to take
but you took it. Sometimes the sky
is better to look at than the ground.

Sometimes the sky is the only place
left to go. When the unthinkable happens
we are forced to think of who we are.
The clouds are thick but full of the only life
that's worth living. Where the gods are is home,
but when the people here try and reel us in
we won't be there. Sometimes knowing so much
is the same as knowing pure nothing.

Another Day

You wake up next to a man built like a chair and you see
someone acting the dog and sitting on him.

You go to a funeral of a dead person and think
all the time of strawberries, because you can smell them
on the air, and in the hair of the girl next to you.

Among the bedding plants in the garden centre by the bypass,
you agree with a complete and ugly stranger
that our young comedians are very very hilarious indeed,
all they need is a few good jokes.

On the way home, you discover that the distant horses
in a field out Linby way,
when you get close up, are stones.

In a book, where you have got lost
wandering among strange and ancient tribes,
you find people breaking the day up into hours,
and circles into degrees.

You stumble across a feeble old man
down on his luck and his knees
and on the point of losing his grip on the empire.

Swallows land on your roof
and you don't know if you should chase them off
or make a quick sketch of the unusual scene.

You find good and evil coming around the corner
like trolley buses on a Saturday night in 1962
and it's so foggy you can't tell which one is yours.

Tonight, a night you were hoping for miracles but settled for sex,
you notice a dark ring surrounding the moon
and stop a policeman to ask if everything is okay,
check that the end of the world isn't arriving.

You discover that policemen, like everybody else
you have ever met, have their shortcomings.

You think about the transmigration of souls,
but not for long.

It is vital to be happy.

Dancing naked in front of the bathroom mirror
is for sad people, you've heard,
but you do it anyway.

You realise that nothing is perfect
except it exist in the mind and not in the physical world.

Seeing Happy

I don't know why I had become so moany.
There'd been mention of a spirit who lived in the walls,
whose presence was like eggs on the underside
of nettles, a small patch of wildness in
an otherwise hopelessly tended plot of world.
Looking out of my window and seeing happy
I immediately wrote down sad, and as for all the hours –
when you totted them up, they would have come to
one or two decent jobs if those little cards
in the Job Centre are anything to go by.

There's nothing I don't know about futile gestures,
like, I would take the canoe out on to the lake
and challenge the sky to cloud heavily up, come on
down, and slug it out, and not notice the dragonflies
being rather marvellous over there above the reeds
or the chaffinches perched aloft airing their one note,
and forget how we would try and count their colours
until they flew off toward the highway and the smoke.

And there would be little notes pinned up around
the house in my handwriting so nobody'd miss
them, but I couldn't swear to having written them
awake. If you read them aloud near a jug of milk
it would go off at once, and it's beyond me to explain
why the world in its weariness would capture me
like this, engulf me in this petty fog,
when I know we're at the beginning of a new age
and there's nothing to be frightened of or blue about.

A Letter In The Afternoon, Including Some Lines By Plautus

Dear 4 O'Clock,

There is an aeroplane passing high
over your head as I write this,
and it's probably full of people,
but are you? Sometimes when you arrive,
only to be gone after a fleeting moment, I think
you are empty as a love poem, and as helpless.
The wind shaking the trees is a bigger person,
and stronger, and could teach both of us
important lessons about patience, and how long
the best things in life take to build
and destroy. The beautiful houses
that graced the white edge of the silver river,
designed by angels. Long hours of sun,
the kind of days that end only when
imagination is exhausted. Suddenly
I'm hungry, as though what I had is gone,
but it isn't time yet to refresh my life.
'The gods confound the man who first found out
how to distinguish hours! Confound him, too,
who in this place set up a sundial,
to cut and hack my days so wretchedly
into small portions. When I was a boy,
my belly was my sundial; one more sure,
truer, and more exact than any of them.
This dial told me when 'twas proper time
to go to dinner, when I had aught to eat.'
But food isn't what I'm writing to you about:
my life is full of clouds and the clouds
fill the sky so the sun doesn't show it's face
all day. Whoever put a mirror in every room

in this house wants kicking: some faces
you want to see, others you don't.
When you get here, I begin to go around
checking doors, looking under piles of debris
for forms of life, trying to chip new ideas
off lumps of impervious rock. It's as if I know
there's not long left to do anything, but
this morning, when I woke too early,
your twin had been gone barely two minutes,
and the world was an empty field
at the gates of which two sentries stood at ease,
smoking cigarettes and not taking notice
of anything. I could have waltzed
right in and had the time of my life,
and nobody would have seen me being myself.

How To Avoid The Subject

If a full stop is a truck stop
what is a semicolon? Answer:
a lay-by, somewhere it's good
to take a short nap in the shade
of an overhanging pause
in a line of argument, temporary
as it always has to be. In such moments
one can suck in a lungful of air,
then spit it out as a lump of ice,
and think about the future.
            And you shouldn't start a life
sentence with the word 'and'
or the other word 'but' (unless
it's a head-butt) but it's okay
if you do. It doesn't matter what's coming
up next: a turn in the road
might open up into a new paragraph
about just about anything, even love.
            And you should always start
a new paragraph a couple of paces
'in' from the side of the road
so you don't get mown down
by a lawnmower or something, they'll
have your toes, those things,
and laugh about it in the shed later.
            And okay, there was nothing
about 'love' in those seven lines,
but then they don't constitute
a paragraph,
rather they consist of what scientists,
call 'matter', as in, 'it doesn't matter',
after which, usually coming behind
carrying the bags, huffing and puffing
because he smokes too many cigarettes,

is ‘much’, which is
what you might call
a late qualifier.

Losing Count In The 20th Century

Nine hundred and ninety nine,
one thousand,
one thousand and one way to look at what you're doing
with your life is from above, though you need
some kind of lifting gear of the mind to do this,

an elevator of the intellect
that drags you from the lead dungeon
where the snakes are stooping low to get through
        the world,
and the drumming of men,
songs that tear through the night like missiles
starting from the edge of a ring of light
and hitting the towers on the horizon
where the gleaming children are concealed in grass,

but you are still going to need a tool kit
        to travel between cities,
some with extravagant towers
and others where it's hard to get a decent cup
        of tea,
because this is what life is like at lakeside
where the air smells sweet of jasmine
and time flies when time wastes,
though all the hours of lead grey sky
are balanced by the celebrations

a hundred or more coloured flags beating their wings,
countless footprints in the wet concrete of
        the new pavement
as if the future events of all the years to come
were wrapped up in a handkerchief and carelessly dropped,
a wholesale misunderstanding of the electronic age

and a gaggle of bozos stumbling out of a tavern,
every word deprived of meaning,
and we had lost our roots,
they were dry like twigs,
and a thief was trying to chain a shadow to a wall,
as if some kind of endeavour
was better than no endeavour at all.

Economic Life

In the fourth year of the reign of our lord King Ratchis,
most excellent man,
I, Alessandro de Sporticiana,
have set aside for you a small piece of meadowland
having at one end the river
and at the other end the meadow of St. Victor.
And just as the governor of the whole world
has made distribution according to the measure of his will,
so I give and concede some portion of land of my rightful possession,
five ploughlands, with all the advantages duly belonging,
with fields, woods, meadows, pastures, waters, mills, fisheries,
fowling-grounds, hunting-grounds, and whatever is contained in it.
And it is to remain freed everywhere for ever from all burdens,
except military service against pagan enemies,
the construction of bridges,
and the fortification or destruction of fortresses.
And if anyone should desire to know why
I have given and freed this gift so devoutly, let him know
that it is chiefly for the love of Almighty God,
and also my consecration which,
through the grace of God, I have received this day,
and for money,
that is, 30 ducats, a gold ring and numerous gemstones,
as I have this day received from you.

I Slow Down For Horses

Because to redecorate the house every two years
or so is one way the team renovates boredom,
        thinkers have a bookshelf
        devoted to telephone directories,
        bus and train timetables, tide tables and almanacs
        instead of knowing anything or asking questions.
A flow chart traces all cash comings and goings
for the current fiscal year,
        and the different colours mean necessity
        or luxury or unavoidable midnight walks
        to the cashpoint in the shopping centre,
        where the street lights illuminate the fog.
And rows of electrical sockets lining each wall
(against which it is okay to huddle in moments of self-pity)
        are because those little adaptors are time bombs
        waiting to go off and blow everything away
        in an angry wind.
To keep hold of every receipt for everything you buy might,
        slimly and elegantly,
        allow one to change what happens.
And because a casual stroll through the capital is unequal
to keeping one's wits about one,
        against stumbling into a gay bar by accident
        and wilting in a hail of optimistic stares.
The other side of the coin
is to wander lonely through the countryside
        shutting every gate, because
        through an open gate storms every horse in the
world,
        followed by slow sheep and cattle,
        and you will never get them back in.
When you remember to stand in the middle of the field
so as not to be struck by lightning,
        because although it looks safe under a tree

it isn't.
And because you look up
and notice that the tops of the trees
are like the hair on a head
it's difficult to say exactly if the person you are thinking of
is ugly or just not particularly attractive.
Which is the slumbering giant
who lay down one day to doze next to a river
and had a city built on his forehead as he slept.

Painting With Sand

It took us an extraordinary long time, almost all our lives,
to discover we are only small in relation to space, the sky
and the universe, looked at from a human animal point of view.
Viewed, on the other hand, through the bottom of an empty
whiskey bottle, we are not only not that small, we are
actually quite big, although somewhat distorted by optics,
the way science does strange things with light and our eyes.
Under the illumination of which knowledge, it's possible
to stand at the edge of the world, with one's feet kissed
by the wet lips of the ocean, your ears lulled by the water's
endless music, to look down and over the edge into the abyss
where, with brand new spectacles, one is able to discern
in frightening clarity a man, evidently older than he looks,
his true age concealed by modern cosmetics and hair colour,
and he's crawling round on his hands and knees, on a beach
exactly like the beach upon which you are standing, under
a sky identical to the sky beneath which you are in awe
of everything in your life which is awful, and he, knowing
that any line he draws in the sand will have expression, is
drawing the sand around him into patterns and shapes that stun
your tired eyes, accustomed as they have become to watery words
that lap weakly at the verge of meaning before they wither away
to nowhere, noises swallowed by the swampy lands between
where you sometimes stand, sometimes sleep, and the horizon.

Those Brazilian Girls Explained

Today there was sun tanning the tops of the hedgerows,
and I couldn't find anybody who would own to being bored,
or a soft toy embarrassed by its knitted heart,
and tomorrow they reckon we're going to get
          a flock of nuns
singing until early evening. This'll be swish,
and a hundred little girls have promised to dance
if there's sufficient reward. A donkey
in a field is being moved indoors to be safe
and not burned up. All creatures great and small
are at risk and we need to be watchful,
because every life is the property of thieves,
as the early Karl Marx suggested.
And now in these uncertain times of struggle
some families have taken to eating dinner
out on the lawns, but there are flies and wasps,
and surveillance cameras day and night; I think
it's enough to be looking forward to the little girls,
because yesterday I was in a car and knew
what roast pork felt like. We sat outside the jewellers
for a couple of hours but all the time I was thinking
about the thieving magpie, how it flits
from windowsill to windowsill and any idea we had
about industry or labour easily evaporates.
Tonight there are plans for a light bulb moon
over the church and a plumed horse under an urban sky,
and I'm going to dream on top of my sheets
about a quiet house in a serene English landscape
with a couple of dancing crazy Brazilian girls
invented because nothing is hotter than invention.

Disco Brilliant

As if to dance sitting down is a way of life,
and not moving when you look at a rock face
is to imitate that rock face, and your chair
in the morning is in the same place as it was
when you got out of it last night and
climbed inside your coffin, but it is not the same
chair, or it has been reupholstered while you slept,
and you might always be the same person.

As if you were to step out into the snow
dressed all in white to complain that nobody
takes notice of you, to write with the toe of
your shoe a note in the thawing flakes then
complain about the absence of a readership,
and building a bonfire on a hilltop
only to return home at dusk having declined
to light the fire so it will still be there tomorrow,
awaiting the spark, as if nobody, nor the wind,
is going to come in the night and carry it off.

As if to dance on your own is okay but
it's a limiting theory and unsatisfactory process,
and there's saying the red light is beautiful alone
but next to the blue each is more than beautiful,
then there's the green and the fish and the trees
are dancing in the great theatre where you have
opened the curtains and six cloud-white horses
complement the piano and the floor shakes.

Our Favourite Man

is like Daffy Duck stuck permanently
at the end of a paintbrush,
waiting for the world
to be filled with colour. He's a forlorn cat
on a loopy trail into the unknown.
Sprawled in a red and white
bathing suit in the sun,
he is a holidaymaker on holiday,
always smiling. On the promenade
with his family, he is in charge
of his family. On the surface of the lake,
he battles to gain control of an oar.
In the portrait above the mantelpiece
his face is expressive, but of what?
You say he is close to tears,
I think he is thinking about being
somewhere else. His arms are crossed,
and you notice how fat and stumpy
are his fingers. Probably
he doesn't play the piano.
Alongside his brother,
it is impossible to say
with any certainty
which is the younger, which the elder.
As he whispers into his girlfriend's ear,
onlookers look politely and tactfully
in the other direction. In snow,
he gazes thoughtfully at the ground,
and he doesn't look himself.
Playing the role of hard-nosed detective,
his life is a mess. Joining in reluctantly
with the party games,
that's a forced smile cracking

across his ageing face.
Clutching a bottle of wine
with both hands, he is a man
walking a tightrope
stretched over nothing. Arms around
his mother's shoulders,
he is eleven again. Squeezed
between friends, he is an impostor.
Silhouetted
against the imposing New York City skyline,
he is sure of himself,
absolutely real.

Jackson Pollock Didn't Look Like His Paintings

Bright and early one morning,
one of those days you open the curtains
and the room gets darker,
and after a couple hours yawning
I tucked my vest in my pants
and my shirt in my trousers and went
and did something. It was either
sawing logs or reviewing a book of poems
for a little poetry magazine: either way
it was exactly like sawing logs,
and I needed a chainsaw and I didn't have one
so I surrendered and went and had a smoke.
Then I made a cup of tea and we sat and talked
for a while, the fire blazing,
but you wouldn't be interested
because talk about hairdressing isn't exactly deep.
The groceries were delivered,
which is a luxury
when the world is being blanked with snow,
as it is now, but as it wasn't then.
Nor was it then when
someone said that I don't look like
my poems, it was some other time, and I thought
that Jackson Pollock didn't look
much like his paintings, but I didn't say it. I added it
to my tiny collection of contradictions and notes,
along with one of those days
I thought something was wrong
but nothing was wrong, but it might get to be wrong
if I thought about it too long.
This happens when you have too much time
on your hands. If this occurs, one way
to spend the day is with a thousand pages of book,

but make sure you wear your reading glasses
if you have them. And one way
of getting the most from your life
is to escape from your life. Dreams can help with this,
and so can aeroplanes and trains.
Later the same day I took a bus to the shops
where I did a little shopping, and on the way home
stopped off for a drink, whiskey with a
drop of water, and a smoke. An old and scruffy bloke
in a dim corner would occasionally
get up out of his seat and shout,
'Who dare rise up from his bed and strike at The Claw?'
and everybody would ignore him.
It was like he wasn't there, living his life.

Wake Up Calls

1. Rude Awakening

It can't be The Man in the Iron Mask
chipping away at the wall of his cell
with a teaspoon he nicked off his dinner tray.
He is too far away for me to be able
to hear him burrowing and muttering
that though the reasons for his incarceration
are persuasive he is not persuaded.
So it must be The Man on the Corner,
mending his garden wall with a trowel
and a chirpy whistle as the sun still dozes.
It's 7:20 a.m.

2. Half A World Awake

The jungle never sleeps, there is always
someone trying to sell you a stolen jeep
or a tablet you drop in the water supply
to stave off the runny tummy. Now
something slips under the bedclothes
(momentarily you recall that promise)
and slides its sleek furriness, velvet
caress, only on the equator, along your
leg, up calf and thigh. But this intemperate
comatose zone! its dreams of Africa!
Don't bite. Cradle of man.
4:27 a.m.

3. Clean Awake

Subtle as a mallet put to the head
of a dragonfly, waste disposal collection is
'contracted out' to a specialist agency;
what happened to the world's loveable rogues?
Here they come: bastards strewing crap and shouts
up and down the street to the roar
of the hoist. And they only call here
once every two weeks so we have two wheelie-bins
but they only ever empty one of them,
as if it'd hurt them or something to do the job
properly. I'm so sick.
It's 6:57 a.m.

4. The Billy Cotton Band Show Wide Awake

Eddie Calvert would be something else,
and Kathy Kay and Kenny Ball & His Jazzmen,
a way of falling asleep on a Saturday night
when you are too young to be out
and too old to be in. And music is sometimes
from a different planet, and happy.
But is the girl next door doing something
abominable to an elephant,
or practising her trumpet? Your guess –
It's 8.05 a.m.

5. The Great Awakening

In this verse is threatened
vengeance, wonderful works,
destruction, walks in slippery

places. There is no want of power
in God to cast wicked men into hell.
Great heaps of light,
chaff before the whirlwind, what are we?
A spider or some loathsome insect,
more abominable in his eyes, you
did not go to hell the last night,
you suffered to awake again in this world.
5.41 a.m.

6. A Wake

The blankets have shuffled to your side
of the bed, as usual. And they have ridden up
the bed so my feet are out in the icy
night, as usual. There are four cats on the bed,
one of which is sprawled across my head,
as usual. There is a dog at the side of the bed,
with its nose in my face as usual. Tomorrow,
or rather, this morning, you are going to
a funeral, as usual. Somebody you never knew
is dead, as usual, and here I am, thinking about it.
6.22 a.m., as usual.

7. 'Are You Awake?'

No.
11.35 a.m.

'As They Lay Battering Of Her With Their Ordnance'

– Points for Discussion and Writing

Poetry is about truth, but this poem
is obviously full of lies. How might it be
compared to everyday discourse? Do you think
the writer of the poem would speak in this way?
The poet writes somewhat out of the daily occasion,
but was he, or is he, completely bound to the present tense?
Discuss the poem's feminism; what effect does the presence
of the male baby have on the statement that
she is 'born among strangers in peculiar hats'?
Can this poem be attacked on feminist grounds?
The poem displays a spirited use of capitalisation,
exclamation, and apostrophe. YES IT DOES! What do you think
this means? Do you know of any other poems
so unashamedly excited by themselves? Why is
performance poetry an appropriate 'literary reference' here?
Discuss irony as a poetic mode. Does this poem ever
break from the ironic mode into meditation
or lyric? Is it daring not to? What is to be made of the line
'he plunged from the bridge into the salvation arms of art'?
The poet is obviously capable of sustaining
a serious poetic mood. Why would he refuse this
mood in this poem? What if the title had been 'Water Buffalo'?
Would it have been more beautiful?
Does this poem have a beginning, middle, and end?
Is there a moral urgency to the poem, as is often seen in satire,
or is the risk of the poem like unto the words of a man
who was going to say something important
but fell off a cliff just as he opened his mouth
for the important utterance?
How might this poem be compared to
William Shakespeare's 'Sonnet XVIII'? (Are such comparisons

odious, or merely frivolous?)
What are the formal constraints under which the poem operates?
Is this a language poem?
Does the import of the poem's last line
render it appropriately placed at the poem's end to provide closure?
Why is the name 'Bob' in quotes?
The title of this poem has a complicated history.
It is based on Loussain's painting 'They Durst Not Board Her'
in which the principal and greatest of four Spanish galliases
is assaulted by divers English pinnaces, hoys, and drumblers.
At the time of the writing of the poem,
the poet was living alone, estranged from his wife and,
in his own words, 'unable to find someone to be my bed-mate.'
The overheard speech is that of Portuguese sailors.
Ask students to discuss the poem
before you reveal this information.

Some Short Poems

THE POEM OF CONVENTION AND REVOLT

This work has no appeal to people in general
and never will have such appeal. So why carry on?
Perhaps because the fighting twins, Convention
and Revolt, are wrecking the kitchen and here,
in this quiet room, one is able to bang their heads
together and make for an entertaining show.

THE POEM OF THE PASSENGER'S EYE

Look at the architecture on that!
The young woman is walking
past the ancient building.

THE POEM OF HEY LOOK! IT'S AN OWL

Hey look! It's an owl. It wasn't there before.
Hey look! It's a rainbow. I really love rainbows.
Hey look! It's two rivers running into one
another, or perhaps one river is running
into another, bigger river.

THE POEM OF THE POSTER

Stick something on a wall to say how I feel
They rip it down
Okay
Rip it down
It remains said

THE POEM OF THE IDEA

There is nothing more dangerous than an idea
in the wrong hands. These are the wrong hands,
and they are on the wrong arms. I have been
accused of being all fingers and thumbs,
but they are wrong, those accusers. They're wrong.

THE POEM OF THE SIMILES

Comparisons are odious.
You are like a tree. A very beautiful

THE POEM OF THE HOME

Kind words purify the house,
stale cooking odours disappear
if you leave the windows open.

But I don't have salt for beans,
and burglars climb in.

THE POEM OF THE BOOK

Life is a book
only a dullard would pick up off the shelf,
and the only use a word has
is to hit someone with. That's what your mates think,
but they're your mates, not mine.

THE POEM OF THE WORLD

All night I thought I could hear the Moon
grumbling about the state
of the world. Then it was chased away, still
grumbling, by the garbage lorry.

THE POEM OF WINTER BIRDS

During the gale the birds wished for bigger wings.
It was Winter.
Seagulls and albatrosses were vanishing.

THE POEM OF THE NIGHT

I couldn't read by moonlight and I didn't want to sit up and talk.

THE POEM OF THE DANCE

I was surrounded by the stifling air
but have become so used to being an Englishman
I'm really bloody good at not dancing
and can't shake this lack of interest.

THE POEM OF THE SHOPPING SPREE

Spend money you don't have. Paste a look
on your face of unalloyed pleasure. This is a lesson
in how to enjoy life before it disappears.

THE POEM OF THE LATE SUPPER

Sitting alone in front of a quiet fire,
watching the flames changing colour. Eating
a supper, on your own, thinking about things.

THE POEM OF THE FAMILY

There is another head inside
my head. To disown a relative
is to step towards a particular freedom.
In crowds you can disappear behind a stranger,
but indoors at home it's you.

THE POEM OF THE BOOK

Go in the Library.
Select a book from the stacks
and steal a life.

THE POEM OF THE OPEN ROAD

There is a spilled load of sugar beet
blocking the open road. Find an alternative route.
The highway leads to the ocean, and
the ocean leads to other oceans, other lands.
The world is full of strangers waiting for you.

THE POEM OF THE CLOCK

He awoke in the middle of the afternoon
and The Clock by the side of the bed was frowning at him.
'What time do you call this?' The Clock asked,
imitating a parent. It was the first and only occasion
he ever heard a clock ask what the time was.

THE POEM OF THREE LINES

In this short poem
nothing very much happens
even at the end.

THE POEM OF THE LIST OF THINGS TO DO

It may be possible to make
all the things you have to do
interesting for another person
to know about, but
whether or not it is worthwhile
is another thing altogether.

THE POEM OF FAME

A way of speaking, a way of keeping silent,
a way of knowing what is good for you and
a way of being a star, rising in the firmament
but acknowledged by only a few of your peers.

THE POEM OF THE NEW YEAR

Accentuate the positive,
something something the negative.
If I don't get off my butt
and sort it out
life is going to fall apart.

THE POEM OF THE FILM

In films, people always know what they are going to say,
and how they are going to behave. It's as if
they've rehearsed their lives and they know what's coming.

THE POEM OF THE MORNING

In this poem, the morning stands for something else.
Let's say it stands for the beginning of a new life.

THE POEM OF THE NAKED MAN

When it rains, the naked man wishes he were not naked.
But then a naked woman appears, also in the rain. Things
aren't so bad

THE POEM OF THE PASSER-BY

How much longer can I live
like a tourist in a garrison town?

THE POEM OF LIFE AND DEATH

We might die today,
or die tomorrow.
We died yesterday,
and forgot to be happy.

THE POEM OF THE PENCILS

We are writing! We are drawing! We are making blank pages more interesting. But when we break, that's sad.
We are useless broken, and can only wait to be sharp again.
Sometimes we are never sharp again, and disappear from the world.

THE POEM OF NOTES

Do go to the Art Gallery.
Do go to the Museum.
Do go to the Library.

Do not go on your own.

THE POEM OF GIRLS OF FLORIDA

Florida looks good in a rear view sort of way.
Coleridge would have loved it down here.
Do not write below this line.

THE POEM OF THE CONTINUING SOAP OPERA

Poetry matters.
Poetry doesn't matter.
Silence matters.
The blank sheet of paper. You can draw on it. Say something.

THE POEM OF THE COUNTRYSIDE

Down in the village they throw mud:
it's not personal, they do it all the time.

THE POEM OF THE PAINTING

She is dressed in a crimson-rose-coloured satin skirt and a white satin bodice and polonaise. Her hat is silver-grey. Her hair is powdered. The upper part of the sky is a dark blue-grey. Behind the heavy trees is a flash of golden light.

THE POEM OF WAGNER

Who rode the seas
of nineteenth century music
with a stormy bluster
worthy of any flying Dutchman.

THE POEM OF WHAT WE WANT

To look forward as well as to look back.
To look forward having learned from looking back.
To look forward and not have to look back.

THE POEM OF HEY LOOK AGAIN!

Hey look! Deer in the middle of the road.
Hey look! The mountains. The smoke from cities.
Hey! A starling, a young star …[1]
Hey look! Look! Look! Hey look! What can you see?

THE POEM OF AN EXCEPTIONAL TALENT

By the age of forty-two it was obvious
he was never going to be a child prodigy.
His parents told him as much,
but he stuffed his ears with cotton wool.

THE POEM OF THE FENCE

Explain how I walk between here and there,
but am always unable to reach you.

THE POEM OF MAGPIES

The magpies are always on this corner, you see them flying
sometimes carrying jewellery in their beaks.

THE POEM OF MENDING FENCES

There is the open window, the view across fields,
the tractor in the field and the farmer on it.
This afternoon he thinks he will mend a fence,
but he won't. He won't even make a start.

THE POEM OF THE HILL COUNTRY

The mountains, with their snowy caps,
remind me of home. But they are bigger
than ours, which are only hills. We do not
think there is anything to be ashamed
of in this, but sometimes we wish
we had a bike that could freewheel uphill.

THE POEM OF 'ON WATER'

On the river bank
there are two kinds of tree.
Those that are the right way up
and those that are upside down.

In my dreams I climb both.

THE POEM OF THE ARTIST AS A YOUNG DUDE

I decided to be a great artist
when my Dad told me he could
get hold of paint at a discount.

THE POEM OF THE SMALL GAP

in the text between page 47 and page 59.
Perhaps leaving out the words is an arty ploy

or maybe it's just nothing happens
in those pages. These days
a story doesn't have to be interesting.

THE POEM OF WASHING

So we expected to be tied to the earth
until we died. There were bends in the passage
of time, and I broke my head going
round one of them. Light bulbs explode
every time I try and shampoo dirt away.

THE POEM OF THE PLAGIARIST

who, said Samuel Taylor Coleridge, rejoices to find his opinions
plumed and winged with the authority of venerable forefathers.

from Chapter 9 of The Autobiography

This was the ~~most miserable~~ happiest period of our life together. The ~~animals~~ children were at their most ~~troublesome~~ playful and a constant source of ~~anguish~~ joy. That July ~~I tried to lose all of them~~ we holidayed in the ~~Welsh mountains~~ sunshine of Florida and had never felt so ~~far from home~~ much at home with one another. It was ~~in this unhappy frame of mind~~ on this trip I began the ~~heap of shit~~ story that became ~~*A List of Fools*~~ *How To Cook A Book,* the novel that ~~precipitated my descent into the underworld of literature~~ some critics regard as my crowning achievement and which was ~~remaindered after only a few weeks in the bookstores~~ ~~serialised on French TV~~ sold to TV companies around the world. I was ~~drinking a lot~~ on a bit of a health and fitness trip at this time, and would ~~stay up half the night hurling abuse at the moon and stars and gorge myself on chocolate cake and burgers~~ run over ten miles a day and eat only organically grown salads – I felt like ~~I didn't have a friend in the world~~ a million dollars, the world was ~~sucking my blood~~ my oyster, my family were ~~the dreck and dross of my life~~ the pearls in the shell, and it was as if the only way to go was ~~down~~ up. ~~I didn't know which way to turn.~~ Little did I know what awaited me as I unstrapped myself from that parachute on the Isle of Wight.

Phenomenology

The sky is always a vaulted ceiling above a circus
of chaos. Leaves stay on
the tree water flows upwards
to the mountain homes paradise
prevails in awkward circumstances.
Rainbows come and go so quiet birds
are clever a hundred yards above us.
Fields are always open cities
sleep giants slumber. The heat from factories warms
eventually and so easily the front rooms of old people.
Beasts make sense in the wild vegetables
reach the market while we lie
abed bread rises. Milk seems so peaceful.
There is always dinner
on the table when we visit our parents. Who controls
what we like and why we like?
How do they hold on to power in a world that is full of surprises?
Fountains of harmony dance next door
to pits where dogs scrap people
appear in happy shows.
Buildings mimic dreams of the houses
of gods nightmares in the night of the dead
architects. Bricks absorb weather
and what happens. And what happens?
The wall stays upright
even when that bloke has smashed his head
into it with real meaning what goes on
in operating theatres is beyond belief.
Who understands the human anatomy?
A blissful heart is ignited by the sun
tired limbs catch fire. Warring factions remain
at distances so great men and women grow old and die
waiting for peace. Memories falter.

Some people forget their own name some people give
everything they own to someone else.
You can shed light on darkness with one finger.
Mountains grow from molehills the tiny honey bee is
gentle as a girl is
gentle.

Endless

as this is. The applause when you have done something
well and made a hall of people happy
and delighted rings in your ears for years, and is still ringing
long after you died and went to hell. But there's always
someone trying to tell you that life is existence – '... *down the town*
a little snow is hanging round and that's exactly how it feels
at the edge of the air's blade until ... 'They also say when you hear
the first tinkling piano of the year, spring can't be far behind, and
these are very proverbial folk I've been listening to talking,
and though they can crack on for what feels like an eternity
their sentences seem always to be travelling,
never setting out from a capital letter
or arriving anywhere in the vicinity of a full stop. Endless
as this is. Anyway, I was pretty surprised
when you died famously because I didn't know
you were alive; in fact, I didn't know you.
We were complete strangers, the familiar is
becoming foreign, and now it will always be like that.

Play

The phone rings
and it's that dumb man again
wasting his time.

                    Life is
crowding in: run away,
they're trying

to make you get a career. Don't
fall over the ugly buildings,
or the people coming out of them.

            Seeing round corners
is astonishingly useful,
to mention shop doorways
where boys and girls mess about
with chemicals I don't understand
is altogether coy.

            The phone rings
but the answering machine clicks in
and the world is hurtling
toward the sun

and I should buy some
dark glasses before summer,
I don't know how I got through
last year.

            Still no hint
of anyone saying anything of
any importance. Sometimes we are

childlike. Or the distance
between us increases.

My head hurts.
It nearly always hurts,

but I read somewhere
how it's through such pain
one comes to
the gates of understanding.

That's what I've read.

5 Famous Women

Elsie Cole

Floated balloons over Torbay
Saying one day she would fly
Balloons all over Britain
Filling the skies with her ideas.
She hasn't done it yet
But she's not dead yet.

Freda Pickering (Europe) plc

Freda Pickering opened The Finger Shop
And waited patiently for her first customer.
3 weeks later she was a millionairette
Having come across sunken treasure
While drowning off the Skegness coast.
Luckily she was saved and her shop too
Though it never opened again except for
Spring cleaning and the Fire Brigade.

George Docherty

Saying out loud at poetry soirées that poetry today is
Awfully depressing and the domain of nitwits is going to
Make you a load of friends, one of whom will be George
Docherty, the woman who invented P:I:C:T:U:R:E poetry,
A poetry that begins with the premise that anything
You can put into words is bound to be untrue, and ends
With the assertion that anyone can enjoy a picture of
A little pony in a field, though to be perfectly honest
The P:I:C:T:U:R:E poetry manifesto doesn't say it
Exactly in those words, but all I can remember is a tree.

Beryl Wells (Mrs.)

'I will skip and I will jump and the Moon will move
when I blow on it.'

Sandra Shakespeare

No point in expressions of anger,
I have invented a machine to rid the world
Of everything that annoys me. It will
Be lonely without you but never mind.

Wishing Wanting Waiting Watching

I slouch in my dark grey chair
and look out the window
only for the darkness to throw me
back towards myself and I reflect
upon the uncovering of arcane facts:
sense of amazement that nobody
knows this stuff: say Hello to the world,
but the world is gone away. I look
at the sky and realise the shining planets
don't proffer the chance of another life.
I pay a visit to the fridge to look
for a chocolate mousse, and when
I take one there's only one left: there
it is on the shelf, standing solitary
in the chilly wilderness. I get out
of the bath and leave wet footprints
all the way down the hall
and into the library where I take down
a well-thumbed copy of Villon's poems
and read a couple of lines
in the original French but don't understand
them. I'm frustrated by history
and tumble head over heels
down the gap between fact
and invention. I am all over
the place, like the knives and forks
in a kitchen recently trashed by someone
fed up looking at the wall. I drag myself
out of bed as if I were clambering off
a crumbling raft on to a sinking ship. I sit
down at the table and study the daily newspapers
and fall asleep within a cloud of boredom.
I walk briskly into the garden

and hold a press conference, tell
the dog and cats, the rabbits and guinea pig,
when things are bad, don't hold your breath
waiting for them to improve.
The beasts nod sagely.
I telephone for a Chinese, order
a 3, a 54, and a 73 and tell them
I'll be there in ten minutes. The car
doesn't start, and it begins
to rain. I telephone the breakdown people
as if I need proof once again
that an hour is an intolerable long time.

From Cuthbert To Cuthwin On The Death Of Bede

He was troubled by weakness
although he remained cheerful and happy
except when slumber overcame him.
Thank God[1] with hands outstretched:
none is wiser than the man who considers
what good or evil he has done.
O King of Glory,
do not leave us orphaned.
And when he reached the words
'Do not leave us orphaned'
he broke into tears and wept much.
In such grace he remained full of joy,
and I do not fear to die.
Thank God with hands outstretched.

He was working to complete two books[2]
worthy of mention,
but what are these among so many?
His breathing became increasingly
laboured, and his feet began to swell.
When dawn broke on Wednesday
he told us, Take your pen and sharpen it
and write quickly. Thank God
with hands outstretched.
Now raise my head in your hands
for it would give me great joy.
In great distress I did as he bid me.
And thus, on the floor of his cell,
he breathed his last.

Thank God with hands outstretched.
His soul was borne by angels
to the longed-for joys of Heaven,

and all who saw and heard
of the death of our father Bede
declared they had never known anyone
end his days in such deep devotion
and peace. Unceasing
thanks to God with hands outstretched.
And although my lack of eloquence
renders this present account brief,
in due course I hope with God's help
to describe all I have seen and heard
more fully.[3]

[1] It is a fearful thing to fall into the hands
of the living God. (Hebrews 10:31)

[2] I do not wish my sons to read anything
untrue, or to labour unprofitably after
my death. (Bishop Isidore of Seville)

[3] My God, I cannot hope to describe all
I have seen and heard and waded through.

I Have Not Given Up Hope But, Let's Face It, The Case Is Hopeless

I have wandered outside, but now I come back in
and have another look around, and I hear
you again, a voice like hope in the eye of the sky,
and so much to look forward to, though I think
I think you are thinking small. I always wondered
what it would be like, to be a blank page someone
else jotted a few notes on and then left you to it.
But of course, that's what I am. But I can't care.
The sun dips down into the night's territory,
and I reckon we have been punished enough.
It's not you I'm thinking of tonight.

A Name Enshrined In Song

Sudden caprice, turn
of the mind, it's wonderful
my eyes are opened and can be winking.
'Entreat me not to leave thee, or to return from following
after thee.' Fortune good or bad follows, I trace
a garage, discover a hotel, and in a twinkling early morning
light is fathomed and unfathomed.
A slight gradient, but I have the energy.

The winds and waves, decisions
waited an entire day. You know how much a day entails:
windings, contortions, slumberings and regrets,
gleaning in the fields, determinations. I go a journey
on a bus through light fog, there is nobody attractive,
cannot read. To see the sky one must have a sky.

Shall I reveal to you
my secret life, viz. I keep finding dead rats on
my floors. And writing Enchantment of Moments,
Cacophonies of Campions, tosh, Poem for Wednesday,
Payment is Due Now, sullenly falter. It is to have experienced
this. And this perchance shall never see you, nor be to you given.
'And it came to pass at midnight, that the man was afraid,
and turned himself: and, behold, a woman lay at his feet.'

Silly, In A Manner Of Speaking

New, the new blonde smile.
I don't think you are beautiful
Music unheard before this.

Discard, this thinking
And the order of books.
Reading, righting, to listen.

Painting brightly
Being here. Coffee, all the
Red lanterns hanging.

I don't think you are beautiful,
A way to fill a day. Turned busy.
See, in the garden sun, pheasant.

The drawing of jade curtains.
Who strolls knowing,
Here and there, beguiling?

I don't think you are
Beautiful, stone.
Elate, our different ways of speaking.

Look, Grand Passion

Look, someone is yelling for someone with a smile
on their face. The someone comes and both are
happy. Soon they intend falling into a restaurant for
espresso and donuts but before that it is important
to go to the bank and look at their money.

Now it is time to fall into the restaurant.
They can't afford the donuts so they have only
the espresso, read the papers, and what the weather is
like on Wall Street. Wall Street is a real street,
she says. I know, he says, I crossed it once.

Look, there's a dark cloud out the window and people
somewhere are going to get that weather, he thinks
but doesn't say. Talk about the weather, she'll consider me
dull. You know, he says, if a man is not calm
he can't make the people around him calm.

You could change the word calm for happy
she says. Look at this I don't understand in the paper:
'The dwarf insists on a quiet place to be
peaceful and alone for the shortness of his life.
"I want to be my friend, look after myself," he says.'

Feeling Unwell, But Heading Off Depression

Laura Fox says to her Larry Fox Hey you Larry
Let's get jobs let's get brains let's get organised
Save our money and book a trip to the planet Venup
Like my cousin from Ireland Patrick O'Mara
Who didn't go to Venup but he went to the Poon
And never came back because he is so virulently happy there
O Larry let's do it let's do it said Laura Fox with her mouth

Which is a cavern where fairies play and delight
Thinks Larry Fox with his insidious usual grasp on reality
As he goes to the refrigerator and helps himself to a can
Of Co-Op Pilsner lager a cheap beer but the best he can afford
And it doesn't taste so bad if you close your eyes
Oh if only common sense would come out of it for once
Her mouth he means as he watches the flies at the waste bin

And on the planet Venup continued Laura it's greatness
I heard the supermarkets never close music has no gravity
You can get your head done without making an appointment
At even the best saloons and everything is red even
Blue birds which I think they ship from here in cages
It's so wonderful to be in love but we must think of our future
One day we will have a baby and what will it think of us

Brahms' 'Motets' thought Larry now there is loveliness
Look at the rain look at the mud on my boots under my nails
Though I do believe there is another world I'm not sure
It would be at all different from this one or if I want to
Go to it at least I know my way around here or at least from here
To the refrigerator and back again and who am I talking to?
And Laura's lips are moving so who is she talking to?

Over The Canal, The Divine

Dear —,

By the time you read this you will have returned to the beginning of your life as if you had a horse and did not simply imagine the horse. You will have found that the answers you needed were like those in a quiz you never quite fathomed, lost in the dazzle of the sun. You will have begun to know how I felt, tracing the footsteps and inkstains of the lovers I once loved in the limelight where the cloudy window opens on leaves on concrete the year round. I hope the textbook on abstractions and how to get a grip of them proved useful.

I implore you to be honest rather than otherwise, dependable as the wind and the music that comes with it as if you were a sailor and did not simply imagine the sea. You will have noticed how, originally, language can be beautiful but there is something going away in it you can never hold. How many times have you wanted to leave and come back, because you have a very hard skin and think nothing of it. One thing I was not taught as a lad was how to be here and I hope I've not left you in the same darkness.

As I write this, nothing is freezing in this quiet month. I have been pleasantly walking out wearing a cherry-coloured hat that once I would not have been seen dead in. Today on the street a very fat person blocked the way but it didn't matter. If you have been adored and did not simply imagine the gibbering idiots many occurrences take on a different slant when it's all over and you are drifting gently into twilight. I can see some scratch marks on the door frame, seeming to have been made by a chisel or similar. Once I would have read them as a possible essay on truth, or a statement equally urbane, but now they are marks, that's all, and I am writing to you about them. Truth dissolves. It goes away. But you know that. I will be, and I know you will be, happy and sad ever after.

Oh, if you can hold back on cashing the cheque until the end of the month it would be good.

Love from —

Dream With Red Fence

Jim Rockford, my head, an exhibit
In a museum, a car rolling over, a girl
Stood looking elegant at a crossing,
A drink half drunk, sun coming up,
Clothes folded neatly, milk always
Being white, a wall of painted pictures.

Cloud massing, a quiet snake, two
Girls on a bus talking, a black telephone,
A line drawn between X and Y, words
On water, cold salad, men leaning
Against a wall, miracles of nature,
Separate curtains, hand on my heart.

A poem about lives, the colour blue,
Horses in a dream, table and chairs,
Envelope, something only you can hear,
The culprit, The Great Wall of China,
Fingerprints on each word, a train,
Something hidden, abandoned light.

Thank You. I'm Coming Out Now.

Don Carlos stood upon the bridge
And composed a poem for the Sun in
His head his life was ebbing away. The
People he had once gathered around him
Were becoming difficult to see because
He was roaming further and further away
From them. He thought of the party
He was going to go to and didn't go.
I must arrange my days differently
Said Don Carlos to the Wind and put that
Line in my poem he added as it delivered
The rain he turned towards home.
Back at the house I have been to the river
And studied the water he said and was
Met by the housekeeper telling him a man
From the Council had called was waiting
In the study she didn't like the look of him
Should she make some tea. Don Carlos looked
At her and heard her made no reply I have
Written words you can see through
Like glass and not like water in my head.
'When next to you I sit in my small way
I burn, but happily, and all dismay
Is banished: I am thus as much alive
As the kestrel on wing before its dive.
All things in daylight are, and the huge air,
I have touched it to prove that I am there.
I must arrange my days differently,
A life has to be saved and urgently
But I will not fear. Sun, look in my eyes,
See how brimming and full they are as lies
Are sent packing and Mistress Truth moves in
To the house I have been decorating

To her taste. One day, Sun, I swear to you
If you sit beside me it is you who
Will burn up like a poet losing rhyme.
I'll put you in my pocket for all time
Like a handkerchief delicately furled
And I'll have nothing to do with the world.'

Eternal Life

Wake and hear on the clock radio the rivers of the world
are fleeing, completely fail to understand, may have
wholly misheard but am immediately reminded of a line
of dialogue in Jack London that goes something like
'I see the river is running away from us again.' Go to make
a cup of tea and return to bed with coffee and chocolate,
listen to the rain fall or, to be exact, land. Don't be any
more precise, it will become annoying. Read once more
Coventry Patmore with all my will, but much against
my heart. Drift off and consider butcher shops, crimplene
and linoleum to no avail but nostalgia pangs on the stroll
to the bathroom where rays of evening sunshine doggedly
illumine sundry bottles of oils and balm on sunshiny
evenings. Lave face, armpits, floor and walls. The stubble
in the fields awash in the rain. A film of dust coats
the mirror, and shall it be silk today or cotton, slovenly
or sharp? Meanwhile, here is one of the four postmen
of the apocalypse assailing as usual the fortifications.
Thank goodness, I have been waiting for this video
for ages: it is called 'Wet and Slippery' and is about
a gorgeous young country gal come to the big city to work
for the water company and directed, it says here,
by the same crew who gave us 'Candy's Little Sister',
for which we are preternaturally grateful. Put to one side,
put to one side. The nation will decide, someone says
on the radio, but don't believe it, switch to tape and delight
in Jeff Buckley's version of Leonard Cohen's 'Hallelujah',
moved to tears so early in the day but no-one will know
so let them flow, let them flow like bloody rain
if that's what you want to do. But you don't,
but you don't. It's clearing, the weather, the town
emerging, clarifying from the cloud and mistiness
that belonged to the night. Sarah was there, in a dream

the substance of which is vanished, she is fleeing
along the corridor but having still the presence of mind
to flick her hair with that flicking action she employs
when she knows or thinks she knows she is watched.
Reminded of pausing a moment to check my reflection
in a car window, a hearse was it, at a funeral was it,
and the rain having stopped as the coffin was lowered
into the ground? Play again 'Hallelujah'. Delight,
the waters recede as time heals, the morning advances,
and the sad road lies so clear, which our solace is.

1st Poem, 1999

I fall asleep as if it is a life after a life I dreamed
and all the doors windows and air vents were bricked
up. Where are you? I remember walking all the way
across a meadow in the wake of horses, hearing
pheasants pleasant in hedgerows. The letter V
of ducks in the sky going somewhere and over there
a scribble of pigeons inventing a new alphabet.
Often there is a thought not yet formed, or
the thought is formed but doesn't want to be
revealed, as if it were a body, or a fit of honesty.
I sprawl in the comfortable bed and think things
that do me no good. Where on earth are you
at the moment? You are the moment. Once I walked
a descent of rocks by rushing waters, the mud
underfoot and the smell of rain on the air.
Homecoming, all the girls were waiting for me
holding their hair away from their faces, turning
everything I could think of saying into hopeless.
That was when I fell asleep with all my lies
around me, and could not explain myself to myself,
so how am I ever to explain myself to the judge
and the jury? Send me out for cobs and I won't come
back, as if that has anything to do with anything.
On the grass I was on my back looking at where
heaven is, higher than the sky, and below me
inside the world there were workers at endeavours
beyond me, and beyond my understanding. And there
were levels of love, degrees of honesty, deeds
of heartbreaking valour, children that would make
you cry, all beyond the reach of my heart. Heaven
remained over and above everything but no more
than a word. I ask in my sleep, where are you now?
In an ideal home in an ideal house and I'm not

there? I seem to wake up and fall asleep with
annoying regularity, except I shall die laughing
because, although everything matters so much
you could scream, nothing matters but the day
that ran in the silence of clouds, the night falling,
some crying, the moment of simple truth,
the nice dream, being with and knowing you.

Explaining Things To Me And Ruth

The best poems are true being made of life and its
difficulties and exultations. Miracles and the ordinary.
In 'Eternal Life' the stubble in the fields is supposed
to echo my few day's beard this is why it's close to
the stuff in the bathroom. The final words of the poem
may be sad but they were written by someone else
and of course that makes no difference they remain
beautiful words. In 'Thank You. I'm Coming Out Now'
Don Carlos is not a real person although many of
the things I make up are true. 'In the study she didn't
like the look of him should she make some tea' would
make more sense if there were some commas or full
stops kicking around but I thought you could slip
some of those in for yourself and feel as if you were
taking part in something. Not you in particular but you
in general, the general reader who probably doesn't
exist but should anyway be ready to do a little work
and perhaps we are talking about quite subtle things but
I figure people who read poems or my poems anyway
and like them will quite like subtle things and quiet
intelligent pleasures. Actually the point of the lack of
punctuation is to contrast the first part of the poem with
the more formal *poem in italics* at the end but it doesn't
matter that much it's just the way it turned out and I
quite liked it. Each of these explanations is true as is
the existence of miracles and the ordinary, of which
I have had my share. But there is no need to explain *us*
having bumped into one another and found much
that was amusing laying around. My gaze just landed
idly on the thing on my desk that holds my pens – a pen
holder I guess you'd have to call it – and in one of the little
compartments there's a couple of rusty paper clips and
staples and three electric fuses I'll never use because

I don't have a clue if they're any good or not. I should
throw all this stuff away but another day maybe
there will surely be days empty enough for such rubbish
but today I'm happy you're my friend and hope you're happy
though all life is full of difficulties as well as exultations.

The Poet Of The Month Club

Why did I join the Joiner's Club of Great Britain?
Why? To meet girls, but all the joiners were blokes
who cared for wood and what could be done
if you go with the grain. It wasn't for me. Why did
I join the Heavenly Songster's Club, when I've known
for years my song is too complicated to learn
and I don't know half the words? Why did I join the
Miserable Club and waste my time there telling jokes?
Why did I join the Chucked Out Into the Street Club?
Why did I join two pieces of string together and
call it a rope? Why did I join the Rope Club,
and go to a lecture about the history
of soap on a rope? Why did I join the Soap Club,
and go to a lecture about the history of soap on a rope
only to find out I'd heard it all before?
Why did I join the Single Men in Search of God Club?
Why did I join the Single Men in Search of Women
Who Aren't Married Club? Why did I join
the I Believe God is a Married Woman
with a Husband and Two Lovely Kids Club?
Why did I join the Single Men in Search of Men Club,
only to find that my cross-country running
experience came in mighty handy? Why did I join
the Solitude Club, and sit there on my own
all evening waiting for the others to show up?
Why did I join the Readers' Club? I expected
intelligent conversation about books, but
everyone just sat there reading. Why did I join
the Give Me My Money Back, I've Been Had Club?
Why was I not suspicious of the enormous
membership fee? Why did I join the My Stupidity
Knows No Bounds Club? I know the bounds
of my stupidity, even though they're way beyond

the horizon, and I should have been ineligible.
Why did I join the Drinkers' Club, and always
miss the meetings because I was too pissed to care?
Why did I join the I've Got a Picture of Marc Bolan
On My Bathroom Wall Club? I'm never
going to meet interesting people that way.
Why did I join the Secret Club, which meets
every Thursday at half past seven in the upstairs
room of The Cross Keys in Upton and I
shouldn't have told you that, should I? Why
did I join the Dried Flowers Club? Why?
Why did I join the Fantasy Club? Or did I?
Why did I join the Cloud Spotters Club? Actually
I'm quite pleased I did, the treasurer has
very nice legs and luckily she's a girl. But
why did I join the Dreamers' Club?
And why did I join the Daydream Club? They
kind of have a crossover of interests, and it's daft
being in both. Why did I join the Philosophy Club?
What was I thinking of? Why did I join
the Girl Guides? Did I believe I would get away
with it? Why did I join the Ramblers Club?
Did I think they would come with me? Why did
I join the Tea Club? Why did I join the Monday Club?
Why did I join the There Is a Hole in the Ground
So Let's Fill It Club? Why did I join the Upside Down
Club, only to find that they only spend a bit of
their time upside down, and the rest of the meeting
getting over it. Why did I join the Six Men
in Trowbridge Club, only to find that it was not real
membership at all but only associate membership,
because six men were already in it and
there were also two on the waiting list. Why
did I join the Hope Club? What did I think
I could bring to it? Why did I join the Black Is White
Club, and not the White Is Black Club? They

meet on the same night in the same room
at the same time, but did I make the right choice?
Why did I join the Daffodil Club? Did I expect
a jocund company? I went to their Spring Ball
but nobody danced, they just lay around
on couches. Why did I join the Poetry Club?
Do I have a self-destructive streak, or what?
Whatever. But it's not true I joined
the Paranoia Club. People just say I did.

Nothing To Write About

I pick up his scent, sing
one of those smiles untrustworthy
and clamber into the back of the car an idiot
rebuilt. Having forsaken dreams
brute reality is so attractive. Most writers
feel it's incredibly difficult to start
even with plenty of time at their disposal – I find myself
writing letters that could easily wait
reading the paper which always depresses me
varnishing my nails
sorting out recipes – *anything* – yet
once I have begun I can hardly bear to
stop

I pick up his scent, swallow party poison
make up a joke and hand it to a friend as if

Books are strewn across the living room floor
and hoovering is impossible. Some of the books
are open and words have tumbled out of them
on to the carpet. 'Unseasonable' is partly under the sofa
and from here looks like unsea,
which is another word for land
A cat curls up
to go to sleep on top of a signed copy of
The Little University of Uxbridge, Bernard Harrow's
first collection of poems, self-published
in large format (12" x 12") with quilted covers
(a motif of autumn leaves) in 1977.
It contains a fine poem called 'Falling Out'
which is about accidentally putting a chair-leg
through the television screen and loads of people
from the poet's favourite programmes tumble

on to his living-room carpet:

```
'Emma Peel is sprawled
and bedazzled
I love her and have longed forever
though never imagined her
only five inches tall
still she is not diminished at all.'
```

Here and there
words are huddled in their sentences
as if they must stick together
('In the autumn of 1810, Coleridge left the Lakes;
and, so far as I am aware, for ever.')
A full moon shining, the ice formed on cars
the fire blazing, dinner simmering in the kitchen.

I pick up, to do this

To do this you will need a typewriter
        (this is long ago I am writing)
You will need a typewriter but you can manage without one for a while
If you are buying a new machine I would suggest
you choose elite type it's in popular use
the letters are smaller than pica
and you will save a lot of paper over the years.

The cat picks his way along a bookshelf
among remarks you would love to utter
jokes you don't understand; on your bench lay ideas
only partly formed. You know how I hate all this shit.
Be a man in a hat, they say. I shall be a man in a hat one day.
Until such time

Can he tell you how sad it is in the whirlpool
Can he tell you how sad in dreams
Can he tell you how sad he has tried to be
Can life be all about little noble moments:

I was 17, and a friend had told me how 'April is the cruellest month' referred to the time when T.S. Eliot played wing-half for Charlton Athletic and he was gutted by a terrible semi-final defeat at the hands of Blackburn Rovers in the spring of 1920. I drew upon this knowledge in a school essay. They had capital punishment in schools in those days, and I am lucky to be alive. So they tell me

If you intend being a writer
you will need an ideas book for noting down a brainwave
the moment it arrives, a note pad – I use A4 lined tear-off blocks
pencils, pencil sharpener and rubber, a ballpoint or fountain pen
paper clips A4 typing paper and copy paper –
It's a good idea to use pastel-tinted copy paper so
you can sort out the pages at a glance
carbon paper (remember, this is long ago I am writing this)
envelopes –
these for writing letters
which I have proved by proving it is
exactly the best way to maintain distances
and I trust it proves the same for you

Oh, I have picked up a marvellous scent
Is there someone lurking in the bushes?
Is there someone sneaking up on me? I thought I had given up
caring. I write:

> In this, one is more smart than one is.
> It's wonderful. (repeat in parentheses several times)
> In 1815 I moved the blue wall;
> this was the subject of much hallucination. Heated discussion
> followed. The car was not invented, my love failed.
> Some baffling remarks are noted in a bed-sitting room.
> One is always learning how to survive life, and may not
> notice another experiencing difficulties. I thought
> this was a discussion programme, but I kept quiet

anyway. You know me, you know
I have to read even if it means I can't view. There we
were: I went to the wake but not the funeral
as I went to the honeymoon but not the wedding;
come to think of it I missed the honeymoon
and only dimly recall the courting.

I may call this poem 'Poems of 1812' for my own pleasure.
If no one gets the joke does it mean it's not funny? If no one gets
the poem, does it mean it's no good? I am conscious
but only of this. Desiring to be a kitten
I cough up and go to the clinic
and counselling and experts and they are thorough:
I feel excellently kittenish but there is (they say)
one more thing:
I am too big and must be shrunk.
They show me the washing machine
and what the boil cycle is capable of.
I run away.
On the promenade at Skegness
I pass the days smoking cigarettes
at last going home by slow train: the fields
are bored but full of life
under a sky I gloom emptily up to.
In my sack there is an apple (I eat it)
a pen with the top missing (I work with it)
a few old tickets and scraps of paper (I travel the world on them)
a schedule (I plan a life by it)
Jasmine's purse (I remember her)
and darkness underpinning everything.
I am there
and I am here.
I am conscious but only of this.

Friday Is A Dope

Sometimes I run out of brain. It's snowing
to the accompaniment of thunder this morning,
I pull myself out of a hole in a world of holes.
The man who lives in my attic is singing
about all that comes between him and the sky,
a song that doesn't once mention the word
'roof'. He is either an idiot or very clever,
I have no way of telling but I like him
so I don't care either way. And how come
my rhubarb flowers? I've never known rhubarb
to flower but it evidently does and I don't
know if this is a good or bad thing,
but I cut the flowering stalks away and
hope this will channel growth into the bits
I want to eat with custard. Sometimes I just
go on my nerve, take a deep breath and
a chance. I never knew ordinary life could be
so exciting, he mused, as they closed the pit
and threw some decent chaps on to the scrap
heap. Jasmine's father is one of them, and
he's scared he'll never work again. As I
drive past the mine this evening everything
is shrouded in low cloud coming to rain, as
if the world is closing down, and this evening
I can't organise myself at home: I spill
cat food across the kitchen floor and
everything is uphill until I discover a bottle
of red wine I opened on Wednesday, it's got
wine in it, enough for a good evening, though
it's cheap and cheerful its cheapness and
cheerfulness is beautifully infectious.
The Ecstasy of St. Theresa
is the favourite record of the man who lives

in my attic, he says it reminds him of life
beyond stairs, and he has come a long way
since being so far away. I look out the sky-
light into the heavens, they are relentless
and dark but streaked with something
I can't explain because it would sound
made up, as if a world were there
that didn't exist but could if it wanted to.

A Different Unknown Person

This is where I live, I live on my own:
you can come in, you can smell my dinner,
see the dog hairs on the carpets, the stains
round the bath, the dust on the shelves.
Will you, I wonder, notice how you notice
everything with so much clarity?
The shapes I understand are all around me,
so the noises fill the buckets, tears fall
nothing like snow. I stand in moonlight, listen
to the explosions made by collapsing colours.
Hordes of Hottentots amass in my backyard:
they should be in Asia if Africa isn't
big enough for them. I can't understand
what they say but I think it's about walking
around and sleeping where you land, waking up
where you dreamed and being alive in your
imagination if not in real life. This is where
I live, you don't know your way to be here,
so I make up stuff and won't ever complain.

A Swashbuckling Adventure

Here is the book I wrote, and the letter
in its envelope. Here are strange creatures
crawling endless shorelines and shapes in
shadowy corners. Here is their name and address.
Here is worry, a scraped living, and
the complete explanations. Here are rocks
and here is the shadow I cast. Here is investigation,
walking, and some pride in ignorance. If this
were not me I would not recognise myself,
and you would not love me. Here's sun up,
my falling, here are your arms. Here is a ship
upon an ocean, here are people, and here are people
jumping into the sea to drown. Here is the rain
that graces the scene, here are droplets of water
disguised as pearls of wisdom. Here is East and West.
Here are all the gods looking the other way.
Here are the barricades in a slow dismantling.
Here is the smoky horizon, here is what is
between us and it, here is a space to fill, here
is time, the shapes of leaves, hedgerows.
Here is dangerous laughter. Here is my fingerprint
on your heart, and here is the invisible mark
for everyone to see. Here the only way to live
life is to risk death, and if not death then misery,
and if not misery then poverty, and if not poverty
despair, and if not despair disappointment,
and if not disappointment only modest satisfaction.
If not any of these things, you have not lived.

Discourse On Cheerfulness

And suddenly in walks William Hazlitt
And think how much of life can be idea and remain only idea
And almost but not quite as suddenly the morning comes
Which is a surprise because it was the night
And its advance was concealed by the hill between us
It's so pleasant to compare my knowledge of geography
With your accumulation of place names and exact distances
Together they approach the complementary
And suddenly in walks Titus Groan
At least it's someone who could be he
The pianist is interrupted in the middle of music
But there is little discontent there hardly ever is
This being a safe place and a warm zone of comfort
And suddenly here's the end of a book that was long distant
And suddenly we are celebrating the cessation of tensions
And suddenly it is alright to be yourself again
We are delighted by trees because we can't begrudge them
Consider all the greens and browns the squirrels and birds
There is nothing to be gained by begrudging them
We are delighted by children because we can't deny them
And suddenly in walks Laurel and Hardy
Looking extremely well considering he's dead
There is so much extraordinary life in death
They are looking for something indisputably funny
And suddenly here is the offer of a job you can't refuse
Although it means travelling to the other side of town
It's not as if I'll be missed because I was never really here
The sun is shining and soon it will have dispersed the fog
And suddenly in walks The Lone Ranger we ask him to leave
And he does so and he is gone he is gone
And we're not going to make the same mistake twice
And we are the best person we know and the worst person we know
We are the best person we know and the worst person we know
We are definitely the best person we know
And the worst person we know

THE MAN IN BLACK

PETER MOORE:

WALES' WORST SERIAL KILLER

'Peter Moore was the man in black,
with black thoughts and the blackest of deeds.'
Alex Carlile, prosecution QC at Moore's trial

'I hold no brief for Moore's way of life.
By his own admission, he is a bad man.'
Eric Somerset-Jones, defence QC at Moore's trial

'He was a dominant homosexual, a violent and
predatory sadist who drew sexual satisfaction
from causing pain and suffering.'
***The Independent*, 12 November 1996**

THE MAN IN BLACK

PETER MOORE: WALES' WORST SERIAL KILLER

DYLAN RHYS JONES

y lolfa

In memory of my father, Tecwyn

First impression: 2020

The publishers wish to acknowledge the support of the Books Council of Wales

Conversations and events detailed in this book have been reconstructed by the author from memory and detailed notes made at the time, with the aim of being as correct as possible. However, they are not verbatim and as they took place over 20 years ago, cannot be taken as 100% accurate.

Cover design: Tanwen Haf
All photos from the author's own collection unless otherwise stated

ISBN: 978 1 912631 27 8

Published and printed in Wales
on paper from well-maintained forests by
Y Lolfa Cyf., Talybont, Ceredigion SY24 5HE
website www.ylolfa.com
e-mail ylolfa@ylolfa.com
tel 01970 832 304
fax 832 782

Acknowledgements

THERE ARE SO many people I wish to thank who have supported and encouraged me in preparing and writing this book. I am so fortunate to have the support of so many family members and friends.

Firstly my thanks go to Y Lolfa and their Head of Publishing Lefi Gruffudd, for their support and encouragement over the twelve months while I was writing this book. I wish to say a special thanks to my editor at Y Lolfa, Carolyn Hodges, for her advice and guidance, her patience with a novice writer such as myself and her skill and expertise. What you read now would have been very different without her words of wisdom.

I would like to thank my friends for their patience and support, especially Eilir and Claire Jones, who have stood by us as a family through thick and thin. To Caren and Glyn Morris and Aled and Llinos Roberts for their friendship at times when it was needed most as well as when times are good. To Vanessa Griffiths and Chris Beasley, my dedicated former colleagues and friends at Coleg Cambria, for standing together and keeping our heads when all about us were losing theirs. I would also like to thank my fellow authors Mared Lewis and Carys Davies for their advice, guidance and unwavering support at times when I was confused and unsure.

To colleagues and former collegues within the Legal profession for their wise words, especially to Lord Alex Carlile of Berriew for his willingness to discuss with me his recollections of the Peter Moore case and confirm certain facts and details of which the intervening years had made me uncertain.

I wish to thank my father, the late Tecwyn Jones, and mother, Eiddwen Jones, for their constant and unflinching support throughout the years and their wise counsel at all times. To my daughter Siriol, you were a blessing the day you arrived and you have made us very proud every day since then. I know you will be a dedicated, principled and successful lawyer.

Finally to my wife Catherine, you have supported me through the good days and the bad, you are wise and loving at all times and I honestly have no idea where I would be without you. This book is a testament to your support, determination and love as much as anything else. *Diolch i ti am bopeth.*

Dylan Rhys Jones
September 2020

Preface

November 2019

It's a dark, slightly damp morning in north Wales. A raw, bone-chilling gust catches me unprepared as I walk the dog along Pensarn beach near Abergele. The tide is nearing its high point and the grey-brown sea churns and swells only a few metres from where I stop and stand for a moment. Twm, my dog, is off on one of his lost causes, chasing a seagull along the beach as I look across the grey stones and pebbles towards Llanddulas and the foaming sea beyond. On a day like this, when it's cold and the stiff breeze catches the spray, and the wind and sand form small tornados and dance across the beach, it seems a very desolate place to be. It's definitely a desolate place to die.

I walk the dog here often. I prefer the days when the tide is far out in the distance and the sun catches the pools of water lying in the miles of undulating sand. But when I'm here in winter, I can only think of one thing, one story; and it's here on the beach in Pensarn where it began. Pensarn beach seems very unassuming to the passer by, who is likely to be driving further into north Wales along the A55 dual carriageway. At high tide it's a pebble beach and at low tide it reveals its miles of flat sand. It has a car park, a couple of small cafés and two small amusement arcades. In summer it will have its fair share of dog walkers and fishermen, and cyclists who stop for a break as they cycle along the coastal pathway, but it's not a popular beach to visit. In winter, locals will venture for a Sunday stroll or a morning dog walk but apart from that, the beach is left to its own devices.

On 18 December 1995 a body was discovered on this beach, lying on the pebbles close to the high-tide mark. It was the body of a man in his late thirties or early forties and he had been stabbed to death. That man was Anthony Davies, who had lived in Llanddulas, only a few miles away from the beach, and I think of him every time I walk my dog here. I didn't know Anthony Davies – in fact I had never met him – but I knew in detail how he died, and the parts I don't know I have imagined over the past 25 years.

For me 2019 had been a difficult year. I had been suffering some heart problems and though I realised that I required some kind of treatment, I had been trying to put the whole thing off and to the back of my mind for a good while. Eventually at the beginning of the year I had an operation, and though I imagined that my recovery would take a few weeks, some unforeseen complications led to me being out of action and away from my work for nearly six months. As many who know me will attest, I'm not at my best when doing nothing and there is only so much daytime TV any sane person can take.

I decided on a whim to do some writing. At the beginning I had no specific plan and no particular subject. Even though someone said somewhere that everyone has a novel in their heads waiting to be written, I didn't think I had one. But there was a subject hiding in the dark recesses somewhere... maybe I was simply attempting to disregard the obvious, perhaps it was all too close and painful? As my health improved and my thoughts of writing a book about something or other began to take form, I started to take long walks with my dog Twm. I felt that doing this would improve both my physical and mental health, and as I walked, I thought.

It seemed to me that this was as good a time as any to begin to face my real demons. Those demons which had been lurking in the dark recesses of my mind and concealing themselves in the shadowy corners of my thoughts and recollections for many years.

Some ten years before I had suffered a serious mental breakdown. Things had been on a downward spiral and I had considered that maybe the world would be a much better place without me cluttering it up. If it hadn't been for my wife and family and my good friends, it's likely I wouldn't be writing this now. During that time of crisis and having been admitted for some time to a psychiatric ward, where I was attempting to recover my equilibrium, I was asked by a counsellor about my demons: those things that haunt me, keep me up at night and shake me to the core. My thoughts turned to December 1995 and to the events surrounding the case of Peter Howard Moore.

I suppose our demons come to us in a variety of forms. What haunts one may not necessarily trouble another. But those demons are very accomplished at catching us out when we least expect it. I always found that mine were very active at about three o'clock in the morning. I would turn over in bed to look at the time on my alarm and there they would be, and when they had caught my eye and got my attention, they were relentless. Memories, thoughts and conversations would be reawakened from the past, tumbling about in my mind like clothes in a washing machine.

Once those demons got hold of me, they appeared to have no intention of relenting. I was plummeting into a deep, dark chasm of despair which would take a considerable amount of time, pain and effort to escape from. In the consulting room, with the counsellor sympathetically assisting, I felt confident enough to reveal those demons, my fears, and the questions and worries I had lived with for years.

I suppose there are some people who go through life without allowing the traumas of the past to affect them. I'm sure there are lawyers, doctors, nurses, police officers and teachers and many others who leave their work at the end of the day and never give the events they've witnessed or the things they've heard a second thought. There may be some, but I'm sure they are rare specimens. How can people not be affected by what they see and hear? How can we be expected to go through life witnessing tragedy, horrors and the worst of human behaviour and remain unaffected by it? When confronted by murder, violence and other criminal conduct, we lawyers are required to present ourselves as detached and unaffected by all we see and hear. We have to look at an event through frosted glass, isolated and removed from the emotion of a situation.

Being a criminal lawyer inevitably results in having to face, on occasion, the most extreme of situations, emotions and circumstances. Situations that you would hope never to experience or witness in your own personal life are thrust upon us second-hand, through our clients and the witnesses involved in a case. Criminal cases involving abuse, sexual violence and rape, murder and manslaughter, cases where victims are vulnerable and defenceless, where perpetrators deliberately target the weak or frail. It's at those times when others ask how these evil people could do such a thing that we lawyers are asked to get involved. When others would rather walk away in fright or revulsion, our job is to walk towards the problem, address the issue, sit in a cell and converse, advise and attempt to reason with people who may be accused of committing the most unreasonable and heinous of acts.

I have sat in cells and interview rooms on many occasions, asking myself why I chose to do such a job. How my hours of studying, examinations and training have resulted in me spending an hour in a cell with a suspect perhaps smelling of strong body odour, maybe affected by drink or drugs, telling me the tragic tale of his misunderstood life. Most of those stories are dreadful, involving family break-up, drug addiction, alcoholism, exclusion from school and rejection from family members and society. We criminal lawyers choose to spend our working lives with these forgotten people, those who live on the fringes, people we pass on the streets without giving them a second glance.

The danger is that we can become immune to those stories, that once you hear the tale of one broken family then you feel you have heard them all. When you've heard one excuse for violence, for assaulting someone, for causing injury to a wife, partner or child, you've heard every version. What we lawyers are exposed to is real life, life at its most basic, raw and primitive, and our job is to deal with it. It's the same for doctors, nurses, police officers and many other public servants – we criminal lawyers are on the front line. Some believe it's a glamorous job, arguing complicated cases in courts and earning vast amounts of money in the process. The reality is far from that: we spend our time in dingy cells and damp-smelling interview rooms with difficult clients at all hours of the day or night and are paid basic Legal Aid rates for the pleasure of doing so. Not many criminal lawyers become rich – we do the work for other reasons. Some of us have become criminal lawyers by design and others by accident: the pull of being an advocate in court can be so strong that many young lawyers leap at the opportunity to do so regularly in the Magistrates' Court at an early stage of their career. Some lawyers discover that once they become ensnared in the system, it doesn't easily release you from its grasp. Until you've become a crumpled, broken mess. 'If you prick us, do we not bleed?' asked Shylock in Shakespeare's *Merchant of Venice*. As far as lawyers are concerned, believe me: in my experience, we do.

So, what motivates us criminal lawyers? It certainly isn't the expectation of making a fortune: that's usually the domain of the big-city lawyers, with their flashy suits, modern offices and expense accounts. In my case it was very simple. I had this hope that I would be able to help someone, an individual or a family who were in difficult circumstances or down on their luck. When I was a student at Aberystwyth University, I recall one of our lecturers telling us that becoming a criminal lawyer would ensure that we would never become rich, but that we would become gatekeepers for the rights of individuals against the power of the state. To an impressionable young lawyer, this seemed a daunting but worthwhile goal to which I should aspire. This was the mid 1980s, the time of Thatcher, the Miners' Strike, Greenham Common, and in Wales the continuation of the battle for language equality. The battle between the individual and the authority of the state seemed a very real and relevant issue. Becoming a criminal lawyer seemed to me to mean that I would be able to contribute in some small way to rectifying some of the injustices in the world. I believe most of us left university with the goal of doing some good in the world.

During my time as a criminal lawyer the question most asked of me was, how do you represent someone you know to be guilty? I suppose most criminal defence lawyers are asked that question at some stage in their careers, and I expect that most have a similar reply. Our system in England and Wales relies on the principle that an accused person is always presumed to be innocent unless proven, beyond reasonable doubt, to be guilty in a court of law. The onus is therefore placed firmly on the prosecution to prove their case, and to do so to a high standard (beyond reasonable doubt). If they fail to do this, then the accused must be found 'not guilty'. The law ensures that anyone accused of a criminal offence has certain rights, and that the investigating authorities must follow certain rules, so as to make the process totally fair. As my lecturer said, our job as criminal lawyers is to be the 'gatekeepers' of our clients' rights. We must challenge and test all the evidence and ensure that our clients are treated fairly and that everything is always done properly.

Of course, if a client admits their guilt to their lawyer, but asks the lawyer to tell the court that they are 'not guilty', then that greatly changes the situation. The lawyer can't continue to represent their client in such circumstances. Over the years all criminal lawyers have had suspicions about clients' stories: assuming that they are lying, or maybe sometimes that they live in a totally different version of reality from the rest of us. But that's not the same as being told outright by them that they are not telling the truth.

A large workload and the resulting problems of pressure, stress and anxiety are facts of life for the busy solicitor. You learn that this is expected from an early stage in your career. Your superiors are looking for you to provide expertise, skills and knowledge but also to work quickly and effectively: it's 'Billing Hours' which, after all, are the key to everything in a busy legal practice. The more you bill, the better you are – or the more profitable you are. This always proved a bit of a problem for a criminal lawyer whose living was more or less dependent on Legal Aid. I began to learn very quickly in my career that you could depend on many things in law, but one thing you certainly couldn't depend upon was Legal Aid.

I had become a Police Station Duty Solicitor and a Court Duty Solicitor very early on in my career. That meant I was regularly 'on call' in case someone who had been arrested required legal advice at the police station. Being a Court Duty Solicitor meant I had to attend a local court on a regular basis and be prepared to advise and sometimes represent defendants who had arrived at court without a solicitor or having not taken any legal advice before the hearing of their case. These defendants were usually a very mixed bunch, from those who didn't care what was happeningto them, to those who didn't understand what was going on. Some would turn up at court knowing that they needed to be there, but having no idea why – that would usually require a conversation with the prosecutor to discover the reason. There would then be a conversation with the client, reminding him or her of any past crimes and misdemeanours and their recent arrest in an attempt to jog their clouded memory.

Peter Moore was not a usual criminal client. He was not the type of personality I would meet in the police cells or in court on a daily basis. He seemed intelligent, well spoken, quiet and calm, considerate of others and polite. He dressed tidily and was punctual for his appointments at my office when he instructed me to deal with the probate of his late mother's estate in the spring of 1994. I never considered him difficult or demanding: he was a model client who was never any trouble.

In 1995 Peter Howard Moore changed my life forever. His name will now forever be associated with the orgy of destructive brutality inflicted upon the communities of north Wales during those final months of 1995. Moore was sentenced by Mr Justice Maurice Kay in November 1996 to four life sentences with no prospect of release. I have battled for years to secure my own release from the grips of the Peter Moore case: writing this book is the final part of that process and hopefully its closing chapter.

Dylan Rhys Jones
in 1995

Introduction

IN NOVEMBER 2019 I realised that it was nearly 24 years since the arrest of Peter Moore. As I considered that fact, I was also aware that if I was ever going to revisit the case and write about my involvement with a man who was called at his trial 'the most dangerous man ever to be in Wales', it should be now. Peter Moore was now in his late seventies and the case had become infamous not only in north Wales but throughout the UK. I had been aware for years that the Peter Moore case and its surrounding circumstances had become notorious – even some of the students in my classes in the local college knew the story of the 'famous case'. Many adults in their forties and fifties in particular recalled the case in detail, remembering the concern which spread across north Wales in the final months of 1995 as the murders were discovered. Those murders remained unsolved for some time and this caused understandable disquiet across many north Wales communities.

This spate of murders happened only a few months after the murder of a 7-year-old girl called Sophie Hook from Cheshire in the north Wales town of Llandudno. Sophie was camping in the garden of her uncle's home, but during the night she disappeared and her body was discovered the following day on a beach near the town. The case sparked an avalanche of media attention, particularly as the suspect, a Howard Hughes from the nearby town of Colwyn Bay, had been linked with previous sex attacks on children. Hughes was convicted of the murder of Sophie Hook in July 1996.

During the final few months of 1995, the North Wales Police were clearly under some pressure. The Sophie Hook murder had put strain on their resources and by September of that same year, these further murders were understandably of great concern. Having only just completed the lengthy investigation surrounding the Sophie Hook case, another murder investigation was likely to stretch manpower and resources beyond anything the North Wales Police had been used to in the past.

The population of north Wales were unused to violent deaths of this nature happening in their area. Nowadays we have become somewhat immune to hearing about stabbings and knife violence occurring on our streets, particularly in our cities. Though of course stabbings were known as a common method of murdering someone 25 years ago, generally knife violence was much rarer than now and as a consequence society was less aware of it as a threat to individuals.

During the second half of 1995, violence and killing became the subject of discussion within communities across north Wales. The local press, who always seemed to prosper in the feeding frenzy of such stories, made the most of the violence and danger they considered we all now faced. We were perceived by some to be in an unprecedented spiral of violence, some became concerned about whether it was safe to venture out at night and whether our families were safe as they went about their daily lives, or if we were likely to be attacked and violently murdered by this unknown killer lurking on our streets.

North Wales is considered a safe and peaceful place to live. Our towns and villages are not free from crime and criminals, but there are, even today, thankfully only a few murders and crime is mostly concentrated in the larger towns such as Wrexham, Rhyl and Colwyn Bay. North Wales is mostly rural, and away from the north-east and the north Wales coast the levels of crime – violent crime in particular – are considered to be low. That's not to say that awful things don't happen: who can forget the case of April Jones in Machynlleth in Mid Wales in October 2012? It was a case that received national and international press attention. 5-year-old April was abducted from outside her home in Machynlleth and then brutally murdered by a 46-year-old local man called Mark Bridger. It was a case that severely affected both the public at large and the police officers who worked on it. Bridger's actions were of the utmost brutality and of such a cold-blooded nature that it remains a case which is beyond all reasoning and belief. What the case did emphasise and confirm is that within all our communities there will forever be potential for the worst forms of barbarism to expose themselves, if given the opportunity. This was true in Machynlleth in October 2012 and the same was true across north Wales in the latter months of 1995.

Revisiting the case of Peter Howard Moore after a period of nearly 25 years was important to me for so many reasons. I had realised that the case had left an enduring effect on me personally. I had for some time begun to question my involvement in the case, the way things had been handled and my failure to get answers regarding some of the most fundamental elements of the case, which remained, in my opinion, unexplained. Even more important was my understanding of the complex nature of my client, Peter Howard Moore. What had caused an unassuming and – to all appearances – respectable business man to commit such terrible crimes? What were his motivations? Were his crimes the product of an evil individual who was destined to act in this way, or was there a more complex explanation for the depravity of his actions?

The case had been difficult and stressful and I found the whole process both physically and mentally exhausting. When the case ended, I was left with the impression that this had been far from an ordinary murder case and that Peter Moore hadn't been an ordinary client.

Getting into the mind of a killer such as Peter Moore, and trying to find answers to questions that had been troubling me for so many years, was to be a challenge. I realised that I needed to contact Peter Moore regarding the events of 1995. I wanted to ask him about how truthful or otherwise he had been with me at that time. I wanted to question his motivation and behaviour at the time. I was keen to know whether, as he was now in his seventies, he would be willing to admit the murders, and whether I could detect some element of contrition in this complex man.

There are so many questions that occur to me when I run the events of December 1995 through my mind. Every criminal lawyer would agree that there are some cases which inevitably take over from everything else you are supposed to be doing. It may be the gravity of the charges or the person who's facing those charges, the families involved, the effect on the individuals or on their family's future which inflates the importance of a particular case and makes it one which demands all of the lawyer's attention. The truth is that those cases stay with you, become part of your DNA, penetrate into your very being as a lawyer and as a person and challenge you with questions and dilemmas which you may be unprepared to face.

The only way to attempt to discover the truth was to approach Peter Moore in the hope that he would be willing to discuss his case with me again after all these years. I contemplated doing this for some months. How would I go about it? What would I say? I wasn't even certain which prison he was in, or even whether he was alive and well, though I suspected I would have heard in the press if he had died. There was a time following the trial in 1996 when I would receive letters from Moore. These letters would usually address the possibility of launching an appeal against both his conviction and sentence and as a result I went to see him in Frankland Prison near Durham to discuss the possibility of an appeal and to consider the written guidance I had received from our QC, Eric Somerset-Jones. The problem that Moore had was the lack of new evidence that would support an appeal against conviction. It was also very likely that any appeal made against the four life sentences he had been given would have to go to the European Court of Human Rights, and that the chance of success was very small.

Since those discussions in late 1996 and early 1997, I had received no further communication from Peter Moore and had had no reason to visit him further. I realised now that in order to progress matters, I would need to contact Moore again. My initial research had led me to discover that Moore was an inmate at HM Prison Wakefield, West Yorkshire. I knew that Wakefield was a large high-security prison and had a number of Category A inmates, which Moore was likely to be among. Category A prisoners are those guilty of murder, manslaughter, rape and kidnap and other grave and serious offences, whose escape would be highly dangerous to the public. Category A prisoners are further divided into three categories: Standard Risk, High Risk and Exceptional Risk. Moore was likely to be in either the middle or higher category and visiting him would therefore mean completing a considerable amount of paperwork so as to become an 'Approved Category A visitor' with specific authority to visit Peter Moore.

In September 2019 I wrote a letter to Peter Moore, addressing it to him at HM Prison Wakefield. I had been deliberating for some time as to what I should say and how to reintroduce myself to him. After nearly 25 years, I had little knowledge of what had happened to him in prison, whether he was in good health and, more than anything else, whether he would have any interest in communicating with me and reliving the events leading up to his imprisonment. I thought it likely that he would be unwilling to return to those days in 1995 and 1996 and that maybe he would have little interest in discussing his case with me. I concluded that it was very possible that I would receive no response to my letter at all, or that alternatively the response I would receive would be short, either from the prison authorities or from Moore, telling me that he was not interested.

I wrote the letter to Moore carefully. I explained a little of my current background and that I was not practising law any more but was a college and university lecturer. I also mentioned that I had been ill recently and that it was this, in part, which had been the catalyst to me beginning to think about writing a book regarding my involvement in his case and my journey before and following his conviction for murder. I explained that my wish was to give a true and honest account of the case and its surrounding circumstances and that I wanted to explain in some detail the process I went through in preparing the case, assessing the evidence and getting his case ready for court. I also wanted to discuss the relationship between us as solicitor and client and how that had developed during the case. I said that I would appreciate the opportunity to discuss his thoughts about that time in 1995 and whether he had considered, over his years of incarceration, how things could have been different for him.

I asked Moore whether he would be willing to meet me. The request was made with a sense of uncertainty and with some trepidation on my part, but I knew that in order to obtain answers to my many lingering questions, we would have to meet.

The letter was sent, and I awaited a response. I was unsure how long such a letter would take to be processed by the prison authorities and then given to Moore to read. I was also unclear, at that stage, how much vetting there would be of any communications sent to the prison and whether the authorities would allow Moore to reply to my letter. As Moore was likely to be a Category A prisoner, sending and receiving mail was likely to be problematic and as I was no longer his solicitor but rather an ordinary member of the public writing to a serious criminal in prison, this might also be an issue of concern.

How many unsolicited letters do people like Moore receive from the public? I wondered. I had heard of people befriending serious criminals in prison, even becoming some sort of a pen pal with them. Whether it is because of some macabre fascination with murderers or a genuine wish to help a 'poor tortured soul', it seems a strange thing to do. It was possible therefore, I concluded, that my letter to Moore could be placed on the 'unwanted crackpot letters' pile and left in some dark corner of a prison office gathering dust.

It was a few weeks before I received my first letter from Peter Moore. It was a jovial, friendly letter, with some detail of his recent health problems and some other brief information about his life. He also confirmed his willingness to discuss his case with me and that he would be willing to meet me when appropriate arrangements could be made. Initially on opening the letter, I was nervous and apprehensive. I was worried that the feelings and emotions I had experienced during and after the case would somehow rush back to overwhelm me. Opening and reading that letter was in some strange way like going back 25 years in a time machine, and via a typed letter from Wakefield Prison, I could hear Moore's voice resonating from the past. The letter's tone was courteous and it suggested to me that, despite the intervening years, Peter Moore may not have changed that much. He asked about my family and about my career over the last 24 years. As I read out the letter to my wife, she remarked that it was as if I was reading a letter from a long-lost friend. I agreed that somehow it did feel that way, but I couldn't explain why.

Having received that initial letter from Moore, it appeared to me that there would likely be an opportunity for me to discuss the case again with him face to face, and finally to get answers to some of those unanswered questions.

Chapter 1

WE LAWYERS ALL dream of that big case. The murder, the manslaughter, the high-profile rape or a case where a famous client desperately wants you to represent him or her, because you are the very best lawyer they can find. That story which hits the headlines and is featured on the TV news. Of course, the majority of us don't get them. We ply our trade day in, day out in police stations, interview rooms and courts with the habitual offenders, the ne'er-do-wells, the addicts and the reckless, listening to their stories, lies and excuses and then presenting those stories to the courts as 'God's honest truth, your Honour.' But even among the ranks of the baggy, worn-out suited, old-time lawyers there is still a hope that, someday, a big case will fall into their laps. As they chat with disaffection about their clients in the smoking area at the back of the court, there remains with each and every one a belief that their big case is only a phone call away.

21 December 1995 could never have been described as an ordinary day. The absurdity of the Christmas holidays was under way and everyone, including our clients, seemed to be busier than usual. With only a few days to go before Christmas, there were still people scurrying around, infected by some demented expectation that everything was to be done by Christmas. There were sales and purchases of properties to be completed, cases to be concluded, matrimonial arrangements regarding access to children over the holidays still to be agreed, and on top of that I still had the fallout from a few disorderly Christmas parties sitting in a police cell somewhere, requiring my attention.

Having been in the office for what seemed like hours, I decided to grab a moment of peace and leave our cauldron of insanity to get a breath of fresh air and a sandwich. As I was leaving through the office reception, the phone rang and the receptionist shouted, 'Dylan, someone wants a word – it sounds urgent.' I was keen for my lunch, some peace and a modicum of silence, and so it was against my better judgement that I went to grab the phone.

'Mr Jones, it's about Peter, Peter Moore.' I didn't recognise the gruff voice on the other end of the line. The caller identified himself as a friend of Peter Moore.

'He's been arrested this morning. I have no idea for what, but I think he may need your help.' I detected worry in the gravelly tones of the caller's voice, and this led me to suspect that he may have known more about the circumstances than he was letting on, but I dismissed my suspicions, concentrated on my instructions and told him I would call the police station and attempt to discover what was going on.

The conversation with the Custody Sergeant at the Llandudno Police Station was brief.

'Mr Jones... yes.... you represent Mr Moore, do you? OK, then you need to get down here as soon as possible, Mr Jones – as in, now. If that's OK with you.' I agreed, collected my things and was on my way. The sandwich would have to wait.

Being called out to see a client at the police station was not an unusual event for a busy criminal lawyer. I had my established clients, who would be in the habit of getting arrested on a regular basis, and others would be referred to me on recommendation, in the hope that I would be able to help them out of whatever criminal predicament they were in. I was also a member of the Duty Solicitor Scheme, which meant I had to be available to any poor and desperate soul who was arrested and required legal advice at the police station. On occasions, this would mean being available day and night. Getting a call-out at 2 o'clock in the morning to attend to a drunk driver, an inebriated fighter or just a plain old confused individual who clearly had no idea what was going on was not unusual.

Choosing to become a criminal specialist is a noble and honourable choice of profession, often accompanied by lofty and well-meaning ambitions to support and assist those less fortunate in society. Those of us who, in my opinion, have made such a virtuous choice are unlikely to be deflected by fame and are certainly not motivated by fortune. They will have been warned by wiser, bloodshot-eyed and exasperated older criminal lawyers of their certain fate as cannon-fodder for demanding amateur lawyers and wide-boy career criminals. They will expect the drunken excuse-merchants and the sad disappointment mummy's-boys shuffling into the office with their tales of mistaken identity and confused intentions. They will have been informed that the truth is never actually the truth and that as criminal lawyers our stock-in-trade is the version most suited to our client's case.

It was a stormy afternoon along the north Wales coast. The sky was a dark grey and the curdled sea foamed and sprayed across the promenade in Llandudno. When I arrived at the police station car park, I paused for a moment, looked out at the storm and considered what I was about to do. I had reasoned in the car that this could be a big case, the message from Peter Moore's friend and the stern response of the Custody Sergeant seemed to suggest that this was something out of the ordinary. When you're told that it's a drunk driver or a shoplifter, after a few months they become cases which hardly get the heart rate racing. The reticence of the Custody Sergeant to go into any detail at least gave an air of mystery to the journey, which was a pleasant diversion before the Christmas holidays. Despite the sense of slight intrigue, I sought to curb my emotions, convincing myself that I would walk into the custody suite at the police station and be told it was a case of speeding on the A55 or driving with excess alcohol.

I thought about calling my wife, who was out somewhere Christmas shopping. If I was going to be a while in the police station, I should at least let her know.

'Cath? Look, where are you now?'

'I'm on my way home from Chester, why? Are you OK?'

'Yes, just been called out to the police station.'

'Well, don't be long. I may want to call you when I'm doing the last bits of Christmas shopping in town, to make sure I'm buying the right stuff.'

'Well, I'll do my best. You know how it is on these call-outs, one thing leads to another and quite suddenly I'm out all afternoon.' She had got used to knowing what a call-out to the police station could mean. It could be an hour; on the other hand it could be five, or even more.

'Well, call me to let me know.'

'Yes, of course,' I said with a sense of relief that I wasn't Christmas shopping with her.

It was still stormy and by now the rain was beating hard on the car windscreen. I struggled for a moment as I pulled my coat on in the car and then collected my things: pen, notebook, all the usual stuff I would need while seeing a client in the police station.

I was 30 years old when the Peter Moore case began. In lawyers' terms, that's young. In fact nowadays, lawyers who are 29 or 30 are only beginning their legal careers after successfully negotiating university, college, training and the various other hurdles required of them. Even in my day, the process of qualifying was challenging and felt lengthy and mind-numbingly difficult at times. Our aspirations were very different to today's highflyers, who aim for pinstriped-suited careers in the City of London or Manchester or Cardiff. Once qualified, my aim was to get a contract with a good local firm of solicitors as an Assistant Solicitor. It was a job title I considered rather inadequate as a newly qualified solicitor who had battled through a degree, examinations, dissertations and then two years of being an Articled Clerk, which was still as Dickensian a role as Uriah Heep's in *David Copperfield*.

At my first firm, my boss was tall and thin with a large moustache which hung over his top lip like a hairy verandah. It was a remnant, I suspected, from times spent as a hippy in the Seventies. He possessed a loud, dramatic voice and a habit of calling me 'Young man' rather than my name, which I suspected he'd forgotten. He was an excellent criminal lawyer and had a loyal following within the area's criminal fraternity. His clients were so loyal that if they were ever under arrest, they would simply ask for him by his first name and everyone in the North Wales Police knew who they meant.

'Yes, yes, son, we'll get him for you now. Just sit tight in that cell and he'll be here in no time.'

He had one weakness: he was without doubt the most disorganised individual I had ever met. His filing methods were slapdash and his diary was kept in what appeared to be hieroglyphics, which neither his secretary nor I could decode. One morning as he arrived at the office, he shouted across the room towards my desk, which was behind the main reception area – in a place chosen, I suspected, so that everyone could keep an eye on me.

'Young man, the Parkin case: the date is up for filing a claim today. Get the file, prepare the documents and get them to the County Court by 4 o'clock.' Bearing in mind that this was a request to an unqualified person, who had never heard of the Parkin case until that moment and, though vaguely aware of the process of filing court documents, had never actually done it for real, it was a steep learning curve. It was the feeling you have when you realise you're unprepared for an exam. That cold, disorientating, sweaty sensation when your stomach churns and you imagine falling into the abyss.

I filed the papers in the court at 3.45 p.m. Another 15 minutes and my boss and his firm would have been sued for negligence. The experience taught me a few lessons. Be organised, don't leave things until the last minute if you can possibly help it and be prepared for the unexpected – and also if you do imagine yourself falling into the abyss, you may not be. All those were to be valuable lessons learnt, as I would discover when dealing with Peter Moore.

I approached the door to the custody suite at Llandudno Police Station and pressed the security communication system. Having identified myself, the large metal door swung open and I was given access, to be greeted by the familiar face of the red-cheeked and jolly Sergeant Davies, one of the Custody Sergeants.

'Hello Mr Jones, and to what do we owe this unexpected pleasure?' Sergeant Davies knew how to keep an upbeat atmosphere in the custody suite, something which was always in great demand during the Christmas period.

'Oh yes,' Davies then said. 'I know why you're here, hold on for a minute.'

Custody was busy. One police officer stood patiently with a young teenager by the Custody Sergeant's desk, waiting for his suspect to be charged, and another couple of suspects, track suited and dull faced, were with their solicitors in what I suspected was a queue. The suspects looked tired, the solicitors looked worse. I found myself at the back of the line.

'Been here long?' I asked the solicitor next to me.

'Two to three hours,' was his answer, with a sigh. He looked down at his notes dejectedly, and asked me, 'What are you here for?'

'I'm not actually sure,' was my truthful reply. As I spoke, I noticed DI Ackerley, who I knew from a previous case some months before, appearing from an office at the back of the custody suite.

'Mr Jones, I think we need to have a chat.' He nodded at me as he spoke.

'Oh hell, you're in trouble,' said the solicitor standing by me, with a chuckle. I followed DI Ackerley into the back office.

DI Peter Ackerley was a detective with both experience and a reputation. He was regarded as thorough, plain-speaking and hard-working and, as a defence solicitor, I knew he was a man who could be trusted and with whom I could work. He was in his early forties, tall and solidly built, like a rugby second row, with a red complexion and a determined look in his eyes. He was full of energy, and that energy was known to be characterised in his investigations as well. If he was heading the case, I needed to have my wits about me, just to keep up with him.

Being a defence solicitor usually requires striking a delicate balance between building a good and effective relationship with the investigating officers and by doing so understanding exactly what's going on during the investigation, and ensuring your client has the utmost trust in the advice you're giving. It's important to understand the quality and strength of the evidence against the client and therefore make sure that your client is accurately advised of how strong or how weak a case the police have. Doing this effectively allows your client, with the benefit of your guidance, to make the most appropriate decisions. Even the toughest of hardened criminals, familiar with every nuance of a police investigation, will need guidance and even some element of cajoling on occasions. I've constantly been surprised by the response of some of my criminal clients. Often it's the hairy, big-shouldered, tattooed thug you will notice crying in the corner of his cell, full of regret and remorse. Meanwhile the scheming and bespectacled scrawny little man will be quietly calculating his next move without anyone suspecting a thing. You learn quickly as a criminal lawyer never to judge a book by its cover.

Whatever the circumstances, guilty or not, the moment of a suspect's arrest and subsequent questioning at the police station is inevitably a moment of crisis and intense stress for that suspect. For many it will be an experience they have never gone through before, though there will be cases when your client has far more experience of the police than you do. Every case is different, because every person is different.

I had realised very early on in my career that my responsibility and approach in the police station was in most cases very simple: it was to listen and advise. I had observed many a lawyer who seemed to have built their reputation upon anything other than those two main pillars. They would arrive at the police station, briefcase in hand and with haste and commotion hanging in the air in their wake. Straining every sinew to be everyone's friend and on first-name terms with all, handing out sweets and cigarettes to their clients and telling them, 'We'll get you out.' This was rarely a successful tactic. Usually it would build up their clients' expectations to such an extent that anything less that complete exoneration would be a massive let-down.

Plying my clients with cigarettes and promises was not my style, and neither was being on first-name terms with them. Unless there was a very good reason, or my client was very young, I would call them Mr, Mrs or Miss. Only in exceptional circumstances would I call them by their first names. In return, I would expect to be called Mr Jones – always. It would always aggravate me to hear a client shouting at his solicitor either in the police station or in the court waiting area, 'Hey Steve, you got a fag, mate?' We are not there to be their mates and, in my opinion, it's crucially important that we are not. I had a client who took to calling me 'mate' or 'chum' every time I saw him. In the end there was no getting around it, I had to tell him, 'Look, just so we understand each other clearly, I'm not your mate: your mate is the one who's been jointly charged with armed robbery with you. He's your mate, I'm your solicitor.' It took the wind out of his sails a bit and he just nodded. We understood each other after that.

DI Peter Ackerley gave a long sigh and sat on the front of the desk in the back office and gestured for me to sit. He scratched his balding head and took a moment, either to gather his thoughts or for dramatic effect.

'What do you know about all this then, Dylan?' he asked me. I shrugged my shoulders.

'Nothing. All I know is that I've been called by a friend of Peter Moore, who tells me that Mr Moore was arrested earlier today and is here, and is requiring my assistance. So here I am.' DI Ackerley nodded. He looked like a doctor who was about to break some very bad news but didn't know exactly how to get started.

'Look, Dylan, it's like this.' He cleared his throat and grabbed a pocketbook from the desk. Referring to his notes, he explained what he believed Moore may well have done and the evidence he had gathered so far to substantiate this belief.

Ackerley explained to me that a victim, a man called Anthony Davies from Llanddulas near Abergele, who was a married man and father of two children, had been discovered by an early-morning dog walker lying on the shale on Pensarn beach near Abergele on the morning of 18 December 1995. The victim had been stabbed in the abdomen, had collapsed from his injuries and died on the beach. Ackerley pointed out that Pensarn beach was a well-known pick-up area for homosexuals and that he was considering a link with the homosexual community. I was aware of this connection: it was after all, a popular joke in the area that you should be careful if you were taking your dog for a walk on Pensarn beach late at night. It was a joke then, maybe not so much now.

Ackerley went on to explain that a trace of blood, which may have belonged to the assailant, had been discovered near the body and that this was in the process of being tested. It was still early days in the use of DNA evidence in criminal cases, but it was available, and could be used in circumstances such as these to identify the presence of another – possibly the assailant – at the scene of a crime. And then there was the issue of identification. A van, fitting the description of Peter Moore's van, had been seen nearby in the late evening or early hours before Davies' body was discovered. Ackerley described a 'tip-off' that the police had received , saying that Moore's name had been given as a potential suspect. It was the identification of that van and this 'tip-off' which had initially led to Moore's arrest. I was told that the police were planning to go to Peter Moore's property in Kinmel Bay near Rhyl to undertake a search – DI Ackerley was awaiting more details of that and would let me know as soon as he could.

'So that's what we have at the moment,' said the Detective Inspector, who appeared relatively satisfied with the situation. He stood up from the desk and I got up to leave.

'One thing,' said Ackerley, grabbing my arm. I turned back to him.

'This man, your client – he's a strange one, isn't he?' He seemed to be asking me rather than telling me. 'Do you know him?'

'Well, he's been a client of mine for a couple of years,' was my reply.

'I can't really make him out, there's just something about him.' I didn't reply. It was up to Ackerley to draw his own conclusions about Moore – I had my own views and I wasn't about to share them with him. He nodded and I wondered what he may be thinking; it was a strange thing for him to say.

'Right,' I said. 'I believe I need to have some time to speak with my client.'

As I waited for an interview room to become available, allowing me some privacy to speak with Moore, I was given tea in a plastic cup, which I drank standing to the side of the custody desk, watching more suspects being checked in. Burglary, criminal damage, some kind of domestic incident – it was a busy afternoon.

'Are you with the murderer?' asked a small scraggy man in his twenties, wearing a shell suit and dirty trainers.

'Mind your own business,' I replied.

Clearly the word had already got around. There was a murderer in the cells, and everyone wanted to know what was happening and – if they were really lucky! – to get a quick look at him. Just to see what he was like. It's always the same: there's a hierarchy of crimes and criminals and on top of the tree are the murderers. Even the gangsters and the drug dealers seem to doff their metaphorical caps to a murderer. To see someone suspected or convicted of such a crime would get all the tongues wagging, and to get to talk to a murder suspect – even passing the time of day – would gain any self-respecting petty criminal some valuable kudos. I could just imagine the scraggy man in his shell suit relaying his adventures to others with similar fashion sense over a pint in some rough pub in Rhyl.

'Yeh, yeh, I spoke to that murderer. I had a chat with him about this and that, you know how it goes.'

The presence of a murder suspect seemed to be big news to everyone. The rumble of the rumour mill was discernible within the police station: police officers were gossiping amongst themselves and so were the suspects. As I stood waiting for an interview room to become available, I could see people nodding in my direction, and in hushed conversations saying, 'He's the murderer's brief.' 'God help him, I wouldn't want to be in a room with a murderer.' But there seemed also to be an ambience of heavy tension – it was different to the usual atmosphere in the police station, as if no one knew what to expect next. And above all a certain reverence: that we all might be in the presence of an actual murderer. A macabre and gruesome celebrity.

I had got to know Peter Howard Moore as a client some two years or so before his arrest. On the face of it, Moore appeared to be a well-spoken, polite and moderately successful businessman. Initially I was instructed by him regarding some debts that were owed to him and after that, some issues regarding the leases of his cinemas. I had understood from Mr Moore that he had been interested in the cinema and the world of film from a very early age. During one consultation in my office, he mentioned how he enjoyed classic films of the Forties and Fifties and other well-known films from the 1960s. He was clearly a total film buff and knew the subject thoroughly, and it wasn't therefore a surprise when I learnt from him that he was attempting to expand his cinema 'empire'.

On leaving school, Peter Moore had at first worked for his father's business, which was run from their home, Darlington House in Kinmel Bay, near Rhyl. Darlington House was quite an imposing and a much larger house than most in Kinmel Bay, standing at the time on the outskirts of the village. Kinmel Bay is just across the River Clwyd from the holiday town of Rhyl and benefited from all the visitors who travelled to Rhyl during the summer. Peter Moore's father ran a business providing gas and other pieces of equipment for the caravans of the vast number of holidaymakers arriving in the area.

It was later that Peter became a cinema owner. He found an opportunity to take over the lease of a small cinema in Bagillt near Holywell, Flintshire in north-east Wales, and then, cinema by cinema, his small empire grew from Bagillt to Holyhead to Blaenau Ffestiniog. As the chain grew, Peter Moore was considered by many to be the saviour of small cinemas in north Wales. His reputation grew to such an extent that the media became interested. There were articles in the local papers about his business ventures and even features on the Welsh news about this local businessman 'saving' small struggling cinemas in north Wales. Peter Moore had become a good news story.

I remember getting home from work one evening. The TV was on and I noticed Peter Moore on the local Welsh news programme.

'Hey, he's my client,' I recall saying. 'He's doing well for himself, isn't he?' And there he was on the screen, being interviewed by the news reporter and demonstrating how to load film into an elderly-looking projector at one of his cinemas. He was dressed in black – black shirt, black trousers – as one would expect a film projectionist to dress, I suppose. I thought nothing of it. He spoke calmly, courteously answering the interviewer's questions with a slightly effeminate lilt to his voice. His accent was English, but I couldn't place it as coming from a particular area. He appeared to be a competent, thoughtful businessman and, of course, his story was a newsworthy tale of success.

During this time, 18 months or so before his arrest, Peter Moore arrived at my office one afternoon during the spring of 1994 wanting to see me as a matter of urgency. He brought with him the sad news of his mother's death. His father had died many years before, but it was clear that his mother's death had affected him greatly. Mr Moore instructed me to deal with the probate of his mother's estate and transfer her assets, which included the property Darlington House, into his name. There was nothing unusual in this request and though understandably saddened by the loss of his mother, I didn't get the impression that Mr Moore was in such a state that his behaviour or state of mind could be affected in any way. I dealt with the issue, there were a few papers to sign, and within a few months after receiving the initial instructions, the matter was at an end. It was simple, straightforward.

Apart from his appearance on the TV news, his attendance at my office to complete his mother's probate papers may well have been the last time I saw Mr Moore until that call-out to the police station on 21 December 1995.

'Mr Jones, we have an interview room available for you now.' I was led by a police officer to one of the few interview rooms at the station.

'Take a seat. I'll go and fetch Mr Moore now.' The room was similar to so many interview rooms at police stations I had been in before. There was a table and four chairs, and a tape recorder to record the formal interviews between the interviewing police officers and the suspect. The only other thing on the table was a laminated document which set out in plain language the suspect's rights at the police station. The walls and the heavy door were covered with cork tiling, in an attempt to create a soundproofed environment. The door had been closed by the police officer when he'd left to fetch Mr Moore, and the room was totally silent. I set my notepad and pens on the table and waited.

I felt almost as if I was waiting to go in the dentist's chair: nervous, expectant, unsure. A knot tightened in my stomach and I noticed I had a nervous, twitching leg that couldn't be stopped. I rearranged my pens and paper a few times, clearing my throat and moving in my chair, looking at the blank walls for any distraction. I had met Mr Moore numerous times: they had been ordinary meetings, nothing exceptional, and I could hardly remember our conversations. But now I was nervous and on edge. What would I say? How should I begin the discussion?

'So, how's things then?' No, maybe not.

'What have you been doing then?' Certainly not.

This initial meeting with a suspect is all about discovering background. Why, when and how he was arrested? Does he know what he is alleged to have done? I needed to explain to him in detail what I had been told by DI Ackerley. It was also necessary to talk about the interview: the procedure, what he was likely to be asked and what rights he as a suspect had in the police station. All formalities had to be addressed, as with any other interview. This interview was the same as others: it had the same format and the same requirements; it was governed by the same regulations. I had sat through hundreds of interviews – surely this was going to be the same. But I was conscious that it was not going to be an ordinary interview.

The door opened. The police officer appeared, followed by another, then Peter Moore and then finally, for good measure, a third officer. I got up and offered to shake my client's hand, and noticed he was handcuffed.

'Do we need these, officers?' I asked, pointing to the cuffs. The lead officer unlocked and removed the handcuffs, then another pulled a chair away from the table and offered it to Mr Moore. 'Unusually attentive,' I thought to myself. Mr Moore and I then shook hands and sat down. The officers left and my client and I sat for a moment in the thick treacle of interview-room silence. I wanted to ensure that the door was properly closed before I began our discussion, so I waited.

'So, Mr Moore, I think I should explain. I was called at lunchtime today by a friend of yours, who told me that you had been arrested and that you required my help?'

Peter Moore (right) at the opening of his cinema in Bagillt (now demolished)

The cinema in Holyhead, Anglesey, formerly owned by Peter Moore

Chapter 2

I ALWAYS FELT that the interview rooms at Llandudno Police Station smelt slightly of damp. There seemed to be little in the way of ventilation and this added to the stifling atmosphere of the room. It was an echoless chamber where conversations and allegations seemed to be absorbed into the walls.

Peter Moore sat across the table from me. He appeared tall and thin, his hair – greying and thin on top – was swept back from his forehead. He was pale, with some stubble on his chin, and wore a black shirt and a pair of black trousers – the outfit of a cinema projectionist.

'I'm glad you're here, Mr Jones,' he said. He was softly spoken and composed. There was no sign of panic, concern or worry. I told him what the police had explained to me about the reasons for his arrest. The body of a man had been discovered on the beach in Pensarn, near Abergele, early that morning. A man had been walking his dog on the beach and had discovered the body lying near the high-tide mark. It appeared that the man had died following a stabbing to his abdomen, though it was unclear at this stage how many times the victim had been stabbed. I had been told that the victim was an Anthony Davies from Llanddulas. Peter Moore listened intently to my description of the victim and the circumstances of his death, nodding a few times but asking no questions. I explained to him that the police had been given the description of a van similar to his van, which, it had been reported, had been seen in the vicinity of the Pensarn beach car park late the previous evening or in the early hours of the morning. It was following this tip-off that the police had arrested Moore.

'Do you know who gave the tip-off?' Moore asked. I didn't – it wouldn't have been information that the police would have been willing to share with me at such an early stage in the investigation. But I wondered if Moore had his suspicions of someone in particular who may have had an axe to grind, and as a result had a vexatious reason to approach the police. I asked him if he suspected anyone. He said that he didn't, but I felt that he may have had a few ideas.

I knew nothing at this stage about Peter Moore's background other than some fairly basic information gleaned from my solicitor-to-client conversations with him over the previous two years or so, which mostly involved his mother's estate. Having dealt with some issues he had with debtors and creditors, I had suspected that he may have been in some financial difficulty, though he had shared little information with me regarding his business. Though his cinemas had received a considerable amount of attention in the local media, I considered, even back then in the mid 1990s, that the small independent cinema business was likely to be vulnerable to the multiplexes which were beginning to appear, even in north Wales. There was something old-fashioned and nostalgic about Peter Moore's cinema business. He had rented a number of old and down-at-heel or previously closed cinemas in small towns across north Wales. I believe he saw it as an opportunity to develop a chain of small independent cinemas which harked back to the great days of Hollywood. Films and cartoons were shown on Saturday mornings to local children, something which hadn't happened in towns such as Holywell, Holyhead and Blaenau Ffestiniog for many years. Local people warmed to the idea of a local cinema aspiring to be something of a hub for communities that had lost some of their identity over recent years, due to unemployment and poverty.

To me, during the previous two years or so, Moore had appeared to be a mild-mannered businessman who kept his appointments, gave his instructions to me clearly and seemed to have a drive to succeed with a business which, though perhaps unlikely at first glance to be one which would succeed, on the face of it was making some positive steps towards success. He would sometimes arrive at my office wearing a large sheepskin coat, which would occasionally make the staff giggle and comment, but other than that there was little about him which was distinctive. Maybe that's why he avoided being arrested for the murders for such a length of time: there seemed to be nothing particularly unusual about him.

As we sat in an interview room at Llandudno Police Station, I began to explain to Moore his legal rights following arrest. I ascertained from him that he hadn't ever been arrested before, made sure that he understood the police procedure for when a suspect was interviewed, what would be said and done by the detectives interviewing him, and what my role in the whole process was to be. Moore took the advice in his stride, asking no questions, appearing to understand what was expected of him and seeming content to be questioned. I then had to ask him the one obvious question which seemed to me essential to clarify before he faced a police interview.

'What do you know about the allegations?' It's the question that every solicitor has to ask a client before an interview. We don't ask, 'Did you do it?' or 'Right, what about this murder, then?' It's necessary to be far more subtle than that. Was it to be a denial of all allegations put to him, an admission of everything or a 'No comment' interview? We had a fair idea of the allegations and I therefore needed to be clear also what Moore thought of these allegations so that I could advise him as to the best approach to take during the interview.

'Mr Jones, I have no idea what's going on here. I have nothing to do with this at all: this is not my doing.' It was a clear, unambiguous denial of the allegations I had described to him.

'Is there a chance that it was your van which was seen at Pensarn beach last night?' I asked. He denied it was his van, telling me that he'd been to his Holyhead cinema that evening and would have been travelling home late, though he was unsure of the exact time. He said that he'd gone straight home and hadn't visited Pensarn beach and therefore it was not possible that it was his van that had been seen. It was Moore's view that whoever the witness may have been had made a mistake concerning the identification of the van. He was adamant that it could not have been him.

Moore's position on the allegations was clear and unequivocal and, as such, my job seemed much easier. If you were not there and it was a case of mistaken identity then, of course, you need to say that as clearly as you can. I was in possession of as much evidence as the police were willing to give me at that particular time; there seemed to be little else to go on at that moment and Moore's denial seemed reasonable. I advised him that at this stage, as it wasn't him at the car park in Pensarn and as he was likely to have been on his way back from his cinema in Holyhead at the time, he should explain that to the police during the interview. Moore seemed to think for a few moments about the advice I had given him, though he didn't ask any questions or betray any emotions. I imagined he was considering his options, so I made some notes and allowed him some time to quietly think. The room was silent, the atmosphere seeming heavy and oppressive. I looked at him, but his eyes seemed unmoved and impassive. Eventually he nodded, as a sign for me to continue.

Though we had met a number of times before, clearly we had never met in such a difficult and stressful situation as this. Moore was suspected of killing a man on a beach by stabbing him, and though the allegations were of the utmost seriousness, Moore seemed dispassionate – even nonchalant – about the situation. Most of my clients, even the ones who had been accused of very serious crimes, would be pacing about the interview room in a frenzy of alarm and confusion after being told that they were being suspected of murder, rape or manslaughter. But that was not Peter Moore. He didn't display any sign of nervousness or distress, but responded calmly to the allegations put to him as if, somehow, they were not shocking to him. He appeared to think about my advice and deliberate his options before saying or doing anything. Some clients would be reeling in a state of bewilderment and astonishment, but I noticed from the beginning that Moore did not respond in that way.

I asked if he was ready for the interview. I had been told that there would be two officers interviewing: DC Dave Morris and DS Mike Guthrie. I knew both as very experienced officers, calm and meticulous in an interview situation. There is none of this good cop, bad cop stuff in reality – what you see on the TV screen is not actually a fair representation of most police interviews.

I have a friend who is a doctor, who says that he can't watch any medical TV drama because the whole thing is normally so divorced from the reality of medical practice that it becomes too irritating to watch. For me, the same thing is true when I watch any TV show or film involving a police investigation, or a courtroom drama. There are usually so many mistakes that for someone who has worked in that environment for any length of time, it makes the whole show unwatchable. It's unlikely an accused person will be faced in interview with two clichéd cops, one nasty bull-faced thug and another timid nice guy: that's not how things work in reality. Police officers wish to get at the truth and it's unlikely that the best way of doing so is trying to be clever or bullying the client into submission.

I would always make a habit of advising my clients before they were to be interviewed in the police station, 'If you don't understand a question asked by the police officer, then tell them you don't understand. Never attempt to answer a question that you don't fully understand – that's when problems begin. If you feel intimidated or scared then tell me and we can have a break for you to calm down and collect your thoughts.'

This isn't a case of pandering to the accused and going soft on them in some way. It's being reasonable, fair and just, and by doing this the police have a better opportunity to get what they want and the accused is treated in a decent, humane manner.

It was a simple and clear piece of advice, which the majority of my clients over the years chose to follow. There were a few characters, of course, who chose not to heed such guidance. Invariably their interviews ended up being car crashes in which they would try to be clever and make a complete mess of things.

Most readers will be familiar with the 'No comment' interview, where the accused is interviewed simply replies 'No comment' to all the questions asked by the interviewing officers, sometimes even when asked for their name or address. This approach can and must be used as a legitimate tactic during a police interview on occasions. Every accused and arrested person is reminded by the police caution that no one has to say anything unless they wish to do so. They have the right to remain totally silent or to say 'No comment' to everything that is asked of them. The responsibility is upon the police, and the prosecution when the matter gets to court, to prove their case 'beyond all reasonable doubt'. But there is a second part to the police caution which some defendants and occasionally lawyers forget. It goes on to state that it may harm a defendant's defence if they don't mention after they have been cautioned something that they later try to rely upon as their defence in court. In other words, when an accused person is arrested and questioned by the police, that is the moment at which they have their opportunity to put forward their defence, reason or alibi. If they fail to do so but give a defence later when they come to trial, the Judge could quite legitimately direct the jury to take it with a pinch of salt and invite them to seriously question whether it's true. This does put some pressure on the accused: they do have a right to remain silent or simply say 'No comment', but that right is limited by the possible assumptions a court could make as a result of them choosing not to speak out when they had the opportunity to do so.

Some criminal lawyers choose to play fast and loose with this right of silence. 'Just say "No comment" to everything, and we'll sort it out later,' they tell their clients. Many would not even discuss much about the circumstances of their client's arrest; they would instruct them to stay silent whatever the case. I suppose most of their clients are repeat offenders and regular customers of the police and know the ropes better than their legal advisors. There are some who have quite boldly told me, before I advise them of anything, 'I'll just go "No comment", yeh?' I would still advise them of their rights and obligations and the implications of giving a 'No comment' interview, but they don't always take that advice. You can lead a horse to water but you can't necessarily make it drink.

Peter Moore was not that type of client. He listened attentively, and though he was quiet, it seemed clear to me that he understood the predicament in which he found himself and was happy, following our discussion, to proceed with the police interview.

There was a knock on the interview room door and DI Ackerley, who was leading the investigation, appeared, wanting a further word with me. I went out into the corridor to speak with him.

'Just thought I would let you know at this stage that we are now arranging, as we speak, to search Mr Moore's home in Kinmel Bay – Darlington House. We have reason to believe that there may be items there relating to the alleged offence.' This reason is usually used in order to search for a weapon or maybe items stolen from the victim, or anything else that could be linked to the offence. I asked DI Ackerley what he was looking for.

'A weapon? A knife? Evidence of blood following the murder.' He was quite candid.

'Have you done a forensic check of the van?' I asked.

'It's being done now,' he replied. I said that I would need some time to explain this development to Moore and discuss it with him before the interview started. Clearly there could well be some implications to his house and van being searched and it would be necessary for him to know what might transpire from that.

I returned to the interview room. Moore was unmoved when I explained that the police were about to go and search his home.

'That's fine,' he said. I went on to explain about the forensic check being done on his van and again Moore seemed at ease with what was going on. There was no panic or concern; it was as if everything was happening somehow as he had expected. As if it was an old film, playing in front of him – a film that he'd seen a hundred times before and whose plot he knew in detail. Nothing seemed to surprise him.

'Are you still happy to go ahead with the interview, Mr Moore?' I asked him.

'Of course,' he replied in a content, self-assured way.

I left the interview room and indicated to the Custody Sergeant that Mr Moore was ready for interview. Within a few moments I was back in the interview room with both interviewing officers, DC Morris and DS Guthrie. There were a few informal moments of small talk as we made ourselves comfortable and the required three tapes were placed in the tape recorder. Then the interview commenced.

Chapter 3

THE INTERVIEW ROOM at Llandudno Police Station was small and stuffy and not a place in which anyone would choose to spend much time. On a rectangular dark brown wooden table was a tape recorder and there were two microphones attached to the walls which were connected to the machine. Peter Moore sat on one side of the table and I sat next to him, with a notebook on my lap in readiness to make my own notes of what was said during the interview. I would receive a copy of the interview tapes in time but making my own notes helped me focus on the interview and allowed me to refer back to questions asked or answers given during the interview, if that became necessary.

On the other side of the table sat the two police officers, Morris and Guthrie, both with notebooks and paperwork in front of them. DC Dave Morris appeared to be in his thirties and was tall with ginger hair and a light complexion. DS Guthrie was more thickset with dark receding hair, and maybe in his forties. They appeared nervous, checking and rechecking the tapes and shuffling papers they had removed from a file. This was a big moment for them: a murder case on their patch and they were the officers chosen to conduct the interview. Every detail needed to be correct, every procedure followed. There were a few moments of throat clearing, adjusting chairs and sitting positions, and then the tape recorder was switched on.

The machine starts with an introductory buzz which lasts for about ten seconds, though sometimes that ten seconds feels much longer. It's that moment of anticipation, nervousness and uncertainty. How will the police approach this matter?

How will the client respond? How will the interview begin? After all, Moore had been calm and measured in everything that he had done and said, but there was no certainty that this would continue – I had no idea how he would react if put under pressure. DC Morris began with the introductions, explaining who he and his colleague were, how they would conduct the interview, what rights Moore had as an interviewee and then a document was handed to him which set out those rights in writing. Moore handed the document to me with a polite smile. DC Morris went on to caution Moore again and asked him whether he understood what the caution meant. Moore said that he did understand and looked at me again for some kind of assurance. This was the first moment of uneasiness I had noticed from Moore: it was as if he wanted to ensure that everything he said was with my approval.

Moore sat by the table with his hands placed on his knees. I noticed that he was sitting straight-backed and other than the flicker of uncertainty he had displayed when being cautioned, he looked directly at DC Morris. He had a pronounced jaw and a long chin, with narrow lips which were fixed shut.

'Mr Moore,' began DC Morris, 'do you understand why you have been arrested today?'

I always found this a rather feeble way of beginning any police interview. It was as if the police office was saying, 'Go on then, you do my job for me, admit to everything.' It became clear though, that Moore would not be taken in by such a simplistic approach.

'I think you'd better explain to me,' was his reply.

A police interview is by its nature a totally artificial process. The police must follow guidelines and procedures set out for them in the Police and Criminal Evidence Act 1984 – they can't just decide to ask questions at any time, anywhere and in any way: there are clear and accepted procedures for everything. Nonetheless, the formality of the process sometimes distracts from the asking and answering of questions. Sometimes banal questions are asked with the intention of lulling the accused person into a false sense of security and safety – some officers begin with a friendly chit-chat as if they're friends having a discussion over a pint in the pub, using first names ('Peter? It's OK if I call you Peter?'). It's as if the conversation is the most natural thing in the world. But of course, we all know as we sit there in the interview room that the whole process is far from being natural.

I would tell my clients to be very careful in an interview. They would be told not to try to beat these expert inquisitors at their own game by trying to be clever, nor to get into some kind of interrogation one-upmanship. I have witnessed some accused individuals attempt this approach, despite my advice. It usually ends up in tears and an appearance in court, and most likely a conviction. A police interview is therefore not an ordinary conversation, despite some police officers' attempts to make it appear as one. These interviews will be dissected into minute pieces, with every word, phrase and inference being tested and interpreted. They will be analysed by the police, the Crown Prosecution Service, solicitors and barristers, and of course the Judge and the twelve members of a jury during a court hearing. It's no wonder some defendants simply say 'No comment' – it would appear to be the easiest and maybe the safest option.

It was surprising how calm Peter Moore appeared as he faced such a stressful situation, a situation which causes many to crumble and capitulate. That didn't appear to be in his nature: he sat calmly as both detectives shuffled through papers and notes at the beginning of the interview. DC Dave Morris then described what the police suspected had happened at Pensarn beach near Abergele during the late evening of 17 December or the early hours of the following morning. He described the victim as being an Anthony Davies, a family man in his late thirties, and explained that Davies had left his home in Llanddulas around 11 p.m. on the evening of 17 December, telling his wife that he was going to visit his aunt, who had just returned home from hospital. It appears that what Anthony Davies actually did was to go to Pensarn beach, where he was stabbed six times in the abdomen and left for dead at the water's edge. His body was discovered the following morning. The information given was consistent with what I had been told earlier, though I was unaware that the victim had been stabbed six times. Mr Moore nodded as if to acknowledge the information given to him, but said nothing.

I made a note in my notebook that there was no response from my client. I also noted that the 'victim had been stabbed 6 times'. My notes seem to emphasise that number '6': it appears that I retraced the writing of that number many times in my notebook most likely because I was dwelling on the actual number of stab wounds. Stabbing someone six times did not seem to me to be accidental, nor an act done in the heat of the moment or during an argument which got out of control. Stabbing someone that many times in the abdomen seemed to me to have been an indication of a more frenzied attack of an uncontrolled nature. I thought that an attack with a knife in the heat of the moment would likely result in one or two stabs before the assailant realised what he was doing. But this was six stabs. This worried me. It appeared, from the description given by DC Morris, that this was an uncontrolled attack of some viciousness. In my mind I was beginning to discount this death being an accident, and started to feel that it may have had a more sinister motivation.

I had heard local gossip in Abergele that the beach in Pensarn was a pick-up spot for homosexuals. I wasn't aware of any offences or incidents which had occurred there at any time in the recent past and had put the gossip down to idle chit-chat, which may have had some foundation in truth. Neither was I aware at that stage of Moore's sexual orientation or proclivities. In our few appointments at my office, I had concluded that he had a slightly effeminate tone of voice but didn't know whether he was gay or not. I knew he wasn't married and that until his mother's death he had lived with her, but that was clearly not an indicator of him being gay.

Neither did I know anything of the background and circumstances of the victim, Anthony Davies. I knew he was from Llanddulas, which is a village only five miles or so from Abergele. It had been explained to me by the police that he had been reported missing in the early hours of 18 December by his wife. What I didn't know was whether Davies was really gay or bisexual and had gone to the beach with a view to meeting other gay people, or whether he was simply going for a late-night bit of fresh air. He was clearly married, but he wouldn't have been the first or the last to have sadly lived a life of lies and deception in this respect.

I concluded that the victim could have been gay and that possibly if Moore – as I suspected – was also gay, they could have known each other, even been in a relationship or met regularly at Pensarn beach. On the other hand, they may have both been at the beach and coincidentally met, having not met before. Maybe things then went wrong somehow: perhaps there had been an argument or a misunderstanding, and Davies was killed. I was unsure whether this was plausible, but it had to be considered as an option. I remained concerned, though, that the number of stab wounds the victim had suffered seemed to suggest something else may have happened. There was no certainty during this interview that Moore was involved, so the theories put forward by the police and considered by myself could still have been mere assumptions.

It's also important to remember that this occurred over 25 years ago. We are familiar nowadays with hearing about knife attacks in UK cities, and even more locally in north Wales. A stabbing seems so common that it hardly makes the news these days, but 25 years ago, a stabbing – though not unheard of – was still an unusual occurrence, particularly in north Wales. People didn't carry knives, so they were less likely to be used as part of an assault. As a consequence, there were elements of this incident which, even in the early days of the investigation, appeared unusual, strange and unnerving.

Peter Moore answered the questions asked of him patiently and calmly. There seemed to be no hesitation or confusion on his part. He denied being on Pensarn beach that evening; he denied approaching or speaking with anyone, Anthony Davies included; it wasn't his van at the scene; it was nothing to do with him. Sometimes during an interview, one will notice a chink in the client's armour. A mistake that has been made, an incorrect statement that exposes the suspect to a line of questioning which leads to an eventual admission. But this was not the case with Peter Moore: he was calm and assured and, at the end of the interview, little progress had been made.

'I think we should have a cup of tea,' said DC Morris, and we all agreed. This gave me an opportunity to discuss things further with my client and also to discover whether there were any further developments in the investigation. The door of the interview was opened and a rush of air, fresher than the stale air of the interview room, rushed in. The corridor outside the room was busy, a few police officers rushed by and within seconds the Custody Sergeant appeared, with the intention of leading Moore back into a holding cell next to the Custody Sergeant's desk.

'Are you alright, Peter?' asked the Custody Sergeant.

'Yes, but I wouldn't mind a bit of fresh air if possible,' Moore replied.

'Give me a minute and I'll put you in the outside yard when the chap who's there has finished his smoke.' Moore nodded and sat in the holding cell.

'A word, Mr Jones?' said the Custody Sergeant as he locked the holding cell door.

The holding cell was a bare room with wooden benches attached to the walls on the left and right of the room. The front wall of the room was made of toughened glass and so was the door, allowing the Custody Sergeant to keep an eye on the room and its occupants. Moore sat on one of the benches and the door was closed.

'I just wanted a word with you to let you know that we may have to wait for a while to restart the interview with your client. DI Ackerley has just called to tell me that they are searching Moore's van and house at this very moment and that he may want to brief the interviewing officers about this before interviewing again.'

I was unsure whether this was ominous or not. If the search was to reveal any evidence, then it was likely to be put to Mr Moore during an interview and he would need to be able to account for it.

Moore was led into the exercise area for a bit of fresh air and I followed him. The air wasn't particularly fresh as it remained thick with the cigarette smoke of the previous occupant. It was still raining, and we went to stand at the far end of the exercise area, where a roof overhang allowed some shelter. We stood for a few moments side by side, sheltering and staring at nothing in particular. The exercise area was simply a small featureless, grey-walled courtyard between police buildings, and about three metres above was a ceiling of steel mesh which gave the whole area the feeling of being in a cage. Cigarette butts and flattened chewing gum littered the floor.

'I have to ask you, Mr Moore,' I said, breaking the silence. 'You will know that the police are searching your house and van at the moment. Is there anything we should be concerned about?'

'No, nothing,' he replied. He then looked at me and shook his head – it was a look of certainty and conviction.

'You realise that I have to ask these questions.' I felt it necessary, for some reason, to explain the reason for my question, so that he realised that I wasn't challenging his honesty but doing my job and covering everything I needed to cover as thoroughly as I could.

'Of course, Mr Jones,' was Moore's reply. 'You need to do your job, I understand that.' He seemed calm, as if he'd been in similar situations before; as if he understood exactly what was going on and what would be happening next. There was a self-assurance, even a confidence that I hadn't encountered in many of my clients. Usually suspects who have been arrested and are in the police station are either intoxicated, unpleasant and threatening to all including their legal advisor, or totally petrified and unable even to speak or move properly in their heightened state of anxiety. You will have some who turn to violence: I recall seeing one person who, having been arrested and placed in a holding cell, had been banging his head against the steel prison door for two hours by the time I arrived at the police station to advise him. There was blood everywhere and an enormous gash in the middle of his forehead which required an immediate visit to A & E. You have others who feign illness, rolling around their cell with a stomach-ache which has come about within seconds of arrival at the police station or demanding a visit from a doctor to get them to prescribe some urgently required medication. And then you have the shouters, those individuals who decide to bang or kick the cell door for hours on end and shout abuse at the Custody Sergeant to try and attract their attention, usually unsuccessfully.

Peter Moore didn't fall into any of these categories. He was calm, collected and took the whole process in his stride, or that was the impression he gave. It was as if he had been through the experience before, though he told me he had not. We remained in silence until the door opened. I was given a mug of tea and Moore was led into the holding room once again, having refused tea himself.

It was nearly 5 o' clock on the custody suite clock – the afternoon had flown by. It was easy to lose track of time in the dark underworld of police custody. Prisoners would go by, shifts would start and finish in a constant conveyor belt of suspects, solicitors and police officers. I had taken a seat in the office behind the custody desk, drinking my tea and contemplating my situation. Police officers went in and out of the office, passing the time of day or sharing a joke or observation.

'Are you with the murder suspect?' they would ask.

'Yes.'

'Oh, good luck then,' they would laugh as they left. I seemed to be the subject of discussion and some amusement within the North Wales Constabulary – was there something I didn't know, or was it perhaps a nervous laugh? Was it possible that I was becoming something of a celebrity within the police station?

'You know, the guy who's representing that murderer. I saw him having a cup of tea just now.'

I thought of calling my wife to let her know what was going on, but at that moment, as I sat in the custody office, I had little idea what actually was going on outside the doors of the custody suite. What further investigations were being carried out? What had the police discovered in Peter Moore's house? How long would I be waiting for the next interviews to begin? There were so many questions, and the calmest individual in the police station seemed to be Peter Moore. As he sat in the holding area alone, seemingly staring at the opposite wall, what did he make of all this?

Chapter 4

'IT'S GOING TO be a while – to be honest, I've no idea when I'll be home.' It wasn't unusual for my wife to receive a call from the police station from me to that effect. She knew by now that the wheels of the law turned slowly and that I relied on others to progress matters. If I was told that I would be waiting half an hour it was likely to be an hour and a half, if I was told two hours, then I might as well make myself comfortable. Criminal lawyers are used to waiting: we wait in the police station, we wait to see our clients in prison, we wait in court for the case to be called. It's a waiting game. Our families know that it's part of our daily lives and so do our colleagues and office staff. 'Sorry, Mr Jones is not available: he's in court at the moment and we don't know when he'll be back' is pretty much the standard answer given by secretaries and receptionists at criminal law practices across the country. Waiting will invariably be followed by periods of frantic and challenging work, and it may be necessary to move from zero to full-on lawyer mode in a matter of minutes, if not seconds.

As I pondered and waited, DC Dave Morris walked into the custody suite. I heard him say, 'Is Mr Jones about?' The Custody Sergeant pointed towards his office as I got up to respond to the call.

'No, no, Mr Jones, you stay there,' Morris said. 'We'll talk in the office.'

We exchanged pleasantries for a few moments and shared a few nervous jokes. It would have been clear to anyone looking at us that we were both on edge, both concerned not to make a mistake – maybe we were both in uncharted waters?

'So, a few developments I thought we should discuss at this stage.' Morris had a large writing pad full of notes in front of him, a pen in his right hand and as he spoke, he began to tick off sections from the pad. He seemed focused on getting all the information he needed to convey across to me as quickly as possible. His face became redder as he spoke, his hands nervously moving from one section to another on the writing pad. I in turn made a note of everything that was said to me. I needed to convey this information to Moore in as complete a form as possible: what the police told me could affect the instructions I received from Moore and as a consequence the advice I then gave to him.

I was told by Morris that near the body on the beach in Pensarn the police had discovered a splash of blood. It might be the victim's, but there was a possibility that it could be Moore's. Morris explained that they were aware of Moore having an injury to his right hand, on the palm between his thumb and his index finger. This had been noted on the custody record on Moore's arrival at the police station. Morris requested that the injury be inspected further by a doctor, and they would be letting me know when they required samples from Moore to discount the blood on the beach as being his.

Clearly this evidence had great significance. Moore denied being on the beach that evening and he and I hadn't as yet discussed the cause of his hand injury – in light of the discovery of the blood spatter, that was now a discussion we needed to have. Moore would need to account for his injury and also I needed to ensure that he realised that if proven to be his, the blood spatter would place him on that beach, not necessarily at the time of the murder, but sometime within the recent past. In that case, he would need to explain how it had got there.

But there was more from DC Morris. I had been previously informed by the Custody Sergeant that the police were in the process of searching Moore's house in Kinmel Bay. In the past Kinmel Bay, with its caravan and holiday parks and its sprawl of small bungalows mostly occupied by retirees from the north-west of England, had relied – like a parasite – on the success of its larger and more well-known host Rhyl. Over recent decades the fortunes of Rhyl had dwindled and as a consequence so had Kinmel Bay, its bungalows now more dishevelled and its shops less prosperous.

Darlington House, the house that had belonged to the Moore family and in which Peter Moore still lived, was somewhat unusual for Kinmel Bay. It clearly had a name which conveyed an air of respectability and importance within the area. Ending the name of your property with 'House' gives it a grandeur and status. In north Wales and many other areas, this is often the habit with commercial buildings housing insurance brokers', lawyers' or accountants' offices: you will find a 'London House', 'Birmingham House' or 'Liverpool House' in many a town in the locality. Often these names are used because of past commercial connections with those towns. 'Darlington House', though, is rarer – my search for a Darlington House in north Wales reveals only one place with such a name: the one in Kinmel Bay, Rhyl. Now that name is forever linked to the name of Peter Howard Moore.

Darlington House was a large grey building on the right before the railway bridge as you drove out of Kinmel Bay along St Asaph Avenue. Initially, I could never really make out if it was a house or a commercial building of some sorts. By the time of Moore's arrest, it appeared mostly unused. The building looked tired and uncared for, the grey paint peeling off the frontage in great swathes as if it was shedding its skin, and the front door, at the corner of the building facing the main road, seemed not to have been opened for years. Rubbish had collected in the doorway and weeds grew between the bottom of the building and the pavement surrounding it. Until I was required to visit Darlington House following Moore being charged, I hadn't realised that it was a fairly large building with about half of it being used for storage and the other half – mainly the rear of the building – as living accommodation. It seemed that the furniture and fixtures in the living area had remained the same for years – maybe things hadn't changed much since the 1950s, when Moore and his parents moved into the house.

DC Morris began to explain what had been revealed during the search at Peter Moore's home. What he said led me to imagine that the walls of Darlington House held sinister and disturbing secrets which were only now going to be revealed.

'You see, Mr Jones, during our initial search of Mr Moore's house, we have come up with a few things which are of concern. There is a knife: it's a large knife, maybe a hunting-type knife, which has some blood traces on it and, clearly, we will need that checked. We will be asking Mr Moore about that knife. Also, we have found a police uniform in the house – it looks like a genuine North Wales Police uniform – and a police helmet and a truncheon as well. Clearly that is of some concern to us. And then we have items of what we would call 'Nazi memorabilia', including a Nazi flag. The search is ongoing, so I'm sure there will be further for us to discuss in time.'

The list of items found were both sinister and strange. There were clearly questions which Moore needed to be asked. It seemed clear to me that the police were making a connection between the attack and the possession of these items, so what I needed from Moore was some explanation as to why he had some of these items in his possession. Of particular concern was the North Wales Police uniform. Clearly the police were worried about how he had he got his hands on this genuine police uniform, and what it was being used for. And of course, the knife: where had he got that from? What had he used it for? It was not illegal to possess some of these items, of course, but it was clear that the police were becoming increasingly suspicious of Moore. I confirmed to DC Morris that I would speak with my client about these discoveries and that once I'd had an opportunity to do so, I assumed Moore would be ready for a further interview.

I went into the holding room where Moore was still sitting and explained to him the current situation and findings following the initial search of his home. He listened intently, seemingly taking in all the facts I had been given by the police. He nodded a few times but said nothing. His eyes looked tired and he clasped and unclasped his hands a number of times as I spoke, as if he was preparing to undertake some manual task.

'But this proves nothing,' Moore said. His voice was clear and unemotional as if, while I was speaking to him, he had thought about every possible scenario and was confident that nothing would implicate him in the murder.

'Well they will want an explanation for why you have the knife, and in particular the police uniform. It goes without saying that they are concerned about that, as they are about everything else.' Moore nodded again,

'I will try and think where I got them from.' His answers again were calm and measured. Maybe he had rehearsed these situations in his mind before, preparing for this – or of course, maybe there was an innocent explanation.

As we finished the discussion, a cup of tea and a meal (which appeared to be from a takeaway somewhere in Llandudno) arrived, courtesy of the Custody Sergeant.

'Come on Peter, teatime,' said the Sergeant in his usual jovial tone. I left Moore to eat his meal and contemplate his future as I returned to the custody back-office with a cup of tea.

I was kept waiting for a long time. The evening seemed to be passing by and every time the office door or the door to the custody area opened, I expected the arrival of someone involved in the investigation. I was left mostly to my own thoughts, though. The information I had been given by the police that afternoon pointed to Peter Moore having been involved in something; whether that was criminal activity or something else which was hidden and unexplained, I couldn't be sure. It appeared to me that his sexuality might be an issue and if so, questions would inevitably be raised as to whether the activities he was involved in were known to those within the gay community in the area or further afield. Then the question was whether these activities where legal or not, whether Moore was involved in something criminal with his police uniform and his knife and the other items discovered in his house. I began to wonder as I sat waiting whether we had somehow discovered a strange underworld in which Moore was involved, which was possibly linked to the murder.

This was a world with which I was totally unfamiliar. A part of society seemed still to be hidden away from mainstream life, despite changes in the law after the Sexual Offences Act 1967, which decriminalised homosexual acts between consenting adults. It was a world which remained hidden in rural Wales, as in many other areas of the UK at that time. My understanding was that at that time, gay people would gravitate towards the larger cities of the north-west of England – in particular Liverpool and Manchester – where they were less stigmatised and could live their lives as they chose.

As a lawyer and an inhabitant of Abergele I had heard that gay people and others would choose to casually meet in dark car parks such as the beach car park in Pensarn. Prosecutions for soliciting and indecent behaviour would sometimes appear in the local courts following what would be described as 'lewd conduct' in the dark corners of these parking areas or lay-bys. We were aware that things went on in these places, but other than a few lines in the local newspaper the *Daily Post* after a court case, little thought was even given to it.

It seemed to me that from the first day of being involved in the Peter Moore case, there were issues which made it anything but straightforward. As I waited for the next interview to begin, it was becoming clear to me that this underworld of which most lawyers and police officers were aware but to which, in the past, they had paid little if any attention, might now be about to be exposed in an unprecedented way. This was not the world of gay people who wanted to live their lives openly and honestly in a community which accepted and valued them, but seemed to be something else: a hidden, clandestine group of people who operated in the shadows and appeared to thrive and feed their desires in that world. A hinterland where people would choose not to adhere to the usual conventions and conduct.

It is sometimes challenging to accept that not everyone lives their lives in the way we and our circle of friends and family choose to do. I suppose we tend to believe that everyone judges the world through very similar perspectives to our own, sharing similar values and standards with us. On the face of it, this view can appear a very arrogant and patronising one. My roots were deep in chapel and Sunday School non-conformist Wales, where even living together out of wedlock was seen as an abomination in the 1960s and 1970s. To some, homosexuality was either unknown or totally misunderstood, as if it was some kind of lifestyle choice made by 'perverted' individuals. Despite this, many of the chapel people would accept some of the congregation such as the two prominent women who had lived together for years, presumably as partners, with no questions asked. It was a strange duality, which would usually lead to suspicion, misconceptions and unfairness and require people to live hidden existences, secreting the truth from everyone they knew.

It seemed to me that the Peter Moore case brought with it a different truth – a truth that, though concealed from the outside world, was a reality to some within our community in north Wales. It appeared a reality which, when revealed, would divulge something disturbing and dark, something which was far less about the choices people make in their lives but rather the things that happen which leave them with no such choices. This, after all, was a case of murder: a man on a beach, stabbed to death.

Chapter 5

IT BECAME CLEAR sometime during the late evening that the police would not be ready to conduct further interviews that day. It seemed that investigations were continuing, and I supposed that the search of Moore's house had been more revealing than I had originally anticipated, or had perhaps led to other lines of enquiry. After a conversation with the Custody Sergeant and a discussion with Moore explaining the situation, I left the custody suite and emerged into a freezing cold night. I took a deep breath, relieved to be out of the stuffy confines of custody. It was good to be outside, with a cold breeze direct from the Irish sea catching my face. I walked slowly to my car as if the whole day had sapped all my energy, leaving me drained. It was nearly 10 o'clock and as I reached my car, I called my wife to tell her I was on my way home.

'Are you OK?' she asked. 'This case has been on every news bulletin – it sounds big.'

'I think it will be,' was my reply. 'I'm knackered.'

After a warning from Catherine to take care on my way home, I rang off and sat in the car for a moment. What a day it had been. I reflected on everything that had happened. The day's conversations and interviews played back in my mind, every word and intonation seemed, as I considered them, to have so many different meanings. Had I understood things properly? Had I responded in the correct way? Had my advice to the client been correct and clear? Did Moore understand what was going on, and was I handling things in the best way possible? I couldn't possibly answer these questions – I had to trust myself, my skills, knowledge and experience and be confident that I was handling things well. I felt a weight of responsibility that evening that I hadn't ever felt before as a lawyer. To a great extent, it's similar to the responsibility felt by any professional person who's trained and prepared for a particular event, which has finally become a reality and it's now time to deliver. I realised even then that I was amongst the few lawyers in north Wales to represent someone accused of a murder, and that every criminal lawyer worth their salt would have wanted that opportunity.

I arrived home to a wife excitedly full of questions, and even though it was late and I was exhausted, we sat together and discussed the implications of what I could be facing if the case against Moore was to result in him being charged. I knew even then that if Moore was charged with murdering Anthony Davies on Pensarn beach, it was likely to be a difficult and challenging case – and being only a few days before Christmas, it was possible that the plans we had made for a family Christmas would change substantially.

The following morning, I was in the office early. It was very possible that I would spend the whole day at the police station, and I needed to ensure that all my other cases were in hand before I left for Llandudno.

My staff arrived at around 8.30 a.m. and instructions were given out, together with explanations as to why I anticipated being out for most of the day. The staff were intrigued by what was happening: they had seen the TV news and also the front page of the local newspaper, both full of the story of Peter Moore's arrest, and knew that it was this case which had kept me out of the office the previous day . Most of them were also acquainted with Peter Moore, having spoken with him on a number of occasions, and this made the whole thing more surprising and also more disturbing. Everybody wanted to know what was happening, what Peter Moore had actually done, and how he was coping and conducting himself at the police station. At that time there was little I could add to the information which my staff had already received from the news, but that didn't prevent them from asking questions.

I decided I would return to the police station by about 9.30 a.m. On the way I called my business partner's office, which was some 17 miles away from mine in a nearby town. I spoke with one of the trainee solicitors there and explained what had been going on. I had thought that my business partner would contact his office sometime before the Christmas break from his holiday on some tropical island or other, and would want to know about the case and my involvement. He hadn't got in touch and the trainee said it was unlikely he would before the Christmas holidays – as it turned out, I heard nothing from him until he came home some weeks later. I realised that as far as dealing with this case was concerned, I was on my own. It was up to me, and maybe it was better that way.

Arriving at the police station, it was clear that things were not the same as usual. A small gaggle of local news journalists had encamped by the front door, which seemed a bit strange as the entrance to the custody area was towards the back of the building. I noticed a few familiar faces amongst them: journalists who would spend most of their times in local Magistrates' Courts, sweeping up stories about burglars, drunks and speeding drivers. This was an enormous story for them. They had just had the Sophie Hook case a few months earlier, and so to get another murder story in such a short period of time would have been beyond their wildest journalistic dreams. One of the journalists I knew saw me as I walked from my car towards the rear of the building.

'Hi Dylan, do you know anything about the murder case?'

I pretended I couldn't hear the question and walked on. I thought that it would be better that way, as to do otherwise and begin making some sort of comment could be detrimental to the case and might result in my office being inundated with telephone enquiries. Better to feign deafness and carry on at speed towards the door of the custody suite, I thought. I pressed the buzzer on the door and got an immediate response to enter. The metal door banged behind me – shutting out a couple of journalists who had come after me, still asking questions – and I was welcomed by the commotion of the Llandudno custody suite. Police officers were milling around and numerous conversations were taking place at the same time. I spotted a few detainees in the holding room looking dejected and bedraggled, and another tracksuited youth stood by the custody desk, shoeless and looking as if he'd been up all night. Equally tired-looking was his solicitor, a familiar if totally exhausted and crestfallen colleague from the local courts, who looked over to me and gave a despondent smile.

'Been here all night?' I mouthed to him. He just shook his head and looked at his client. No words were needed – I knew how he felt. It's the unseen part of a criminal lawyer's work: getting up in the small hours and trying to reason with some drunk or drugged-up individual about their senseless violence or ridiculous behaviour. Sometimes it's difficult not to blurt out, 'You total idiot, why do you think behaving in this way is acceptable? Grow up, you moron.' It's more likely you will say, 'Right John, so you're in a little bother here. What have you been up to? Was it someone else's fault? Of course, so let's see if we can have a chat with the police officer.'

I waited patiently until I could catch the eye of one of the police officers and ask if I could see my client for a quick chat. I wanted to ensure that Moore was fine after a night in the cells and that nothing had changed from our conversation the previous evening. Though I had no further information from the investigation team at that time, it was important – on a human level, if nothing else – to ensure that my client was fit and well. I was led to his cell, and as the door was opened, I could see that Moore had been given a change of clothes and was now wearing the police-issue grey sweatshirt and sweatpants and a pair of greying white socks. A pair of blue flip-flops had been placed by the bed.

As I entered the cell, Moore got up again to shake my hand. I urged him to sit on his bed and as he did, I asked him if he'd had breakfast and been given some toiletries to shower and shave if he wanted. He confirmed he was fine. He asked if I had spoken further with the police about the case and I confirmed that I planned to do so and then speak to him again before any further interviews. I explained that my intention was to discover what the police were intending to do next, whether there were any developments after the search of the house and additionally if they were now able to provide me with information regarding the forensic examination undertaken at the beach in Pensarn. Moore seemed content with what was to be done and as I left the cell, I assured him I would return with further information.

I was surprised by how calm Moore appeared: he wasn't panicking and didn't appear stressed, worried or concerned at all about his situation.

'Maybe this was a massive mistake, maybe Moore was simply in the wrong place at the wrong time?' I thought. Wasn't it just totally inconceivable that someone who had committed a murder would sit in a police cell a few days later, serenely perched on the cell bed, sipping from a plastic teacup? The composure of this man was surprising – he seemed to be calmer than me. My brain was racing at a hundred miles an hour and though I attempted outwardly to appear to be the measure of professionalism, I actually felt that I was in uncharted territory and that as a result I was making things up as I went along, juggling plates and awaiting the inevitability of them beginning to crash to the floor all around me.

As I left the cell and returned to the main custody area, I spotted DC Dave Morris appearing from the offices in the police station.

'Dave – a word, if possible?' I asked and pointed to a quiet corner in the custody suite. 'What's the situation? I need some information so I can advise my client properly – are there any meaningful developments that I need to know about?' Dave looked at me and hesitated, as if he had something to say but had been told not to tell me, it intrigued me and I urged him on, explaining that I needed as much information as possible about the allegations against my client.

'I think you'd better have a word with Detective Superintendent Eric Jones. He's heading some aspects of this, and I think he's the man in the know!' I got the feeling that Dave was 'in the know' as well and that a chat with Eric Jones would be necessary as soon as possible. It was explained to me that DSI Eric Jones was expected over from Bangor soon and Dave promised to ask if he could come and speak with me upon his arrival.

This conversation with Dave was intriguing. I felt that there was something going on behind the scenes, and that strict instructions had been given that I wasn't to be told about it. It appeared to me that there had been some developments which affected the case and that DSI Jones was involved in those before coming over to Llandudno.

My approach with the police was always to play with a 'straight bat'. I would avoid trying to be 'clever' or to 'trick' them during their investigation. It was always my belief that if I played fair with them, they would equally treat me and – more importantly – my client fairly, and this would result in a reasonable and just conclusion. This didn't always happen, but I would always point out to my clients that if we were all civil to each other, at least this would make the process easier to endure, even if we didn't agree with everything that was happening. In the end, the final decision would rest with the courts and the jury.

In this respect I had decided to approach the Peter Moore case the same way as any other: I would be as honest and open as I could be with the police, and I expected this to be reciprocated. Information was the key in this case as it was in any other, and I was determined to get as much of it as I could, so as to present my client with the best advice and the clearest of choices.

I was offered a mug of tea by one of the officers.

'White, no sugar, isn't it, Mr Jones?' said the officer as he handed me the mug. As a regular, they knew how I took my tea by now.

I waited expectantly for some time, idly observing the constant conveyor belt of police officers and criminals arriving. Some hoodlums were complaining and protesting their innocence, and others struggled against burly officers as they aggressively threatened all in their path.

Eventually, after what seemed like hours, DSI Eric Jones arrived. I knew him from previous cases – he was known for leading the investigation into the murder of Sophie Hook in Llandudno about six months before and brought many years of experience and knowledge to the investigation. I knew he would be thorough, but also fair, and I was confident that even at this early stage in the investigation of the Anthony Davies murder, I would be party to as much information as it was possible to give me.

I spotted Eric Jones entering the custody area from the main police station. He looked stern and perturbed. He fixed me with his eyes across the busy custody suite and nodded towards the office, mouthing 'Let's have a word' as he turned. I followed him into the office and he closed the door behind me. I got the sense that this was about to be a very serious conversation.

'Dylan, how's things?' He offered me a seat and went to sit at the side of the office desk.

'Well, I'll be better when I know what's going on.'

He smiled. 'Where do I start?' There was a feeling of an impending change in the atmosphere in this case, from serious to very serious and beyond.

'We feel we have substantial evidence against your client regarding the Anthony Davies murder. We can place his van at the scene and we may have some blood of his near the body, though we're still waiting for the results on that. Then there's the search of the house,' Jones added. It appeared that more was to be added to the list I'd already been given of items found at the house.

'So, Dylan, when detectives arrived yesterday at Mr Moore's house to execute a search warrant, they discovered a substantial assortment of sexual equipment, including rubber gags and handcuffs. There was a collection of Nazi flags and what appeared to be military uniforms, including two German-style military caps and a pair of long black leather boots.' He went on to describe the police helmet, truncheon and police sergeant's uniform also discovered in the house, as had been mentioned to me by DC Dave Morris the previous day.

'Interestingly,' DSI Eric Jones continued, 'on the sideboard we noticed that there were two copies of the *Daily Post* where an account of Anthony Davies' murder investigation was carried as the lead story.'

My opinion of what I'd heard so far was that there was nothing particularly shocking which directly linked Peter Moore to the murder on Pensarn beach. The fact that he was in possession of Nazi memorabilia and a police uniform was neither here or there in terms of the case and having a copy of a recent *Daily Post* was not surprising as many people in the area would have been shocked and surprised by the murder and would have wanted to read more about the investigation. But there was more to come from DSI Jones.

'You see, Dylan, we believe that this investigation needs to be expanded to consider wider options.' 'Wider options' sounded interesting – worrying, even.

'What exactly does "wider options" mean?' I asked.

'Other crimes, other murders. We must consider this as a possibility.'

I was aware that there remained two unsolved murders which had occurred on the island of Anglesey some months before. I had also heard that someone had been arrested for those murders in the recent past.

'Do you mean the Anglesey murders?' I asked.

'We have to keep an open mind on this,' was DSI Jones' reply. It wasn't a definitive response, but clearly the police had found or were looking for connections between the murders on Anglesey and the recent murder on Pensarn beach.

There were some things which occurred to me immediately on hearing this news. Firstly, as I had been representing Peter Moore for around two years and knew that he was having business and financial problems, I knew in some detail the extent of his business interests. I knew that the small cinemas in which he had some interest or other were spread over north Wales from Bagillt near Holywell in north-east Wales to Holyhead in the north-west of Anglesey. He lived in Kinmel Bay near Rhyl, and had told me that he would regularly travel across north Wales to visit his cinemas. What this suggested to me was that Moore was very likely to have been visiting Anglesey during the period in which the murders there had happened, on more or less a daily basis. That gave him ample opportunity, I supposed, to commit the murders.

There was one thing that did confuse me as I received this information from DSI Jones. I had been under the impression that someone had already been arrested for the Anglesey murders – it had been widely publicised in the news that someone had confessed. I asked Jones about this.

'Look, at the moment we have to keep an open mind. That's all I'm prepared to say.'

His response was short and to the point. I got the feeling that I may be on sensitive ground. Either the man in custody and linked to these two Anglesey murders was proving to be somewhat problematic, or alternatively evidence had been found in Moore's house suggesting he'd had something to do with these murders. The difficulty I had was knowing that someone had admitted to the murders already. I decided at this stage not to pursue the matter any further but made a note of my conversation with Eric Jones as I believed that it might have some significance in the future.

I needed to speak with Peter Moore again. I had to inform him of the developments and the likelihood that he was going to be questioned not only regarding the Pensarn murder but also the two murders in Anglesey. I wondered what his response would be to this revelation. He had been so calm and collected in his reaction to everything so far, and even though he'd looked tired when I'd seen him earlier in his cell, he still appeared tranquil and unperturbed by everything happening around him. I thought that maybe he had switched off his emotions completely and detached himself from the allegations that had been made about him – possibly that was his way of coping with stressful situations. I had no knowledge of Moore's past and it was possible that withdrawing into a state of disengagement was his natural instinct.

Clearly things were getting serious: the stakes were already high, and the police were now making links with another two murders. Sometimes a criminal lawyer will begin to suspect the police of becoming involved in some kind of 'fishing expedition', making a trawl of unsolved crimes in the hope that they may be able to clear up those offences and pin them on the suspect. This didn't appear to me to be one of those instances. I dwelt on the situation, concerned about what would develop following the most recent revelations. What if these new allegations against Moore were true? If he had killed three people, then what exactly was I dealing with here? Was Moore some kind of sociopath or psychopath who had been free for years to travel around north Wales? He didn't strike me as being a psychopathic killer, but on reflection, I'd never knowingly met a psychopath before so had nothing with which to make a comparison.

After some waiting around, I was able to return to the cell to speak with Moore. I had planned my approach. I intended to be straightforward and quite clinical: everything I'd been told by Eric Jones would be passed on to my client, even the comment that at this stage the police were 'keeping an open mind' – whatever that might mean.

After listening quietly to what I had to say, Moore nodded calmly.

'I thought they would begin talking about those murders. Hasn't somebody been arrested for them?' he asked me.

'Yes, that's what I believed. It was some time ago – to be honest with you, I have no more information on what happened to him, it's just what I saw on the news,' I replied. I promised to look further into these murders, and also the situation regarding the arrested man. I then asked Moore the obvious question.

'Do you know anything about these murders in Anglesey?' Moore shook his head.

'Nothing,' he replied.

I promised to find out more and then left the cell, telling him to be patient as I was sure the police would be ready to interview him again very soon.

I knew the clock was ticking and Moore's time in custody was gradually coming to an end, unless the investigating officer, Detective Superintendent Eric Jones, was able to apply in the local Magistrates' Court for an extension to the detention time in custody. Moore had been in custody for over 24 hours. An initial short extension had been granted by the Police Superintendent, but by 10 p.m. that evening, it would be necessary for Moore to have been placed before a Magistrates' Court and the application for an extension made. The alternative would be to charge him, but the way things were going, I suspected that this would be very unlikely. I believed that the investigation was becoming bigger and more complex than either the police or, for that matter, myself had anticipated. The one thing the police haven't got in any big investigation is time; a valuable commodity in any criminal investigation. I was beginning to get the feeling that it was a commodity that the North Wales Police were running out of very quickly.

It was some point in the early afternoon when the police came back to speak with me. Eric Jones was keen to point out that they were working as quickly as they could, but that there were effectively three investigations being brought into one and this made things more complicated. I was told that Moore would be interviewed further, and DC Morris and DS Guthrie would be ready to proceed with those interviews sometime during the afternoon. It was also necessary to apply for an extension to the custody time limits and the police had already spoken with the Crown Prosecution Service with the intention of arranging for this application to be made that evening at a local court. It was clear that we had another long day ahead of us.

Peter Moore was brought into the interview room and I asked for a few moments with him to explain the situation before the interview started. It was important that he knew that due to the apparent extension of the investigation, he would be taking a trip to a local Magistrates' Court sometime during the evening for the police to make their extension application. He seemed to understand and only appeared concerned about whether he would be getting something to eat before or after the court hearing. I told Moore I would find out, thinking that he clearly had a better appetite than I did. He sat in the interview room as the police officers organised the cassettes to be placed in the tape recorder, and then DS Guthrie left the room and returned with a large bag which I assumed contained numerous exhibits. Clearly questions were to be asked about items discovered at Moore's house before they then started to address the issue of the Anglesey murders. Moore looked at me and gave a slight shrug of the shoulders – it was as if he didn't really care about what questions were going to be asked of him, as if he had prepared for this.

'Are we ready, gentlemen?' asked DC Morris as he went to close the large interview room door. Everyone nodded in agreement and the tape recorder was switched on, its irritating buzz elongating ten seconds to what felt like minutes.

Peter Moore – mugshot
(Wikimedia Commons)

Chapter 6

THE DULLNESS OF the atmosphere in the interview room felt cloying. The soundproofing on the walls and door seemed to hold everything – the conversation, a cough, the shuffling of papers or the rustling of the evidence bags – in its echoless chamber. It made the whole process feel unreal, as if the four of us in the room were acting out some prepared script.

The formal introductions were made for the tape. Both officers were again on one side of the table, sitting in the same seats as in the first interview. Moore sat opposite them with me next to him, balancing a notebook on my knee.

DC Morris began with a summary of what the police had been doing since Moore's arrest, in particular at Moore's house. A number of items had been recovered from the house and it was their intention to question Moore as to what these items were, what they had been used for and where he had acquired them. Moore nodded, looking unperturbed. Then, like conjurors in a macabre magic show, the police officers began one by one to reveal the items contained in the large plastic evidence bag. Each item revealed was in an individual container or plastic bag, labelled with its own evidence reference number.

The first item out of the bag was a knife. It was in a long, hard plastic container and was placed on the table before Moore with some flair by DC Morris.

'So, this is the first exhibit.' Morris read out the full reference number. 'It's a single-bladed knife – what could be described as a hunting knife, with a wooden handle.' Morris explained that the knife had been discovered in a bag in Moore's house during the search.

'Anything you can say about this knife?' There was an expectant tone in Morris' voice, as if he expected a full explanation of how the knife had found its way into Darlington House. The interview room fell silent. Morris gave time for Moore to fill the emptiness with a reply, to fall into the trap of talking when time was given for him to talk. I knew already that Moore would be too shrewd, too wily to fall into that simple interviewer's trap. He didn't. The silence hung there expectantly for a further few moments, throats were cleared, and we moved uneasily in our chairs.

'Is this your knife, Peter?' asked Morris.

'Yes, it is,' Moore replied, in a very matter of fact way.

'Can you tell me about it?'

'It's a knife I bought some weeks ago from the hunting shop on Elwy Street in Rhyl.' Moore then explained that he'd needed a knife for his work in his cinemas and decided that a multipurpose hunting knife would do the job. He said he knew when he saw this knife in the shop that it would 'fit the bill', and so had bought it.

I was unsure if this was a particularly convincing explanation. I couldn't imagine that many cinema proprietors went around with large hunting knives. Neither was I certain that Moore was actually making much of an effort to give a credible explanation for his possession of that knife.

'Is this the best you can do, Peter?' I thought to myself, as I noted down his answer in my notebook. I was expecting something more reasoned and believable – surely he would have anticipated, as soon as he knew the police were searching his house, that the knife would be found?

DC Morris explained that the knife was going to be tested forensically for blood and asked whether Moore wanted to say anything further at this stage about the knife. Moore just shook his head. He seemed calm and unconcerned about what was possibly an exhibit which could link him to the murder in Pensarn. It was as if he had already considered some get-out clause which I couldn't see. Maybe he was simply unwilling to share with either the police or me the reason why he believed the mounting evidence against him for the murder of Anthony Davies was irrelevant.

Morris and Guthrie worked their way through the large evidence bag. There were some handcuffs and the police uniform, which was of particular interest. What did he use these for? Why did he possess these items? Moore deflected all the questions: some were not his, others he would use occasionally, but he did not go out in the police uniform.

'What about the Nazi flag and other similar paraphernalia?' Morris asked. 'Why do you have these?'

Moore was once again dismissive of all questions, batting away any suggestions that his interest in such things was linked in any way with unpleasant or illegal practices. He was interested in these things, he said, because of his interest in films and their links to history, but he wasn't willing to volunteer anything else. It was clear that the police were attempting to make links between the possession of these items and the murder of Anthony Davies and the Anglesey murders, without directly mentioning them.

Moore continued dismissing the items discovered in his house one by one as DS Guthrie continued revealing them from the large plastic bag.

The truncheon was revealed. What had Moore used this for? Where had he got it? How long had he had it? And what about the newspaper articles he appeared to have collected about the Anthony Davies murder? Why was he so interested in this?

Peter Moore was not the type of client to capitulate to difficult questions. He seemed more calculating than many I had met before, not looking towards me with a look of alarm when an awkward line of questioning was presented to him as many would. but seeming to take it all in his stride. I continued to note his replies as the officers ran through the list of items discovered in his house, but Moore seemed to have nothing much to say. His answers were short, sometime evasive and at other times seemingly calculated to confuse. The atmosphere in the room had become tense: the police officers were not getting what they wanted. Moore squirmed out of every trap they set, answering direct questions in a cagey and vague manner. He seemed devious and slippery at times, and then oblique and elusive. It was as if I was watching a wild animal wriggling its way out of a hunter's snare. Moore seemed to rely on his instincts, even sometimes appearing to me a few steps ahead of the detectives. They were getting nowhere with him.

The afternoon proceeded with one interview after another, repetitively following the same theme. At a certain point, as we were taking a break and having a cup of tea, with Peter Moore back in his cell, DSI Eric Jones appeared once again, wanting a chat. He had a map of Anglesey and laid it out on a table by the custody desk.

'Dylan, have a look at this,' he said, pointing to the map. 'These are the locations of the two murders on the island. One in Caergeiliog near Holyhead, the other on the Llangefni junction of the A55.' I could see that there were two areas marked on the map, both very near the A55, which cuts across Anglesey from the Menai Straights to Holyhead, a road which Peter Moore would have taken on a regular, sometimes daily, basis to his cinema in Holyhead.

'What have you got, other than the locations, to pin this on Moore?' I asked. 'I thought you had a man in custody for these murders.' Eric Jones looked a bit uncomfortable at my line of questioning: they must have had sufficient evidence to arrest this man in Anglesey, so why were they bothering about Moore?

'Look, that man may have taken us in the wrong direction in this investigation. In the circumstances, we must look at these two murders again and that's what we're doing. Moore was travelling past both murder scenes daily, so it's very likely we can place him at the scene. There are also similarities between the Anthony Davies murder and those on the island. Multiple stabbings, they are all men – maybe gay men – and we have a knife which could have been used in all three offences. There are too many coincidences here for us to ignore the possibility that Moore is a serial killer.'

Eric Jones looked at me, and I'm sure he would have noticed my reaction to the statement he'd made. I was shocked. I knew this was a complex and distressing case and that the allegations made against Moore were disturbing, but a serial killer? It was the first time that the phrase had been used, and it brought with it connotations which, so far, I hadn't considered.

Serial killers, in my mind, were people like Dennis Nilsen, Peter Sutcliffe and Fred and Rosemary West. A cinema owner from Kinmel Bay couldn't possibly be viewed in the same category as them, could he? Was it possible that there was a serial killer living amongst us in north Wales? Was it possible that I was his lawyer and that my job was to represent him? I'd realised from the beginning that this case was likely to be challenging, but now it appeared enormous, daunting – even horrifying.

I sat down in the interview room to gather my thoughts and drink my mug of tea quietly. Questions and doubts fired through my mind. I was an ordinary market-town lawyer, not some big-time hotshot – what business did I have dealing with a case like this? Was I up to it? Was I capable of dealing with this? This was becoming a larger, more complicated case than most criminal lawyers would ever get close to in their careers, and I couldn't avoid the doubts and uncertainties that were infiltrating my thoughts.

I thought about the evidence. Other than the fact that Peter Moore had been driving past the scenes of both Anglesey murders before and after they had occurred, and that they were stabbings of males, was there any other evidence to link the Anthony Davies murder to them, or Moore to the Anglesey locations? This hadn't as yet been presented to me and I believed that before advising Moore I would require a clearer picture. I noticed that DI Gareth Jones, the leading investigator in the Caergeiliog murder, had arrived at the police station and ventured a few words with him in an attempt to get more information. Jones seemed a little defensive, which was probably not be surprising. He explained that they had arrested a man on Anglesey in connection with the two murders, but that he was a man who had proved unreliable in the past and that they were now of the view that there may be connections between Moore and both murder scenes which would make him a clear suspect.

'And what are those connections?' I asked. 'I need to advise him regarding your suspicions and get his instructions, so I need to know what evidence you believe you have.'

Gareth Jones explained that they were in the process of undertaking forensic test on items found at the murder scenes, and also pointed out that there were similarities in the Anglesey stabbings and the Pensarn beach stabbing. The first Anglesey victim was a man called John Henry Roberts, a 56 year old who lived in a dilapidated house on the outskirts of the village of Caergeiliog, some five miles from Holyhead. Roberts' body had been discovered by a concerned neighbour who hadn't seen him for a few days. He'd called at his house to discover Roberts dead in the front yard, having been stabbed numerous times in the chest and abdomen and also about thirteen times in the buttocks. The manner of this killing was unusual and strange – there was a suggestion that the stabbing had been frenzied, but it was also bizarre. The victim had had his trousers pulled down and the attacker had stabbed him in the buttocks, many times. Stabbing a victim in the buttocks seems peculiar, and may suggest that by demeaning the body of his victim as he was dying or dead, the assailant was achieving some kind of sexual pleasure. My subsequent research showed that this is a sadomasochistic practice called piquerism, whereby the attacker gains sexual pleasure by penetrating the skin of another person with a sharp object – usually the breasts, buttocks or groin. This practice is sometimes performed by the attacker post-mortem and may involve anything from a small pin prick to multiple stab wounds to an area of the victim's body considered erotic by the attacker, and becomes part of the repertoire of many sadists, depending on their progress along the 'sadistic learning curve'. I wondered whether the police's discoveries at Moore's home were an indication of the dark life he actually led. This attack and murder worried me, and during the investigation my research about it pointed to this murder possibly being the key to the whole investigation.

Another strange element of this murder was apparently the fascination that John Henry Roberts had for Nazi memorabilia. DSI Gareth Jones explained that Roberts had a number of Nazi mementos in his house, including a swastika flag. He explained that the search of Peter Moore's house had also discovered a flag and similar items. Jones surmised that there could therefore be a connection between the two men because of this shared interest, and questioned whether this had somehow brought them together.

The second murder in Anglesey, I was told, was that of a man called Keith Randles. He was a 49-year-old family man from the Chester area who had been working as a nightwatchman at a work site on the junction of the A55 with the road leading to Llangefni. There had been roadworks there for some time and Randles had been employed to keep an eye on the plant and equipment during the hours of darkness. Sometime during the night of 29 November 1995 or the early hours of the following morning, someone had approached the caravan where Randles was staying in the roadworks compound. The following morning at about 7.30 a.m. as workmen arrived at the site, they discovered Randles' body. He too had been stabbed.

These two murders, which were close to each other in both location and time, seemed to have caused the police some difficulty. There didn't seem to be any clear link between them other than that both were on Anglesey and near the A55. It was clear that Henry Roberts was gay, but Randles was a family man and there was no evidence of him being gay. They were both middle-aged men but, other than this, there appeared to be no clear indication of why both had been selected as victims and brutally stabbed. It appeared that following the murder of Anthony Davies in Pensarn, a clearer link could be made between him and Roberts due to Roberts' homosexuality and Davies' murder at a gay pick-up spot, and the police considered that these murders were the actions of one man. They believed that the man was Peter Moore.

I could follow the reasoning in the explanation given by DI Gareth Jones. I could see that there seemed to be some clear links between certain elements of each of those murders, and there seemed to be a common element in the presence of the A55, which runs all the way across the north Wales coast and across Anglesey. I wondered whether Moore knew these men and whether a firmer connection could be established between them rather than the randomness of the location of their murders near the A55. They were middle-aged and I wondered whether that in itself could be a connection. Moore was also middle aged, about 49 years old at the time, so it was something all three victims and Moore had in common. What seemed absent from the information given to me by DI Gareth Jones at the time was any clear evidence placing Moore at either Henry Roberts' house at Caergeiliog or in the compound near the Llangefni junction on the A55. It was possible that the trace of blood found on Pensarn beach could link Moore to the scene of the Davies murder, but was there anything putting him in either of the other two locations? So far Gareth Jones had given me nothing.

It was time to speak to Peter Moore again. I needed to convey to him exactly what I had been told by the police and advise him as to how I believed this affected his position. Moore was brought into the interview room near the custody desk. It was clear that most of the officers in the police station knew that he was a man potentially facing three murder charges and, as such, there seemed to be an unnatural aura around him affecting the police officers dealing with him. It may have been that everyone recognised that this was potentially a big case and therefore required an attention to detail above and beyond what would be usual. Nobody wanted to mess this one up, so everyone acted as if they'd been told by some superior somewhere that everything must be done by the book.

As the interview room door closed, Peter Moore still looked calm and collected. He confirmed that he felt fine and that he had been looked after adequately in the police cells. I then related to Moore the conversation I'd had with DI Gareth Jones, the suspicions he had and the links, tenuous as they seemed, with the murders in Anglesey. As I spoke, Moore nodded. He didn't appear flustered or confused, just listened intently to all the information I was able to give him. He would scratch his head occasionally and flatten his receding hair with the palm of his right hand. His fingers were long and thin, his fingernails tidily cut. His long, thin chin was now covered in greying stubble. He leaned forward on the table that was between us as I spoke. As he leaned forward, I noticed his eyes: staring, concentrating, deep-set, bluish-grey. I wondered what he was thinking. I asked if he had understood everything and whether he had any questions, but he didn't and was happy to go ahead with the next interview. Moore seemed confident and self-assured – he had the air of someone keeping a secret, or that of a gambler who believed that he had one card which would win the hand, but was playing the long game, waiting. I increasingly felt as if he was in control of proceedings and I was a mere player in what was for him a grander and far more perilous enterprise. I got the feeling during that discussion that he believed the uniformed police, the detectives, myself and all others involved to be subservient to him: he was in control. He liked being in control.

I asked if he wanted a cup of tea and he said he didn't. I thought that cutting the tension a little would help – I needed tea even if he didn't. We sat in the interview room in relative silence as I sipped my tea from a cream-coloured plastic cup. When we did speak, it wasn't about the case; we talked about the weather.

'They were promising snow someday soon.'

'Maybe we'll have a white Christmas.'

'We haven't had one of those for a few years.'

The conversation was awkward, stunted, artificial. What do you talk about with someone suspected of killing three people? I suppose you talk about ordinary stuff. The strange thing is that, despite murderers or suspected murderers being portrayed as monsters, their ordinary chat about the mundane is most likely to be the same as ours. They may well enjoy a white Christmas as much as anyone else. Our conversation floated from one banal comment to another, and we laughed on hearing the protests of one youth being asked to empty his pockets by the Custody Sergeant and then the youth's vain attempts to explain away two blocks of cannabis resin.

'I don't know where that came from, boss! No, seriously I don't. Oh, yes – maybe my mate asked me to look after something for him. Yeh, that was it...'

Moore shook his head as we laughed at the youth's doomed performance.

'Kids nowadays,' he said.

After waiting a while in silence, DC Dave Morris entered the interview room and asked if we were ready for the next interview. Within minutes the cassettes were in the tape recorder and the interview preliminaries were being read out by Morris and Guthrie. What happened was what I expected: the interviewing officers confirmed their intention to question Moore about the two murders in Anglesey. They proceeded by giving Moore dates and some details of the murders as I had previously outlined to him and, once this was done, they asked for his response. Moore seemed disinterested, even dismissing the suggestion that he could be involved. He shook his head and said that he knew nothing of either incident. Both Morris and Guthrie appeared to expect his response.

'Look Peter, you've denied the murder on Pensarn beach and we know you're involved in that one, so why should we think you're telling us the truth now?' said Morris.

The process of questioning suspects in these circumstances involves a considerable amount of sparring and shadow boxing. Usually one of the officers, Morris in this case, goes gently through the allegations, sometimes skirting around the main issues and just touching on one or two things and then, rather than pushing the issue further and labouring the point, moves on to something else. Sometimes you can see that they're trying to gain the confidence of the suspect and then lulling them into a false sense of security and confidence. Usually the setting of a metaphorical trap can be spotted a mile away. Peter Moore was defensive and unwilling to volunteer much information. He stuck to the story that he knew nothing of the assaults other than what he had read in the *Daily Post*.

'Do you know the locations of the murders?'

'Have you driven past the locations?'

'Do you know Henry Roberts?'

'You must have driven past the murder scenes on numerous occasions?'

Each enquiry was fended away with a nonchalant shrug. There didn't seem to be any chink in his armour and there seemed to be no indication from Moore that he had any knowledge of the victims or how they were killed.

Through a series of interviews that afternoon, the same issues were raised again and again. The similarities in the ages of all three victims, the method by which they had been murdered, the closeness of each murder to the A55 and the apparent fact that two of the victims may have been gay. Of course, the clear fact that each murder was on Peter Moore's route to his cinema in Holyhead was emphasised. Was that a simple coincidence? the detectives asked. And what about the knife that he admitted buying from the hunting shop in Rhyl, did he realise that the knife would be tested for blood traces? If had been used in a number of murders, was it possible that traces of all the victims' blood remained on the knife? Moore appeared unfazed.

At the end of the last interview of the afternoon we stayed in the interview room, reflecting on the previous couple of hours. I asked Moore if he was happy with how things had gone.

'Of course,' he replied. 'I've stuck to the truth, so I'm OK.'

It was a resolute response, confident and unyielding. I was even beginning to be convinced by his performance myself. I asked him if he'd like a break and something to eat, he said he would and we got up to leave the interview room. As we did, DSI Eric Jones appeared in the doorway.

'Gentlemen, it's our intention to continue to hold Mr Moore for questioning at this stage. As the PACE [Police and Criminal Evidence Act] clock is running, you will know, Mr Jones, that it will be necessary to make an application to the Magistrates' Court to extend Mr Moore's custody period. My intention is to arrange for that to be done as soon as possible.'

My calculations were that it would be necessary to bring Mr Moore before the Magistrates during that forthcoming evening, otherwise if they were unable to charge him, he would have to be released at about 10 p.m. It was five o'clock, so the police needed to act quickly. By the time I'd spoken with the Custody Sergeant about getting Mr Moore a meal, confirmation had come through that there would be a court hearing at the Colwyn Bay Magistrates' Court at 8 p.m. I said my farewells to my client, assuring him I would be at the court in ample time that evening before the hearing. A phone call to my wife and then a visit to my (by now neglected) office to discover how many phone calls I would need to attend to, and then I would have to get to Court.

Time moves so quickly when you're involved in cases of this nature. Hours of interviewing blend into one, phone calls and enquiries come one after another, and very often it's difficult to know the time of day when most of it is spent in the unnatural light of the windowless custody suite. Leaving the police station gave me a blast of fresh air: it was a chilly evening and the promised snow hung heavily in the wind. I filled my lungs with the cold air as I walked to my car. Having been shut up all day in the heavy atmosphere of the police station, the breeze, though icy, was an invigorating heady rush of freedom for which I was thankful.

I drove back to my office along the coast road. The sea to my left was coal-black with a few boat lights reflecting on the glistening water. There was a calmness that I craved after the insanity of the day, and though the darkness of the sea seemed sinister, I could fall under its spell and be haunted by its calm mystery. Maybe I was simply tired, browbeaten by the constant talk of violence, stabbing, killing and murder. Now though, was not the time to stop. As I drove, I gathered myself for the next step: what did I need to say, what further advice did I need to give my client, what observations would I make to the court about the investigation so far? What would I say to the court? What, more importantly at this stage of the investigation, should I be saying on my client's behalf to the press, if they were there? Alternatively, should I stay quiet, stay in the shadows and try not to rock the boat or make any fanciful declarations which could be misconstrued at a later stage? There were some lawyers I knew who would make a show of it and start grandstanding as much for their own benefit as their client's. I had to focus on what would benefit Peter Moore at this stage – as his defence lawyer, my prime consideration was his interests. His approach was that all this was nothing to do with him, he wasn't there, it was none of his doing. My approach needed to be as simple, straightforward and clear. This was not show business and it wasn't a film, though occasionally I felt as if I was starring in one. This was real-life criminal law, numerous lives had been affected – even Moore's life was being affected, rightly or wrongly – and at that moment my duty, as his lawyer, was to him.

The A55 in Anglesey, with Snowdonia in the background
Phil Williams (CC BY-SA/Wikimedia Commons)

Sign to Caergeiliog near Holyhead, located by the derelict house of John Henry Roberts

Chapter 7

ON THE EVENING of 23 December 1995, I arrived at Colwyn Bay Magistrates' Court early. I considered it important to arrive before Moore was brought in the police van from Llandudno Police Station, allowing enough time to discuss any outstanding issues prior to the hearing. The local press had arrived before me: I saw a few familiar faces standing outside the front door of the court and gave them a nod as I walked in.

'You got this one then, Dylan?' asked Brian from the local newspaper. He knew I was Moore's lawyer before he'd asked – it was a way of breaking the ice and getting me to engage.

'Of course,' was my reply.

'Keep me posted on what's going on, will you?' Brian then added. I laughed in response – as if I was going to begin offering him and his colleagues tip-offs at this stage! I was convinced that they'd already been digging into the Peter Moore story, contacting his friends and people that he may have known through his business. They may have hoped to get me on-side as well but I had no intention of playing that game at that moment, though I knew I may need them in the future.

The Magistrates' Court in Colwyn Bay was a red-brick Victorian building attached to the town's police station. There was a lingering smell of old polish and varnish, ingrained not only into the wood but into the whole atmosphere of the building. The courtroom itself was a large wood-panelled room with a celling of intricate water-stained plasterwork. There was a lingering smell of damp mixed in with the polish, which hung heavily in the air. At the front of the court was a high pedestal bench of church-like proportions, where the Chair of the Magistrates and two colleagues would sit. In front of this pulpit was an extraordinarily large table. Located immediately beneath the Magistrates at this table was the Magistrates' Clerk's seat and adjacent to that was where the prosecuting and defending lawyers would take their places when their cases were called. The table was always strewn with well-thumbed criminal law books, some with long-forgotten page markers, reminders of the many legal battles which had been fought in this courtroom through the decades.

As I entered the court, I took a deep breath. The place was library quiet. At the large table sat the Crown Prosecution Service prosecutor, looking at some paperwork. She looked up as I entered, and smiled. It was Nita Dowell, the most experienced CPS lawyer in north Wales. I was glad to see her as I knew from past experience that we could work together.

'Nita! It's nice to see a friendly face.' She laughed a jolly full-throated laugh, which made me chuckle as well. There's this impression given in the media and often on television detective series that lawyers for the defence and prosecution never get on and are at each other's throats from the word go. Maybe it makes good TV, but it's hardly ever true. We are all there to do a job of work: our roles are both important and our criminal system would not properly function without effective prosecution and skilful defence lawyers. In most cases they know each other – they may have been to university or law college together and some will have worked at the same law firms in the past. They will often have shared hours of coffee and idle courtroom banter as they hang around criminal courts waiting for verdicts or cases to be called.

'I heard you were on this one,' Nita said as I walked towards the big table.

'Someone's got to do it, and that man is me,' I replied with a laugh.

'Well, it looks as if you have your work cut out with this guy – it seems Mr Moore has been quite a busy man.'

'I haven't seen much evidence to prove that yet,' was my reply. 'You need to get the evidence, no point making assumptions.' She laughed.

'Come on, Mr Jones, you know as well as I do that this man is a killer.'

'Well, that's the point: at the moment I don't,' I said. We left it at that – no harm in a bit of shadow boxing at this stage; both of us knew where we stood and what needed to be done.

The purpose of the hearing was very limited: the prosecutor was applying to the Magistrates to extend the custody detention period. Moore had been in custody for nearly 36 hours and for him to be held longer, the CPS would need to prove that they needed to detain him for more time without charging him so as to enable the police to question him further and undertake more enquiries. In the circumstances and in view of the severity of the allegations against Moore, it was not particularly difficult to prove to the Magistrates that the police required more time to investigate. They had clear reasons for suspecting Moore, but needed time to gather further evidence and statements and to question him at greater length, so any objections I might make to this request were, in my opinion, likely to be rejected. Nita's application for an extension of Moore's detention period was therefore very easy. Nonetheless, the formal application had to be made and Moore had to be presented before the Magistrates for the formalities to be completed properly.

As we spoke, a Court Usher arrived from somewhere and announced that Peter Moore had arrived by police van at the police station next door. I walked round to the entrance to the cells at the rear of the police station, where a small scrum of journalists and photographers were jostling for position to get the slightest view of Moore leaving the van and entering the police station. I caught the eye of one of the police officers who was ushering Moore inside, and he pushed me ahead of him and through the door into the relative calm of the small custody area in the police station.

Moore was checked into the custody area and we were given a room to chat for a while before the proceedings began. I explained what was going to happen, what application the prosecution would be making and the reasons behind the application. I also explained that there was little point in us objecting to the application. I set out the situation with the evidence as it was, and what it was likely the police would be doing next. Peter Moore confirmed that he understood the situation, and I returned to the courtroom.

By then the Court Clerk had arrived. He was one of the senior Clerks on the circuit and clearly there had been some jostling as to who was the most senior and most experienced to deal with such a case as Moore's. Derek Jones had clearly won, or had pulled rank. Derek was a jolly and considerate Clerk, always making sure that lawyers were treated fairly, but he also did everything by the book, and he seemed to know the Magistrates' rules and regulations from back to front. There would be no opportunity in this hearing to try and blind the Magistrates with science – not that it was my intention to do so on this occasion.

'Are you raising any objections to the prosecution's application, Mr Jones?' asked Derek, with a slight chuckle in his voice.

'Any point in me doing so?' I countered.

'Well, that's up to you, Mr Jones,' said Derek. 'I suppose the question is, when do you want to get to bed this evening?' The three of us laughed. We all knew what was going to happen during this hearing and that it was likely to be over as soon as it had begun.

As we were laughing, a bell was rung by the Magistrates in their retiring room, which usually meant they wished to speak with the Court Clerk. Derek leapt to attention and disappeared through a door behind the bench. Within a minute or so he returned, and behind him appeared three Magistrates, who all looked slightly annoyed to have had their evening disturbed in this way. They sat in their usual seats on the bench. The Chair of the Magistrates, a former schoolteacher, seemed to have the look of someone who was about to hand out a lengthy period of detention. On one side of him sat a middle-aged female Magistrate that I had seen in court but never heard speak (and wondered whether she could!) and on the other side a younger male Magistrate, who I believe was a businessman of some sort. They took their places and sat, poised, with pens at the ready. Derek the Clerk was busy calling the police station, requesting that Peter Moore be brought into the dock from the cells beneath the courtroom. The court sat in an extended moment of embarrassed silence and throat clearing, then the heavy door between the cells and the stairs could be heard opening with a loud creak, some keys could be heard engaging locks and then muffled conversations before a police officer appeared in the dock followed by the prisoner, Peter Moore, and another police officer behind him, I turned toward Moore as he was placed by both officers at the front of the small dock, facing the Magistrates. I noticed that his hands were positioned in front of him and he was still wearing handcuffs. As it is custom to remove the handcuffs of every accused person in the court dock who has not yet been found guilty, I nodded at one of the officers and mouthed 'handcuffs', but he pretended he hadn't seen me.

I got to my feet.

'Your Worships, it is customary to remove handcuffs when the accused is in the dock. I wonder if you would agree to give permission for this to be done.' The Chair of the Magistrates looked left and right to each of his colleagues and then, with the look of someone who had been asked to give up his spleen to save the life of the Yorkshire Ripper, he nodded towards me and then added in as quiet a voice as possible, 'Yes, Mr Jones.'

The handcuffs were removed and Moore adjusted himself in the dock, rubbing both wrists as they were released . I looked at him to check that he was fine.

'Could you please confirm your full name and address?' asked Derek, the Court Clerk.

'Peter Howard Moore, Darlington House, St Asaph Avenue, Kinmel Bay, Rhyl, Denbighshire.' The reply was given in a measured, quiet tone, as if he was speaking in church. I could see he was directing his answers to the Chair of the Magistrates, looking directly at him. The Chairman looked down at his notebook and made a note of the defendant's name – it seemed that he couldn't or wouldn't make eye contact with Moore.

Moore was invited to sit down and Nita the prosecutor stood up and addressed the Magistrates, explaining why the police were applying to extend the custody time period. Copious notes were again being made by the Chair, with a few nods of the head and grunts of agreement as Nita spoke. A brief description was given of where the investigation had reached and what was to be done next, and the anticipated timeframe of all the investigatory procedures. I was then invited to speak.

My speech was short and to the point. I had no particular observations to make at this stage regarding the police investigation, I was aware of the direction it was taking, having spoken to the Detective Superintendent in charge, and did not see any merit or purpose in objecting to the police's application.

The Chair of the Magistrates consulted his colleagues and they confirmed their agreement with a nod each.

'Then we allow the extension of the custody time in this matter as requested by the police,' announced the Chair, and then asked Derek whether there was anything else he wanted them to do.

'No, Your Worships,' said Derek and the three Magistrates scuttled through their door and no doubt back home for some supper and to relay the gossip to their husbands or wives of the evening they heard a case involving a serial killer.

I looked back at Peter Moore as the Magistrates were leaving the court. He looked grey and a little dishevelled in his police-issue grey sweatshirt and jogging pants. Maybe, I thought, it was the colour of what he was wearing which made him look so pale. His eyes looked red and the stubble on his chin added to the overall grey effect. I considered whether he'd changed between the afternoon and the evening, maybe even that he looked older.

'I'll see you tomorrow morning,' I said to Moore as he was turning to be escorted from the dock and back down the stairs to the cells. He turned to me and gave me a thumbs up.

'See you then,' he said as he disappeared down the stairs.

By the time I left the court building, it was after nine in the evening. The previously cold breeze had become even colder and was biting as I walked to my car. I looked back down the road and saw the police van pulling out from the rear of the police station, with Peter Moore on board. I considered how he might be feeling in the back of the van, returning to his cell in Llandudno Police Station. A few days ago, he would have been at home, and now his fate was the subject of investigation, press reports and rumour, and his destination was a featureless cell with a built-in metal toilet.

I called my wife to tell her I was on my way home. She was at my parents' house in Denbigh, so I promised to pick her up. I'd driven home along the north Wales coast and up the Vale of Clwyd countless times, but on this evening it felt different. There were so many questions and uncertainties piling up in my mind. I wanted to ensure that everything that required my attention regarding the case was addressed, and a list of priorities was forming in my mind as I drove. Much depended the following few days. I knew that the investigation would run into Christmas Day and probably Boxing Day, and it was already becoming apparent that if Moore was going to be charged with a number of murders it would mean a substantial amount of work in the near future. How would I run my office and deal with all my other clients? How much time would it take to deal with a case of this type? How much support and assistance would I receive from my colleagues at my firm? These were all questions that worried me.

It felt at the time as if there was no one else I could rely on as an advisor or counsel – it was me, alone, making the decisions. I was drawing on every bit of knowledge and experience I had, but I was still young (in my early thirties) and though I had a good few years of experience, this was on a totally different level. I reasoned to myself that this would be true of any north Wales lawyer and of most lawyers in the country. This was not a usual case – all of this was out of the ordinary for all involved. Peter Moore was not a normal client.

I thought about what Moore had been accused of doing. It wasn't a case of stabbing someone once or twice: it appeared frenzied, crazy even – out-of-control attacks which had killed three men in a most vicious way. Did those actions fit with the person I knew as my client, Peter Moore? I couldn't be sure – I had doubts and concerns. Did he look like a cold-blooded killer? No, in my opinion he didn't. But maybe that made the whole thing worse. If he was a killer then his ordinariness, his normality as an ordinary face in the crowd, made him and the allegations against him even stranger and more bizarre, and possibly even more chilling.

I arrived in Denbigh and drove up Park Street to my parents' house. It felt darker than usual, though the pale light of the streetlights was still reflected on the wet road in orange pools. The street was empty and there was not a single soul about as I arrived. I noticed my parents' gates were closed and so I pulled in from the road and parked in the mouth of their driveway. I began to get out of the car, opening the driver-side door. As I got up from the seat, I felt a sensation of someone running up the road towards the car and me. I hadn't heard anything, no rushing footsteps or heavy breathing – there was nothing distinguishable from the cold breeze gusting into my face as I got out of my car. I hesitated for a moment, then went to shut the car door – but as I held the handle of the car door, I froze. I had the distinct sensation of somebody approaching me, this time at speed. He was rushing up the street, a knife in his hand, and as he approached, he was raising the hand and holding the knife above his head. He moved faster and faster, but I couldn't move; I stayed rooted to the spot, holding the car door handle, waiting, expecting the blow of the knife as it was struck with force into my back.

The terror must have lasted for a few brief seconds, though at the time it felt like minutes. The panic ebbed and as if a ghost of some evil being had passed right through me, I shivered with both fear and disbelief at what I had just experienced. It was as real an experience as everything else that had occurred in the previous 36 hours. I had felt the fear and the helplessness of those victims in Caergeiliog, in the compound near the A55 and on the beach in Pensarn. I had experienced what I believed to be the reality of knowing that you were about to be stabbed and the paralytic terror of expecting the blow of the assailant's knife, of expecting to be killed.

I couldn't understand what had happened to me that evening, and to this day it remains a mystery. Maybe it was my mind playing evil tricks on me. Maybe I needed to experience the unbridled terror of someone expecting an attacker's knife to come down on them so as to give me an insight into what the victims had experienced in their final moments. Possibly it was my unconscious playing with my emotions, testing me – asking whether I was really up for this challenge.

I reached my parents' front door and was told that I looked exhausted, and I agreed that I needed my bed. I chose not to mention the incident by the car. I may never have mentioned it again, had it not been for this book.

Chapter 8

I'D ONLY HAD a couple of hours' sleep by the time my phone began ringing on my bedside table. I flailed around for a few seconds before I found it.

'Yes,' I answered, in a semi-conscious state.

'Mr Jones?' enquired a stern-sounding voice at the other end. I grunted my confirmation.

'It's the Llandudno custody here, we have a bit of a situation with your client, Mr Moore. He's called one of my colleagues into his cell and told him that he wanted to make a full admission.'

This got my attention – I was wide awake and sitting up in bed immediately.

'A full admission? What are you talking about?' It didn't make any sense. I was beginning to think that I was still dreaming – I had only seen Moore a few hours before at the Magistrates' Court hearing and there had been no mention of an admission; he had appeared as resolute and calm as he had been ever since his arrest. I couldn't understand what would have led him to such a change of mind, within a few hours.

'You need to come over here as soon as possible, Mr Jones.' I agreed, put the phone down and leapt out of bed, despite only having had a few hours' sleep. I had planned to be back in the police station for further interviews later that morning, but to receive a call at 1.40 a.m. was beyond anything I had considered possible. I grabbed whatever clothes were closest – a pair of jeans, T shirt and jumper – and put on a warm coat. My wife turned over in the bed as I looked back into the bedroom before setting off. I was unsure if she even knew I was leaving, but I didn't want to wake her.

I drove back to Llandudno, and it started to snow lightly as I drove along the Vale of Clwyd. 'That's all I need,' I thought – a heavy snowfall could cause me difficulty going back and forth to the police station and maybe affect the whole investigation. And then there was this 'admission'... I hadn't been given any details by the Custody Sergeant of what exactly Moore had said or even what the circumstances of this apparent admission had been. In the interviews, Moore had been adamant that he'd had nothing to do with the murders and that he knew nothing about them. No matter what the police had said, Moore hadn't wavered at all during his questioning; he'd stuck resolutely, even stubbornly, to his story.

I'd always believed that I had an inner sense of when a client was lying. There were the obvious 'lie-merchants', who seemed to twitch and bungle through their lies with the lack of subtly of a criminal Mr Bean, the unthinking liar who seemed to lie as if it were their second nature and they couldn't help themselves. Occasionally one would encounter a liar who had spent their lives lying but didn't have the ability to do it well, and so they were caught out time and time again as a result. Once in a while an impressive liar would turn up, one who believed in their own lies; someone who – having convinced themselves – had no difficulty persuading others with their untruths, but there were never many of those about. They were always the most self-serving and manipulative people and could be found in many walks of life, not only in the criminal fraternity – some of them were lawyers! It was very possible that Moore was one of these individuals and the most dangerous type. If that was the case, I knew that I needed to tread very carefully.

I arrived at Llandudno Police Station at about 2.30 a.m. By this time, the snow was heavier and even in the seaside town of Llandudno, I could see tyre tracks through the snow that had settled in the police station car park. It had also got colder since I'd left home and a biting wind from the north caught my breath for a second or two as I got out of my car. I rushed to the custody suite door and pressed the buzzer. Usually I would need to identify myself but on this occasion no questions were asked, the door immediately opened.

'Mr Jones.' Dave Morris was waiting for me with a concerned expression. 'We've been waiting for you.' The custody suite was warm, and a number of detectives were milling around, talking to each other. I was ushered into the office and offered a seat. This was clearly going to be serious. One officer came in with a mug of tea for me, and was asked to shut the office door as he left.

'So, thanks for rushing in. As you've heard, things have taken a bit of a turn and we did need to respond to that as soon as possible, as you'll understand.' I agreed and got my notebook out of my briefcase. I was then told by Morris that the Custody Sergeant was best placed to explain the situation which had developed during the early hours of the morning.

'Yes, Mr Jones.' The Sergeant stood poised in front of Morris and me, holding a written copy of the custody record. It was as if he was about to read out a poem or do a reading at church. He took a deep breath and began.

'You will know, Mr Jones, that the hearing at Colwyn Bay Magistrates' Court came to an end at around 9 o'clock yesterday evening. The prisoner returned by police van to the police station here in Llandudno, arriving here...' he consulted the record again, 'at 21.45.' The Custody Sergeant then looked over to Morris and myself, initially I thought for some sort of sign of approval, so I gave him a nod and noted the time on my notepad.

'Mr Moore was then asked whether he wanted a cup of tea, which he declined, but he did ask for a writing pad and a pen or pencil, which we provided to him.'

'In his cell?' I asked. The Custody Sergeant confirmed this.

'Yes, Mr Jones. We then put him in his cell at 22.00 and the door was closed. I checked him again at least every 30 mins or so. He was writing at 22.30, 23.00, 23.28 and again at 23.45.

I then checked him again at 00.10 and he was sleeping. Still sleeping at 00.30 hours and at 01.00 hours, and then he set off the alarm in his cell at 01.23 hours and I went to see him. I made a contemporaneous note on the custody record of what then transpired.' The Sergeant began to read from the custody record itself.

'At 01.23 hours, having received an alarm call from the cell of the prisoner Peter Howard Moore, I attended the cell and spoke with the prisoner. He confirmed that he was in good health and had been sleeping for a while. He then said to me, 'I want to make an admission with regard to the crimes that I have committed.' At this point I cautioned the prisoner and then he continued, 'I want to speak with someone so I can make a full admission to four murders. There were two murders in Anglesey, another on the beach in Pensarn, and another of a man from Liverpool who I killed in the Clocaenog Forest near Ruthin. I have drawn a diagram to show where I left this man's body in the forest.' There was a lull in the Sergeant's performance; it may have been that he expected a reaction. Clearly DC Morris was aware of this development. I decided to make a note in my notepad and attempt to contain my incredulity with an air of professional indifference, but it didn't work. I must have looked shocked, and I wouldn't be surprised if I was sitting there with my mouth wide open, attempting to come to terms with the information I'd just been given. I think I may have said, 'Bloody hell, what the fuck have we got here?' I can't recall a reply from anyone – I think we remained silent for a moment or so just to attempt to absorb the information – it's as much as we all could do.

'So, gentlemen, where do we go from here?' I finally asked, just to break the silence. It was clear that I needed to speak with Moore and that everything reported by the Custody Sergeant needed to be verified and advice then given to Moore as to the effect of this admission he'd made – if that's what it was – and what he should do next. Clearly the whole situation seemed to be changing, and what had appeared to be disputed allegations a few hours earlier might now be agreed facts.

'Well, we will need to immediately interview Mr Moore, obviously,' said DC Morris. We agreed that I should have some time to consult fully with my client and then we would proceed to a formal interview, subject to what Moore said to me.

I asked to see Mr Moore in the interview room and as the Custody Sergeant went to fetch him, I went to the room to get my notes and my head prepared for what was ahead of me.

This was a unique situation. As criminal lawyers, we're used to dealing with unusual and unexpected scenarios, allegations and circumstances, but I doubted whether the situation which I was now facing had been the experience of many in the past. I was representing someone who could potentially be called a 'serial killer' – an alarming if not horrifying term, a term which held many chilling associations. Serial killers are infamous, portrayed by the media as subhuman incarnations of the devil. They are thought of as callous, soulless, even feral beings, living on the edges, preying on the weak and defenceless. We know their names and their crimes and the swollen, bloated modern myths about them seem to grow and expand from one day to another. We give some of them nicknames dehumanising them further – 'The Yorkshire Ripper', 'The Kindly Killer', 'Doctor Death' – which seems to change them into objects rather than people, as if they are from a different world. Their tales are macabre legends told to others so as to chill the blood and unsettle the mind of the listeners. Fred and Rosemary West raping, torturing and murdering their victims and then burying them in the cellar or garden of their house in Gloucester. Dennis Nilsen, the apparently affable Scotsman who lured young men to his London flat, where he would strangle or drown them, then keep the victim's body for a lengthy time before dissecting them and burning their remains or flushing them down his toilet. It was this class of crime and this type of criminal we could now be dealing with in the case of Peter Moore.

Sitting in the interview room waiting for the appearance of Moore, I steeled myself for whatever might face me. Had this apparent admission changed Moore? Had the revelation that he'd killed four people unleashed some monster which until now had been hidden under the polite and courteous façade of a north Wales cinema owner and businessman? Was I about to meet the real Peter Howard Moore?

I was deep in thought when Moore appeared at the doorway of the interview room. I must have slightly jumped in my seat when I saw him standing there, looking down at me.

'Mr Jones, good of you to come at this unearthly hour. I'm really sorry that you've had to be dragged out now, it's very unfortunate.' His remarks were polite and considerate, delivered in a polite and respectful manner. He looked the same as he had the last time I'd seen him – perhaps his grey stubble seemed a little longer and his eyes redder, with dark shadows becoming more apparent around them. His mouth wore the same neutral grin. I was never too sure whether he was grinning or not: he appeared sometimes to have the look of someone who had found something amusing but would rather keep it to himself, an inner grin which was only exposed by a slight turn in the side of his mouth. It was a look which I sometimes found disconcerting and perplexing. Maybe that's why he did it.

Moore sat in the same chair as he had in each of his previous interviews and placed his hands on the table between me and him. I looked at my notebook, where I had noted everything the Custody Sergeant had told me earlier. I noticed his hands were clasped; he had long narrow, slender fingers and tidy, maybe even manicured nails. His hands betrayed no stress or nervousness; they seemed resolute and determined in their positioning. Were these the hands of a killer? Had these hands held a knife as it plunged into the abdomen of his victim and then wielded it in a frenzied attack until the defenceless victim lay dead in a pool of his own blood?

It's unusual to share a room with someone who's an accused serial killer. In one way it's a privilege, if a nauseating one, to have the opportunity to sit opposite such a person and be able to stare directly into his eyes and ask the question, did you murder those people? A discussion about murder at any time is difficult – at 3 a.m. it's even more challenging. I read out my notes of the statement from the Custody Sergeant and asked Moore to verify that the conversation had taken place. He confirmed that it had. He said he hadn't slept much after returning from the court hearing the previous evening and had been thinking about his situation. His comments were made in a measured and calm way. It's the way anyone would have reacted if faced by a difficult or challenging problem, they would have thought about it, maybe been unable to sleep or settle down and then in the early hours come up with a solution on how to proceed. In our ordinary lives these are not unusual situations – we all experience sleepless nights, worrying about things which usually turn out to be trivial. The main difference was that in Moore's case, this was not an ordinary problem and he seemed not to be an ordinary person, even though he may have attempted to resolve his issue in a fairly ordinary way. I wondered if this told me something about Moore, and whether understanding his thinking processes would give me a deeper understanding of the man.

'So, do you want to tell me about the murders?' I enquired. He nodded but simply repeated what he had told the Custody Sergeant earlier.

'I want to admit to four murders, as I mentioned to the police officer. They are the two men in Anglesey, one on the beach in Pensarn and another in the Clocaenog Forest.' I made a note, which was more or less identical to the one I'd made earlier when speaking with the custody officer.

'OK,' I said. 'anything else?' Moore shook his head but then hesitated for a moment. He unclasped his hands and reached for something in the right pocket of his police-issue joggers. He took out a piece of paper which was folded neatly, and began to unfold it as he spoke.

'I've drawn a plan of where I left the body in the Clocaenog Forest. As you may know, the place is large with Forestry roads going everywhere, so I've shown on my plan, as far as I can recall,' – he pushed the unfolded handwritten map across the table to me – 'where the body was left.'

I looked at the map on the desk. It was drawn in some detail, showing the main road and the turning into Forestry Commission land, and after that a route through a maze of Forestry roads to point marked with an X. As I looked at the map, Moore reached over and pointed to the X.

'I think that's where the body was. I put it down an embankment from the road, I think on the right-hand side.'

'Was it there that the man was killed?' I asked.

'I killed him on the roadway and then took his body over to the side of the road out of the way.' I made a note in my notebook; as I did, the silence hung in the room. It seemed that we were both conscious of the seriousness of what was being said and how important it was to get the details correct. I was shocked by what I had been told, but remained silent for a moment and continued to make my notes. The silence ached in the room – it was like an itch that you dared not scratch. The normal human response on being told by a person in the same room as you that they had murdered someone and effectively dumped them in a ditch on the side of the road would be to recoil in absolute horror. Being a lawyer in those circumstances asked for a totally different reaction. It meant detachment and disengagement from any emotion. I needed to know the story of how these murders had been committed and, more importantly, why. I needed to obtain as many facts as possible.

I began to enquire about the circumstances of each murder. Moore, though, seemed resistant to my questioning and somewhat evasive: the more I tried to elicit information from him, the more unyielding he appeared to become. I advised him of the legal situation, what making an admission meant as far as a court case was concerned, the implications of what he had decided to do, and his options during the forthcoming interview. He could continue and make an admission, or he could remain silent. I asked if he understood the process and the situation he was now in; he confirmed that he did and that he wished to make a full admission to the police along the lines of what he had told them earlier.

'You do understand, Mr Moore, that the police will want details of every murder?'

He nodded, but seemed to have nothing else he wanted to say to me. I asked whether he was feeling fine and if he required a break before going into the interview. Moore said he was fine and would prefer to carry on and get the whole thing over with. I looked at him across the table, a grey man in many ways. He looked placid, serene even, as he sat with his hands clasped once again, looking back at me. What was he thinking? What did he think of me?

I wanted to ask at that moment, why did you do these things? But he seemed to have resolved that he would unburden himself to the police in the interview, so maybe my intervention at this stage was not needed. Was he prepared to tell them why he had murdered these men? I was uncertain if he was going to do that, and whether the police would be satisfied with the answers they got from him. Time would tell.

Chapter 9

It was nearly 3.30 a.m. by the time everyone was ready for the interview. As Peter Moore and I sat in the interview room waiting, with the door by then open, I could see a number of detectives and police officers scuttling around nervously, huddling in groups. DI Peter Ackerley appeared. He was now in charge of the whole investigation, having taken overall control of what was now probably four murder investigations. Ackerley was a tall man in his early forties with a rugged complexion and a look of determination as he paced around the custody suite. He acknowledged me with a nod and a 'Mr Jones' as he passed the open door of the interview room.

DC Morris and DS Guthrie appeared in the throng of consulting police officers, with bundles of papers and what appeared to be notes. There was an air of impatience about the place – they were like two boxers eager to get into the ring as they received their last words of encouragement from Ackerley. This was the 'big one' for them, professionally. It may have been the moment they had been dreaming about since they first became detectives. I'm sure all of us felt our senses were heightened and our minds in overdrive: this could be a career-defining moment and each one of us needed to perform to the best of our abilities, even at 3.30 a.m. on Christmas Eve morning.

'What are they doing out there?' Moore enquired, his back to the open door.

'Preparing,' I replied. He chuckled and then we both said nothing and waited in silence.

DC Morris was the first to enter the interview room.

'Gentlemen, are we ready for the interview?'

'Yes, I think we are,' I replied. DS Guthrie then arrived, overloaded with evidence bags and documents, which he began to organise around the desk.

'Peter, do you feel OK to go ahead with this interview?' Morris asked.

'Yes, of course,' Moore answered, his voice soft and muted. He clasped his hands on the desk in front of him again and cleared his throat.

'Do you want a glass of water, Peter?' asked Morris.

'No, thank you,' Moore replied.

Morris began removing the plastic wrappers from the cassettes. The process seemed to take an eternity, and the rustling of the plastic wrappers filled the room like nervous static. The door was now shut and in our echoless chamber we waited for the tape recorder to be loaded. It was as if we were all watching some religious devotion undertaken by Morris in exaggerated movements, apparently to demonstrate to all present that everything was above board and being done properly. It was not the time to mess up.

'Ready, then?' Morris asked, looking at each one of us present for affirmation. We all agreed. The red button on the tape recorder was pressed and for a few seconds all four of us sat motionless as the machine let out its preliminary elongated loud buzz.

'My name is Detective Constable Dave Morris. This interview is being conducted at Llandudno Police Station on 24 December 1995. Present is Peter Howard Moore – can you confirm your date of birth, Mr Moore?'

'Yes, 19 September 1946.'

'And your address, Mr Moore?'

'Darlington House, St Asaph Avenue, Kinmel Bay, Rhyl.'

'Thank you, Mr Moore. Also present are –'

'DS Mike Guthrie.'

'And Mr Moore's solicitor – could you also confirm your role during the interview, please?' Morris gave me a nod.

'Dylan Rhys Jones. I'm here as Mr Moore's legal advisor.'

'Thank you. The time is now 03.32 hours,' Morris responded. Papers were then shuffled once again as Morris and Guthrie found the document they required. It was the custody record, a copy of which both had. Morris explained that he was referring to the custody record and in particular the entry in the record completed by Sergeant Davies, the Custody Sergeant, at 01.28 hours on the morning of 24 December 1995. Morris then read out the entry in the record.

'Mr Moore, according to what Sergeant Davies has noted here, you have stated that you wish to make an admission. Will you explain to us, for the tape, what exactly you wish to say?'

The tension in the room was palpable: the detectives had no idea whether Moore would repeat his admission. They wanted to ensure that at least everything that had been said to the Custody Sergeant at 1.23 a.m. was repeated to them. If they could get more information, more detail of the crimes, that would be even better, but they needed Moore to talk.

Neither of the detectives knew the effect that my involvement in the situation would have had on Moore. He might have changed his mind after seeing me, or just clamp up and say nothing. For all both detectives knew, they could now be facing a 'No comment' interview and be left to do the best they could with the admission made to the Custody Sergeant. There was a lot hanging on this interview, and there was a feeling that it was make or break.

I sat in my usual chair next to Moore, pen poised on my notepad. I'd decided from the beginning of the Peter Moore interviews that I would take all my notes using my fountain pen – I believed that I wrote much more tidily and quickly with a fountain pen, and I needed to get every word that was said during the interview process. My own notes would be important: I would need to refer to them later when preparing for the trial, and though a written record of the taped interview would be produced in time, my notes and my impressions of all that was said would be crucial.

Moore took his time responding to Morris' question. He was patient and measured, and it even appeared that he was prepared to extend his moment in the limelight as long as he possibly could. He looked around at the three of us, looking eagerly towards him. Morris, Guthrie and I waited, expectantly.

'Well, as I told the Sergeant earlier,' began Moore, 'I want to admit to both of the murders in Anglesey, the murder on Pensarn beach and also I want to admit to another murder that you don't know about, which I committed in the Clocaenog Forest near Ruthin.' It was what he'd said to the Sergeant earlier, more or less word for word, as if he'd prepared his statement beforehand in readiness for this confrontation. It seemed to me to be a speech rather than a confession, delivered in his calm, slightly effeminate, polite voice. He looked directly at Morris when he spoke and remained motionless with his hands still clasped on the desk when he finished.

Clearly this was not enough for either detective. They needed as much detail as they could elicit from Moore and a straightforward statement in very general terms would not suffice. I suspected that Moore knew this, but I got the feeling that he wanted to toy with them and wouldn't be volunteering further information until the detectives had squirmed a little. Moore hadn't been willing to go into any great detail with me when I had spoken with him earlier; it was clear that this was how he'd decided to approach things. There's no doubt that at that moment Moore felt in complete control of the situation: we were all puppets dancing to his tune.

'Well, Peter, thank you for that information. We appreciate that you are candid and willing to help, so you will also understand that we'll need more detail from you so we can verify what you're saying? I'm sure you understand that,

Peter?' Morris had clearly decided on the polite and patient approach. There was no good cop/ bad cop here – they wanted him to remain calm and co-operative, and irritating Moore at this stage was very unlikely to help them.

'Of course,' said Moore. Morris then continued.

'So, what about the first murder in Anglesey? The victim was a John Henry Roberts, a 56-year-old man from the village of Caergeiliog near Holyhead. He was killed sometime between 22 and 25 September 1995 at his home in Caergeiliog. What can you tell me about this murder then, Peter?'

Peter Moore didn't immediately respond, and the interview room remained silent in anticipation of what was about to be said. Morris' question hung in the air as Moore seemed to gather himself for the answer.

'Well, I've travelled a lot along the north Wales coast and to Holyhead, where I have one of my cinemas. I pass that village, which is by Holyhead, regularly and some time ago I noticed the house on the edge of the village, because of its bad condition more than anything else.'

Moore explained further in his measured, passive tone. There was no dramatic explanation of the circumstances; things were said in a monotone with no emotion at all. He continued by saying that he had been intrigued by the house for some time and had decided to have a closer look. I felt this was a strange thing for Moore to say – it would be a strange thing for anyone to do. It appeared an unusual and somewhat sinister explanation. Moore continued.

'So one day I stopped in the village and I wandered to the property for a look. There was a yard in front of the house, and the house looked in a bad condition. As I got into the yard, a man came out of the house and began shouting at me.'

'Can you describe the man?'

'Yes – he was in his late fifties or early sixties, he looked untidy, he was wearing untidy and dirty clothes, he had a beard and unkempt hair, and he was shouting at me.'

'What was he shouting?' asked DS Guthrie.

'He was shouting, "I am not Jewish, I am not a Jew."'

'Why would he be shouting that?' asked Morris.

'Because I was wearing dark clothes and I was wearing a German sort of Nazi-style cap.'

'Why would you have done that?'

'To scare him,' answered Moore calmly. 'I think he thought I was a Nazi and he was trying to persuade me that he wasn't Jewish.'

'Do you think he felt threatened?'

'Maybe, yes. Certainly, he did – I was holding a knife.'

'So you were going to kill him, Peter?' asked Morris.

'Yes,' answered Moore, without hesitation.

'Why would you want to kill him?'

'For fun.' said Moore. There was a hesitation, from everyone in the room. I suspected that Morris couldn't respond, and for a second or two I sat with my fountain pen hanging in my hand above the page, uncertain if I'd actually heard what I knew I had heard. I then considered writing Moore's answer down on my notepad – maybe it would allow me to make more sense of what I'd heard? What were we dealing with here? I contemplated, as I attempted to put on paper what in all honesty I was struggling to process. Did he really say that he'd killed 'for fun'? It was horrifying, and I suspect that the two police officers also found it difficult to comprehend, but we were professionals and it was impossible for us to recoil at what we had heard. We needed to press on with the interview.

'What happened when you got into the yard, Peter?' Morris asked.

'He was shouting at me and telling me he was not Jewish, so at that point I approached him with the knife and stabbed him.'

'How many times did you stab him?'

'I don't know.'

'Was it once or many times?'

'It was many times, numerous times in the front. He then fell onto his front in the yard.'

'What did you then do?'

'I pulled down his trousers and then stabbed him many times in the buttocks.'

'Why did you do that?'

'I don't know.'

'How many times did you stab him there?'

'Many times.'

I was by now becoming even more troubled and concerned. This man in whose company we sat in the interview room was describing behaviour which was strange, frightening and sickening. He was beginning to take us into the realms of the most alarming and notorious murderers in the United Kingdom, of deeds and people that are known by many and become the stuff of 'modern legends'. I wondered whether any of us in that interview room were prepared for the journey we were about to take into the dark mind of Peter Moore.

'What did you then do, after you'd stabbed him, Peter?' Morris asked.

'I left him in the yard and went back to my car.'

'How did you feel after you left him?'

'I was fine, no problem.'

'Did you regret what you'd done?'

'No.'

'What about the next murder in Anglesey?' It appeared that Morris had decided (or had been directed) to rush through the murders as quickly as possible so as to get as many covered as he could during this interview. No detail was necessary at this stage. 'Just get the all the admissions' was what I suspected he'd probably been instructed by DI Ackerley, so now Morris was moving on to the next murder, which had been committed a month or so later.

'This man's name was Keith Randles. He was a 49-year-old man from Cheshire who was working as a nightwatchman on some roadworks near the junction of the A55 and the A5114 turning to Llangefni. Do you know where I mean, Peter?'

'Yes, I do,' Moore confirmed.

'So, tell me what happened there, Peter.'

Once again there was no immediate reply. We all sat quietly and I felt a knot forming in my stomach, fearing what I was about to hear next. Patiently, Moore replied.

'I'd seen the work there for some time and when travelling home, I'd noticed a light in a caravan in the compound late at night. I thought that there may be someone staying in the caravan overnight – a nightwatchman or one of the workers. When I was returning from Holyhead late one evening – I would usually lock up the Holyhead cinema – I decided to have a look. I drove off the A55 and parked my van in the mouth of the turning into the compound. I then went into the compound and approached the caravan, which had its light on.'

Morris intervened.

'What were you wearing, Peter?'

'My black clothes that I usually wear for work, the clothes that a projectionist would usually wear. Black clothes.'

'Yes. So you went to the caravan, which had its light on?'

'Yes, and I knocked on the caravan door.'

'Tell me what happened then.'

'The man answered the door and I dragged him out of the caravan. He saw that I had a knife and then he began to plead with me not to kill him.'

'Why did he begin pleading?'

'I think he knew I was going to kill him. He told me that he had a wife and family and looked a bit nonplussed about it all.'

'What happened then?'

'He asked me why I was killing him as I stabbed him, and I said that it was for fun.'

'You stabbed him twelve times, Peter.' Morris said. Moore looked unmoved by this fact.

'Maybe!' was his only response.

'What happened then?'

'He fell to the floor. I just thought it was a job well done, and left and returned to my van.'

The atmosphere had changed in the interview room. It had gone from a degree of excitement on hearing these admissions to a realisation of how brutal these deaths had been. I imagined the sheer terror of a victim who knew that he was about to be killed and had no alternative but to plead for his life, being told that he was being stabbed 'for fun'. I wondered about that – can someone actually kill someone for fun? Can the act of stabbing someone twelve times, as with Randles, be seen by even the most callous of killers as fun? Possibly the word 'fun' was being used by Moore instead of something deeper and more sinister that couldn't be properly explained either by him or ourselves as witnesses to this admission. At that time, in the heat of the interview, it may have been easier for Moore to use that word as an excuse for what he had done. Possibly it's the only way Moore could describe the elation he may have experienced from killing. Murder for 'fun' seemed too simple, too uncomplicated an explanation. It appeared so cruel and grim as to nearly dehumanise the act of murdering another human being in cold blood. It made Moore appear less of a man and more of a monster.

'Can I ask you about the next murder?' Morris continued.

'Yes, that was the man I picked up from Liverpool.'

'What was his name?'

'I don't know.'

'Tell me what happened.'

'I went to a nightclub, a gay nightclub in Liverpool. I picked up a man there who was looking for sex. He was very drunk. He wanted me to drive him back to his place in Birkenhead, but I drove him back to north Wales instead.'

'Had you decided to kill him?'

'Yes. I think he realised that I was going to kill him on the way to north Wales and he tried to escape from the van as it was moving, but I managed to restrain him. He was drunk and a drug addict. I think he got a bit frightened, actually.'

'What did you do?'

'I drove to Clocaenog Forest and killed him there.'

'Did you stab him?'

'Yes, I did.'

'What did you do with his body?'

'I hid it down a bank at the side of the Forestry road. I've drawn a map of the Forestry and indicated where I think I placed the body. It's the best I can do.' Moore removed his hand-drawn map from his pocket, unfolded it and flattened it out on the desk. He then pointed at the cross he'd marked on the map, where he believed the victim's body had been disposed of.

'It's there, as far as I can remember.' Both Morris and Guthrie studied the map for a moment or two.

'When did this murder happen?' asked Guthrie.

'I'm not sure. Sometime in November, I would think.'

'Peter, we're going to have to take this map – I'm sure you'll understand – and get someone to look into this, if that's OK?'

'Yes, of course,' agreed Moore. The map was then taken by Guthrie and placed on top of a pile of papers.

'And what about the final murder, which was on the 17th or early hours of the 18th of December this year, on Pensarn beach in Abergele?'

There was silence for a few seconds. It was as if the whole process had taken the wind out of Moore's sails and he needed a few moments to gather himself – not that there was any sign of emotion or regret. His face, his eyes and his composure seemed unaffected by all this talk of murder and his recollections of the past few months.

'Yes,' Moore finally said. 'Of course, the murder on Pensarn beach.' I looked down at my notepad again. I felt it a comfort to take detailed notes during what was clearly a harrowing and disturbing experience for both myself and the detectives. As for Moore, he appeared to be coping reasonably well with the process.

'You do know that the car park near the beach in Pensarn is a well-known cruising place for gay people?' he enquired.

'We do,' confirmed Morris.

'So, I would go there on my way home from Holyhead sometimes, and on returning home – it must have been, as you said, on 17 December – I went to Pensarn and walked onto the beach. There was a man there. He was not far from the sea and as he turned round, I noticed that he was exposing himself to me. I walked up to him and stabbed him in the abdomen.'

'How many times did you stab him?'

'I don't know. A number of times, I suppose.'

'What did you do then?'

'I left him. He was near the shoreline.'

'Was he dead?'

'I think he was alive when I left him. I'm not sure.'

'Why did you stab him?'

'I don't know.' Moore responded. The reply hung in the heavy air of the interview room and remained there for a few moments as we contemplated it. There was no contrition or concern for the victim; it was as if Davies hadn't even existed. It was an incident which had happened and then concluded, and even if not forgotten by Moore, then it had at least been placed by him in some dark place in his mind which he would visit only rarely to replay his crimes.

And now we were getting into unknown territory. Morris and Guthrie had covered the murders mentioned by Moore during his admission to the Custody Sergeant, but could there be more? Had this killing spree started in September

1995 or sooner? There was a need to ensure that everything was on the table. There was a danger in this approach: the police could very well be tempted to use Moore to clear up any outstanding murders across north Wales over many years. As Moore seemed in the mood to admit to his own misdeeds, he might get carried away and admit to things that were nothing to do with him – the 'in for a penny, in for a pound' attitude of saying, 'Well, if I'm admitting to four, I might as well admit to some others.' This would put Moore in dangerous territory and I wanted to ensure that we didn't fall into that trap.

'So, Peter, is there anything else you want to admit to us at this stage?' Morris asked. The fishing expedition had begun.

'I think we need to be careful that we focus on the investigation in question, Mr Moore,' I interjected. He looked over to me and nodded and gave me half a smile. It was the type of smile that wasn't born out of happiness or agreement but rather of sympathy.

'Over a period of some twenty years or so I have assaulted many men, usually in the Conwy Valley area. When driving around, I would sometimes notice someone walking along the road late at night and I would stop and attack them.'

'How would you attack them, Peter?'

'I would assault them with a police truncheon and strike them on the body and their heads many times. Usually I would be dressed as a policeman or in a Nazi uniform or something similar, just to scare them. I heard that a few of these men had been seriously injured after the attacks.'

'Did you kill any of them?'

'No, I didn't, I just assaulted them.'

'Why did you do this?'

'I got pleasure out of it.'

'Did you get aroused?'

'Yes, I usually did.'

'Did you attack them sexually?'

'No, but I would sometimes masturbate on them and then leave.' These were graphic and horrific descriptions of incidents which had occurred over many years. Moore was unable to recall specific instances: they seemed to have been blurred into one or two which remained detailed in his memory.

I was aware that there had been incidents of men having been attacked over a number of years in the Conwy Valley. On one or two occasions the victims had sustained serious injuries, but the perpetrator had never been arrested. I guessed that it would be impossible to verify whether Moore's admission of 'around twenty men' was correct or not. Some victims had reported incidents to the police, but others would very likely have kept quiet because of embarrassment or unease about admitting that such an incident had happened to them, in particular due to the sexual nature of some of the attacks.

I also knew that there was one old, unsolved murder in the Conwy Valley and as soon as I heard reference to attacks in that area, I suspected that the detectives would be onto that old case.

'So, you haven't murdered any of your victims in the Conwy Valley, Peter?' asked Morris. Moore was onto that suggestion without hesitation.

'If you're thinking about that unsolved murder, then that's nothing to do with me. I know the one you're thinking about, it's that old one in the barn. I'm afraid that's got nothing to do with me.' He smiled. He knew what the police were trying to do – of course they had a duty to ask those questions, but Moore seemed to be satisfied that he had addressed their suggestion. By being adamant in his denial of any involvement in the Conwy Valley murder, Moore did, though, create greater certainty in my mind of how genuine his admissions to the other four murders had been. It appeared to me that he was willing to hold his hands up and admit to the crimes he had committed, but was unwilling to accept anything else.

This interview was far from being concluded. The detectives had got Moore to admit to four murders and around twenty or so serious assaults, some of a sexual nature, but there were still questions to be asked.

'Peter, can you tell me if you've murdered or planned to murder anyone else?' The fishing expedition continued. What was Moore going to admit to next? I was concerned by this approach and waited for Moore's response.

'I thought of murdering a man in Llangefni, but by the time I got back to where he was, he'd disappeared,' said Moore, in a matter-of-fact way.

'Tell me what happened,' said Morris.

'I was driving home from Holyhead late one evening and decided to take the turn off the A55 near Llangefni and drive into the town.'

'Can you recall when this was?'

'No, I can't. Sometime in November, I suppose. I drove into the town and as I was driving, I noticed a man walking along the pavement, maybe going home from the pub or something. By then it was about 11.45 p.m. So I decided that I was going to kill him. I drove through Llangefni and around the one-way system to get back to where I'd seen the man, but by the time I'd got back there, he'd gone. So I drove home.'

'If you had found the man, would you have killed him?' asked Morris.

'Yes.' Moore replied in an emotionless and impassive way. I couldn't come to terms with the stolid and blunt manner in which Moore delivered the description of his actions. It was if these were the mundane acts of someone who neither cared nor had dwelt on their behaviour afterwards. It was a desensitised description from a cold-blooded killer who seemed to have no understanding of the effect that his actions had on others.

It appeared to me, from the descriptions given by Moore, that he was someone who acted sometimes in a planned and calculating way and at other times adopted a random method of attacking his victims. In either case, his appetites drove him to commit worsening acts of extreme violence, originating from his bleakest and darkest desires. I began to realise as I sat next to Moore in the interview room, that if what we were hearing was true, then Peter Moore could perhaps no longer control that dark inner being, driving him from one violent and brutal deed to another. From the attacks in the Conwy Valley, in a worsening spiral of depravity, Moore had now reached a point where he was driven to kill. Maybe Moore himself had become the victim of his own desires and compulsions, now with no choice but to kill so as to feed the ravenous monster which was now controlling him.

'Any other similar incidents to that, Peter?' Morris asked.

'No, I think that's it,' he said. 'Apart from the bank manager,' he then said, as an aside.

'Tell me about the bank manager, Peter,' said Morris.

'Well, as Mr Jones knows,' Moore looked at me and I acknowledged the look, 'I've had some difficult financial problems in the last few months with the cinemas and I'd been in some discussions with the HSBC Bank about my debt with them, which was causing me some concern. I got to feeling that the HSBC weren't that helpful and they were putting me under pressure. I decided to make an appointment to see the manager in the HSBC Bank branch in Abergele and as a final flurry, so to speak, I was going to kill him in the bank's consulting room and then wait for the police to be called.'

'Had you decided when you were going to do this, Peter?'

'Soon, I suppose, but I hadn't decided on a date. I would have done it if you hadn't arrested me.'

The matter-of-fact way in which this information was delivered was shocking. This wasn't to be an impulsive act in which Moore would succumb to his wants and his appetites; this was a plan, or a 'final flurry', as Moore had described it, where his most evil and depraved self would display itself to everyone in the most wicked and public of acts. There would be no hiding if this deed had been committed – he was prepared to wait for the police to arrive as the bank manager lay dead or dying in the consulting room. I've tried to imagine the scene if Moore had executed his plan. I knew many of the staff at the bank in question, including the manager, and the horrors that they and their families would have faced if Moore had succeeded are unimaginable.

I have reflected often on whether what Moore said during this interview was true. Was it a case of bravado: the man had his audience and took his opportunity to perform, like an actor on celluloid before a captive cinema audience? Could all of this have been a sham, a show? The two detectives and I were cast as the gullible audience, ready to lap up the gory details of the admissions of a horrific killer in some B-movie, just for Moore's pleasure. The three of us were shocked, horrified and captivated by the performance we'd witnessed. But was it all true?

'How did you feel when you killed your victims, Peter?' asked Morris.

'It was easy. Just like a knife through butter.'

I found it difficult to make a note at this point. I felt unsure if I had actually heard what Moore had said. Morris' question was about how Moore felt emotionally when killing his victims, whether he felt regret or pain or sympathy, or anything. Moore had taken the question differently: he concentrated on the process, the physical act of plunging a knife into someone else, and to him, the act had been easy. On reflection, that may have been the cornerstone of the whole interview, the insight that was needed into the real Peter Moore: the fact that he didn't even consider the emotional context of his actions but rather the deed itself, the process of killing. When he had done it once, how easy he had found the act of stabbing someone again and again.

'Like a knife through butter.'

It was a chilling admission, delivered by Moore as if he was describing a mundane, easily forgotten action of daily life. To him, it appeared meaningless.

The interview proceeded towards its end. Morris asked about newspapers found at Moore's house. Why had he collected them? Moore explained that he had wanted to keep up with the investigation, especially in Anglesey, where he had noticed that another man had been arrested for the two murders. The knife which had been discovered in his house: was it likely that the blood of all four victims could be found on it? Moore acknowledged the possibility. Would there be anyone else's blood on the knife? It was unlikely, thought Moore.

Guthrie then revealed a number of other items which had been discovered at Moore's property. These appeared to be belongings of each of the murder victims. They had been recovered by the police from the fishpond at the back of Moore's home. There were watches, wallets and credit cards. I was aware that serial killers may have an urge to take items of a personal nature from the bodies of their victims. Looking at a victim's watch, wallet or other personal possessions would fuel the killer with the ecstasy, euphoria and possibly, in Moore's case, the sexual arousal and satisfaction experienced during the process of stabbing and killing his victim. Possessing an object would allow a killer to relive that moment repeatedly.

I looked at the items recovered from the garden pond held up by DS Guthrie. They looked incongruous and alien, things which on their own carried little significance. Their context and what they represented to Moore clearly had more meaning, as he identified each of the items held up by Guthrie and explained who they belonged to. It was like looking through the belongings of someone lying in a coma next to you: it was invasive and intrusive and felt as if it was something we shouldn't be doing.

'Is there anything else you want to mention at this stage, Peter?' asked Morris.

'No, thank you,' said Moore.

'In that case, we'll close the interview now. I'm sure we'll have more questions for you tomorrow.'

There was a moment of silence, and I detected a short sigh from Moore. Maybe he was tired, or possibly it was relief.

The tape was switched off. I made a note of the time: it was 4.15 a.m. The interview had lasted just under 45 minutes and we had covered over twenty assaults, four murders and two planned murders. Not bad for 45 minutes' work, I thought. DC Morris completed the formalities by sealing and signing each of the recorded tapes and as this was being done, DS Guthrie opened the interview room door, a stream of fresher air entering the room.

'Sergeant, could you take Mr Moore to his cell, please?' Guthrie asked the Custody Sergeant. The Sergeant responded immediately by escorting Moore from the interview room and back down the corridor to his cell.

I placed my notepad on the desk and sat back in my chair. It was only then that I noticed that both police officers were doing the same.

'I can honestly say that I don't think I will ever experience an interview like that one again. That was a complete one-off,' said Morris.

'Un-bloody-believable,' said Guthrie.

For a few moments the three of us sat in complete silence in the interview room, each of us staring straight ahead somewhere, trying to come to terms with what we'd just heard.

'I've got cups of tea for you guys,' said a police officer, bringing a tray with three mugs of tea into the room. I was a relief to have a cuppa. The three of us remained in the interview room, drinking our tea and talking about what had just happened. Because of what we'd gone through, it made little sense to immediately leave and go home. Staying and discussing the interview with others who had shared the experience appeared the correct thing to do.

When a group of people share an extreme experience together, the circumstances and the emotions of that experience bring those individuals together, as only they can really understand what they went through. This interview in the early hours of 24 December 1995 was an extreme experience. I sat sipping my tea, exhausted, not because of the early hour – the adrenalin surging through my system took care of my physical tiredness – but because of what I had heard. I felt mentally drained.

The silence in the room was a blessing. The three of us simply needed to recover from what had happened. Some would expect a solicitor and two detectives to resolutely be on opposite sides, keeping their feelings to themselves, unwilling to reveal their thoughts and impressions. But this felt different from the ordinary. It was as if the whole experience had been so overwhelming, so extreme, that the three of us as human beings needed some time to gather our thoughts and come to terms with it all.

I suppose it was the calmness and composure of Moore as he told his story and gave reasons for his actions that I found most shocking. His descriptions of killing someone were told in assured, dispassionate terms. He made the process of killing sound easy; the process of physically stabbing a person straightforward. Moore was subsequently described at his trial as a cold killer and that was true; it struck me during the interview that he had made killing an emotionless, simple and efficient process. Moore was ruthless in feeding a need in the darkest recesses of his psyche stimulated by violence, control and ultimately death. I believed then that Moore had enjoyed what he had done, that he believed it was a job well done and that he'd fed his demons in an effective way. The act of killing was like putting 'a knife through butter' and the pleasure he gained from killing appeared immeasurable.

It's no wonder DC Morris, DS Guthrie and I were in a state exhaustion and astonishment after what we'd heard. They were both experienced detectives and I had been at many an interview – it wasn't the first time we had listened to gruesome tales from suspects at interviews and it wasn't the first time we'd been woken up at 1.30 a.m. and asked to deal with people who appeared strange or violent, or even psychotic, but this interview was undoubtedly a first for us all.

After finishing our mugs of tea and discussing the way forward, it was decided that the detectives would need to fully debrief their team in the morning about developments during the night and that we would meet again for further interviews around lunchtime on what was now Christmas Eve.

We left the interview room, still shaking our heads with astonishment and disbelief, and made our way into the cold early morning. I walked over to my car, filling my lungs with the freezing air. It felt refreshing and invigorating, and made me feel alive. What a case, I thought to myself – how did this happen to me? How have I, this lad from north Wales who liked singing, acting and performing on stage as a boy, found myself in the middle of all this? It seemed unbelievable – not only that I was dealing with such a case, but that these murders had happened in north Wales.

It was nearly 4.45 a.m. by the time I started driving home. My mind was racing. I couldn't help but think about what was likely to happen over the next few months. I considered how I would handle such a big case, and what help I would need to deal with my current caseload and my responsibilities as a partner in the firm.

I decided to drive to my office, more for the comfort of knowing what had being going on during the past few days than to do any work. The place was dark and peaceful and it felt comforting to be somewhere I knew so well, though at an unfamiliar time. I looked at some notes of phone messages that had been left on the reception desk: newspaper and TV news desks asking about the case and my involvement.

'Please call us back'

'Get back ASAP.'

'Call me urgently.'

'Can we have an interview with you? Call today.'

Little did they know.

Then I noticed the other messages – the ones which had nothing to do with the Peter Moore case. That was the problem with being a small firm: there was nobody willing or able to help. I had a former partner still working at my office, but he restricted himself to probate, wills and some conveyancing, and my business partner – away on one of his long-haul holidays – was unlikely to care about my caseload and current predicament. In reality it was just me. I had to do this alone. I didn't mind doing the work and putting in the hours, and I didn't worry about taking on such a responsibility. I was young, enthusiastic and I realised that I'd been given a rare opportunity. I decided, as I sat by my desk in a dark office that morning, that this was my time. I had trained for this, I had worked for this, and now I'd been given an opportunity to show what I could do and be the best lawyer I could be.

Chapter 10

I ARRIVED HOME that morning at about 6.30 a.m. By that time, it had started to lightly snow and brisk, chilling gusts blew the small snowflakes into a wild flurry. It was nice to get into the warmth of the house. I dropped my bag in the hallway and went into the kitchen to boil the kettle – I needed a coffee and something to eat. As I poured the coffee, my wife appeared at the kitchen door.

'Is it now you're returning? You've been up all night?'

'Yes,' I replied. 'What a night! I just can't believe it.' She wanted to know what had happened, so we sat down and between bites of toast and sips of coffee I went through the night's events. The story seemed even more unbelievable when it was retold, and the admissions made by Moore and the way he presented himself seemed even more frightening as I reflected upon them further. Then there were some obvious questions that needed to be considered.

'Where do you go from here? What's going to happen now?' she asked.

I had to confess that I wasn't too sure. It was clear that the police would need to interview Moore further and would need to get into far more detail about each murder if they could. It was also likely that they would be looking into the numerous assaults he had mentioned, and it was even possible they would try and address other issues during their questioning, such as the outstanding Conwy Valley murder. They had enough time to look into these issues as the Magistrates had given them the custody time extension they required.

'So, what about tomorrow?' Cath asked.

'What about it?'

'It's Christmas Day! We have all the family coming here for lunch – I've bought enough food to feed the whole street.'

'Oh yes, Christmas. It wasn't in the forefront of my mind, sorry. Well, I suppose the show must go on. He'll have to be interviewed sometime tomorrow if he hasn't been charged today, which I think is unlikely. I'll have to see what happens tomorrow.' It didn't seem a particularly satisfactory answer, but it was the best I could do at the time. She gave me a hug. I knew that she understood me better than anyone and that she would accept that this case was important to me and that I wanted to do my best, Christmas or not.

We talked for some time about the case, my concerns and worries, and resolved to take one day at a time.

'Let's see what happens today and then make some decisions this evening. Is that OK with you?' she said. 'Whenever I see you this evening!' she added, with a laugh. Ever understanding, ever supportive, it was always a comfort to know she was on my side.

Having showered and changed, I returned to the office. I hadn't really registered that I'd had very little sleep the previous night. The snow was still falling as I drove; it appeared to be a bit heavier and I was driving in tracks left by previous vehicles for most of the way. This worried me. I needed to make sure that I could attend all the interviews in Llandudno – I had nobody in the firm who could adequately deputise for me. I needed to get there come what may, so if the weather and the road conditions deteriorated, I would have a problem.

I reached the office and, having not seen my staff since the day Moore was arrested, they all wanted to know what was going on. The gossips and storytellers had been doing their rounds in Abergele and my staff seemed to be in the middle, being asked questions by people and called by press and TV journalists. I decided that we should get together and talk things through. There were obvious concerns, in particular about what should and could be said, so I felt it was important that we discussed our approach.

'I think we should decide to stick to a consistent line,' I said. 'Let's face it, we don't know what exactly will happen in the next few days and therefore let's agree to tell people only what they'll already know anyway. Yes, Peter Moore is our client; yes, he has been arrested but at the moment has not been charged, and the police are continuing with their enquiries.'

'What if the press or TV phone again?'

'Then we give them the same message as well. That's all you know at the moment. There could well be further developments in the next couple of days, but at the moment that's the story.'

We all agreed that this was the best approach and if there were any other issues then they should come through me. There was one more problem which caused concern: the office drinks party at lunchtime on Christmas Eve – something of a tradition for all offices in town. Unfortunately, I suspected that the event would be proceeding without me this particular year, but the office would shut as usual on at 12 noon on Christmas Eve, allowing office staff to go to the nearest pub.

Sometime during the morning, I received a call from Llandudno custody to inform me that Peter Moore would be interviewed again at 1 p.m. I did as much as I could in the office that morning, but had trouble concentrating. The snow continued to build up in the streets, so I called the police station to check the weather in Llandudno.

'Not too bad here, Mr Jones,' said the Sergeant.

I decided to leave for Llandudno sooner rather than later. By the time I got onto the A55 expressway, I was driving in deep ruts and the snow was coming down heavily. The sea was dark grey and foaming and the clouds were low. It appeared to have closed in for the day. I managed to park on the road near the police station – it seemed that most road users were making their way home for a cosy Christmas Eve. I was heading in the other direction, having no idea when I would see my family.

'Bit nasty out there, Mr Jones,' said the jovial Custody Sergeant as I walked in. 'We could all be stuck here for Christmas,' he added. 'I've got some chicken sandwiches in the fridge if you fancy them, but that's about all. Not much of a Christmas dinner!' We both laughed, and I hoped his prophecy would not come true.

I asked to see Moore and went into the interview room to wait for him. I intended to go through the previous night's interview with him and advise him as to what I believed the police would be asking during the interviews that day. I wanted Moore to realise that the police would need more details of the murders he had admitted to during the early-morning interview, and that they would return to each one of them and want to go through every part of the incident step by step. Every detail was important, even though Moore may consider them trivial.

Moore arrived at the doorway of the interview room, escorted by the Custody Sergeant.

'There you are, Mr Moore,' the Sergeant said. 'Fancy a cup of tea, either of you?'

I declined and so did Moore. He looked tired as he sat down, his face was drained and his movement slower and more lethargic than earlier that morning. He sat down with a sigh and didn't appear to wish to engage much in conversation.

'Everything OK, Mr Moore?' I asked. 'Are you feeling alright this morning? It was a late night for us all.'

'Yes, thank you,' Moore replied politely, 'I'm OK.' His voice seemed quieter and more sombre. There appeared to be less of the bravado and a greater amount of thought and reflection behind that quiet voice.

'What I want to do before today's interviews is go through –'

But before I could finish my sentence, Moore held up his right hand. I assumed it was to stop me from speaking, but he looked like a child in a classroom trying to answer a teacher's question.

'Mr Jones, can I mention one thing before you begin?'

'Of course.'

'About yesterday's interview, the one in the early hours.'

'Yes,' I responded with some hesitation, 'what about it?'

'Well the thing is, Mr Jones, it wasn't true.' I didn't understand. I'd been stopped in mid-flow and maybe that was the reason why I was struggling with what Moore had said.

'What part of it wasn't true?' I asked – I truly didn't understand.

'All of it, Mr Jones. All of it wasn't true.'

It's very likely at this point that I may have looked as if I was about to be knocked down by a bus. I was finding it difficult to comprehend what Moore was telling me. I had been awake for most of the previous night listening to Moore explaining in great detail how he had assaulted and murdered people across north Wales and now, only a few hours later, I was being told that none of what I had heard was true. It was as if I was in the middle of some kind of life-sized game.

I had spent time after the interview thinking about what had been said and possible strategies for how Moore should approach the forthcoming interviews. I had considered many options, but I hadn't considered this one. What I was now being told was that he intended to make a complete U-turn, that he'd lied to me and the detectives earlier, and that he was now prepared to tell the truth.

As lawyers, we are used to clients, other lawyers and sometimes police officers playing games. We're familiar with the bluff and double-bluff tactics necessary when working as a criminal lawyer. We accept daily the games that are played in the police stations and the courts: the system allows for that and in some ways, it's what's expected of us. This game seemed to involve higher stakes: it was being played with lives and emotions. I believed I deserved an explanation.

'Are you telling me that what you told us yesterday during the interview is not true, Mr Moore?' I asked, in what I believe was a very steely tone of voice.

'It wasn't true. I was having you on.'

'Why would you want to do that?' I was incredulous, and it showed.

'Because I was protecting someone. I was protecting the real murderer.'

This was a problem. It was causing me confusion and it was likely to perplex, baffle and frankly anger the police even more. It was important that he realised that having given reasonably detailed information about four murders, which the police were no doubt in the process of attempting to verify, changing his story would most likely prove very complicated. What if all the details given by Moore were found by the police to be correct? How could he explain the knife and the victims' possessions at his house? How could he explain having knowledge of all those assaults in the Conwy Valley? Was he going to say that the person he was protecting had told him all this, or that he was acting on that person's instructions?

And what about me? Where did I stand in all of this? What exactly were my instructions from my client? Things were becoming so convoluted and confusing that it was difficult to know my direction of travel in this case. Could I still represent Moore in these circumstances, or should I hand the case over to someone else? It wasn't an idea I particularly relished, but what was the right thing to do?

These recent developments had raised so many questions. I began to challenge Moore about his change of mind, and as a consequence his change of instructions. Moore remained calm and resolute and spoke as if he had come upon some great epiphany during the early morning after the interview, which had now compelled him to finally tell the truth. Moore explained that he had hidden the truth until now due to loyalty to his friend, who he called Jason. He had been friends with Jason for some months, and had become aware of his wrongdoings and had agreed with him to hide this secret. Moore told me that Jason lived and worked as a waiter or porter in a hotel in Llandudno, but he had no address for him and could give no details of his whereabouts. He knew Jason was a killer, but because of what he now described as loyalty to him, had decided to protect his friend and that was the reason why he'd lied during the interview.

Did I believe him? I listened intently to his story: it didn't sound like a hurried tale that had been constructed on a whim in the early hours. Moore had clearly given it some thought and consideration. If it was a true story, it seemed strange that nothing about Jason had been mentioned before, even as a friend or a companion. Jason hadn't featured in any of the background information to the four murders. It seemed that the police couldn't at this stage provide much in the way of forensic evidence to place Moore at the scenes of any of the murders, other than maybe the Pensarn murder if the blood on the beach turned out to be his, but there hadn't been any suggestion of anyone else being present.

I needed to be clear firstly what Moore's instructions were to me. Was Moore now going to tell the police that everything was down to Jason? Did he realise how implausible that would sound, in light of the interview in the early hours? Did Moore understand that the police would be asking him about why his story had changed and how that would look if the case went to court?

I wanted to know if Moore could now give some more information about Jason. As he was now apparently disclosing his friend's identity, it was important for Moore to provide as much information as he could, to prove Jason's existence. I emphasised that as he had now told the secret about his friend's involvement, my duty to Moore as my client was to advise him to tell the truth, though I suspected that if Jason was real, Moore's loyalty would remain with him.

Moore listened to my advice but didn't contribute much to the discussion – a nod here, an acknowledgement there was all he seemed to be prepared to add. I hoped that he understood the predicament he was now facing. After our one-sided discussion, I asked him whether he was ready for the interview. He said that he was and I popped my head around the interview room door and told the Custody Sergeant that we were ready to proceed.

'I'm afraid Mr Moore will have to return to his cell for a while. There's been a delay, so you're going to have to sit tight for the moment,' said the Custody Sergeant. Moore was taken back to his cell and I took a seat by the desk in the interview room. The door was wide open so I could see what was going on, and I exchanged a few words with some of the police officers as they went about their work.

'Are you going to see any of Christmas Day tomorrow?' asked one.

'Not too sure about that!' was my reply. We both laughed, but in all honesty after the recent revelations, it was difficult to know what the next few hours would hold. I couldn't think about Christmas Day. I wondered about the delay and what was so urgent as to affect the planned interviews. It was possible that the information given by Moore in the early-morning interview had led to the police considering other murders, including the Conwy Valley murder, which might require further investigation at this stage.

I wondered how the police would take Moore's U-turn. Would they respond in the same way as I had? I must have looked totally shocked. I always prided myself on being able to use my acting skills to hide my true emotions when dealing with a case, but this situation had been quite different. What had happened for him to change his story? Was Moore playing games with us all, for his own macabre amusement?

A couple of mugs of tea later, Guthrie arrived.

'Just thought we'd have a quick word before the interview,' said Guthrie, closing the interview room door behind him.

'We've been to where Moore showed that he'd disposed of the body in Clocaenog Forest. We can confirm that a body has been found in that area, though it's a bit early to give you any more details of this at the moment.'

'So the map drawn by Moore was accurate?' I asked.

'Yes, it was pretty well spot on, fair play,' said Guthrie.

'OK,' I said, 'as we're talking, I think it's important for me to mention to you that the instructions from my client have changed.'

'Changed?' asked Guthrie. 'What do you mean?'

'My instructions are that what you were told in the early-hours interview was a complete pack of lies.'

'Lies?' Guthrie laughed as he spoke.

'Yes, all lies. My instructions from my client are that he didn't commit any of the murders but that he has actually been covering up for his friend Jason.'

'Jason who?' Guthrie said. 'Who the hell is Jason?'

'Your guess is as good as mine,' I replied.

'Well, bloody hell,' said Guthrie in astonishment. 'I'd better have a word with Dave.' And off he went to speak with Dave Morris and also, I suspect, DI Peter Ackerley.

Morris and Guthrie returned after about half an hour, indicating that they were now ready to proceed with the interview. Both looked slightly flustered and somewhat confused by the course this investigation was taking. Moore was escorted into the interview room and took his usual seat. When the preliminaries and introductions were over, Morris began by telling Moore that following the admissions made in the early hours and the plan drawn by Moore, the police had been to Clocaenog Forest and discovered a body more or less at the point indicated by Moore on his plan. Moore looked unmoved. He clasped his hands again on the desk and slowly nodded confirmation that he understood what had happened.

'Is there anything you want to say about this, Peter?' asked Morris. Moore paused. It was a lengthy and deliberate pause, agonisingly drawing out the tension growing in the room.

'What I told you in the interview last night was not true.'

'Not true, Peter?' responded Morris, pretending, I suspect, that he didn't understand what Moore was talking about. 'You'll have to explain to me, because I don't understand what you mean.'

'The whole thing was made up. It wasn't true. I didn't murder those people. I have been covering up for a friend of mine who was the real murderer, and that's why I lied.' There were a few grunts and groans by the detectives and shuffling of papers as they adjusted to the new situation. Moore didn't flinch; he stared unblinking at DC Morris.

'So let me get this right, Peter: you're telling us that you didn't murder these people but that you know who did murder them, and it was a friend of yours and you've been protecting him. Is that right?'

'Yes, that's correct.'

'So, Peter, who is this friend of yours? What's his name?' asked Morris, his pen poised on his notepad ready to write it down.

'His name is Jason.' Morris and Guthrie – and I, for that matter – wrote down the name 'Jason'.

'Right. So, Jason what? What's his second name?' Morris pressed on.

'I don't know. I just know him as Jason,' was Moore's brief and stony reply.

'Jason?' Morris said. 'But you don't know what his second name is?'

'That's right.'

'Isn't that a bit strange? You don't know his second name? Where does he live? His address – do you have it?' Morris continued.

'No, sorry, I don't have an address. I think he lives in Llandudno. Maybe?' Moore's impassive, unemotional response to these questions seemed childish and ill-thought out, as if he didn't care what answer he gave. I looked at his hands on the desk: they didn't move. He didn't appear to be nervous or worried. His eyes seemed to be focused directly on Morris – no flicker or movement, like a lizard studying its prey before pouncing – and his thin lips were pursed, waiting for a response from his inquisitor. We seemed to be all waiting to see what was going to happen or be said next. There were so many questions that needed to be asked and Moore appeared ready to fend off each question with a bland answer of little, if any, substance. It appeared that Moore was now unable to recall much, even though his performance in the early hours had seemed full of vivid recollections. It may have been plausible that he was protecting someone, and it was certainly believable that he may not have been alone when the murders were committed – these were horrific acts and two men may conceivably have collaborated in carrying them out. But there was no evidence of a 'Jason' being present, and if he had been, I would have expected Moore to have made more of an effort to persuade the police of this now that he had named Jason as the 'actual' murderer.

Both detectives sought to get from Moore a description of Jason, his address and his possible whereabouts. They asked questions about where Jason worked and where he came from. From what Moore said, it seemed that Jason was younger than Moore, that he had dark hair and possibly that he worked in a hotel in Llandudno. Moore had no address and neither did he have any other information which may have assisted the police in tracing Jason. It's possible of course, that Moore was just unlucky: if there really was a Jason and if he was a manipulative and devious individual, then he may have been careful what information he gave Moore or have been unwilling to give him correct information so as to hide his real identity. Moore, though lacking in detail about Jason, spoke about him as if he was a real person, not a product of his imagination. Maybe for Moore, Jason was a reality.

I subsequently discovered that the police, on the instigation of the prosecution counsel Alex Carlile QC, had undertaken a full search for anyone called Jason in the Llandudno area. They requested from every hotel and guest house an inventory of the names of all past and present employees. There was no Jason to be found. It would have been possible for Jason, if he did exist, to have been a shrewd and clever operator and made sure that if he was working in Llandudno, he gave his employers an assumed name and identity. Alternatively, there can be no certainty that the elusive Jason would have given his real name to Moore.

Moore spent most of the rest of the day bypassing any question which would directly link him to the murders. He would sidestep any enquiry regarding his presence at any of the murder scenes, avoid answering any question linking him to the possessions of the victims discovered at his home and was unwilling to elaborate on the reasons why he had a police uniform, a truncheon, a Nazi cap and other similar items. It became difficult for Moore to explain away some of the answers he had given previously, and some of the minutiae which by now was being confirmed by the police investigation.

Moore attempted to explain how he had originally met Jason and then got to know him. Moore said that he was involved with a circle of gay men in north-east Wales who would meet each other casually or in a gay club. Moore specifically mentioned one underground club on the Wirral which he and others had frequented. Moore believed that it was through this circle of friends that he had initially come into contact with Jason. It sounded a strange circle of people from the descriptions given by Moore. They were a group who would casually meet, but what went on during these meetings was mostly left by Moore to the imagination, despite the police's questioning and pushing for more detail.

It was clear that whether he was a serial killer or not, Moore had inhabited a sexually promiscuous and deviant world for some time before the murders began. He said that he had a propensity for domination, dressing in military-style uniforms and assaulting and hurting others. He derived pleasure from causing pain and it appeared that his circle shared similar impulses and lived in a world where torturing others gave them pleasure and sexual gratification. Moore recounted an incident in one of his cinemas where a group of his friends met for sex and where his police truncheon was used by him to penetrate a man who had been picked up by one of the other participants. It appeared to be a world where victims, many of whom may have been vulnerable people, were passed around from one to another. Moore mentioned with some delight and exuberance the regular participation of someone he described as a 'hermaphrodite' within this circle – Moore described him as 'a very popular guy'. The world Moore inhabited appeared degrading and depraved to an outsider, but he spoke about these incidents as if they were ordinary meetings of ordinary people involved in everyday mundane activities.

I found the way Moore spoke of these incidents shocking and difficult to reconcile with the man who sat before us. It appeared to me that we had come across a hidden world involving a number of men in north Wales who led their lives influenced by conduct of an extreme and nefarious sexual nature. As one would expect, the information that this underworld existed seemed to greatly interest the detectives. Moore's involvement and openness about it appeared to open a path for the police to investigate further wrongdoing and question whether murder and violence was commonplace within this group of men.

The interviews continued with Moore dismissing his involvement in any of the four murders and blaming them on his friend Jason. He asserted that he'd been told about them by Jason, he knew the locations of the murders because of Jason but he had no interest in breaching the trust Jason had put in him. He was in a relationship with Jason and as far as Moore was concerned, that trust was more important than anything.

Obviously I was concerned that Moore's explanation did not appear plausible. It left so many questions unanswered, in particular regarding the admissions he had made earlier. It was difficult for me to accept that he actually believed what he was saying, and I was struggling to reconcile the detail given by Moore in earlier interviews with this story. That early-morning interview, and the way he had delivered his account in such a cold and callous way, couldn't be forgotten.

By early evening we were all tired. The detectives seemed to be going round in circles with their questioning, Moore appeared to give shorter answers on every occasion and I was struggling to keep my eyes open and my notes were getting more and more illegible.

'I think we all need a rest,' said Morris. We all agreed enthusiastically.

With the formalities of sealing the interview tapes completed, the detectives and I discussed when we would reconvene, bearing in mind it was Christmas Day the following day. We all had families and thought about the possibility of conducting some interviews in the morning, around 10 a.m., which might allow us to return home in the early afternoon to spend the rest of Christmas Day with our families. As we were discussing our possible approach, Moore intervened.

'Yes, gentlemen, I think you should spend some time with your families on Christmas Day. Don't mind me, I'll be OK.' It seemed a surprisingly polite and thoughtful remark from someone suspected of being a serial killer. Strangely, it seemed sincere and heartfelt. Clearly he had a vested interest, in that by not facing further lengthy questioning, he would avoid the need to continue with his Jason story and the difficulties that was causing him. But for a moment, after spending hours on the horrors that Moore may have inflicted on his victims, there was a glimpse of a humanity – a considerate and sympathetic being appearing from the abomination and evil of the previous few days. That was the contradiction of Peter Moore.

We agreed to reconvene for a further interview at 10 a.m. on Christmas morning. As I left the police station, it became clear that it had been snowing for most of the day and now, by early evening, the snow was thick on the ground and causing very difficult driving conditions. Driving home would take time, but it gave me an opportunity to think about the day's developments and what Moore had said, how he had behaved and how the case was progressing. It was clear that Moore displayed many confusing and contradictory characteristics, from the most violent and depraved to considerate and affable. We are all full of contradictions and exhibit them on more or less a daily basis, so why should Moore be any different? It was the extremes of his contradictory behaviour which appeared so shocking, from the caring and charming businessman to the destructive predator. Moore was a complicated and perplexing individual.

Chapter 11

CHRISTMAS DAY DAWNED with a blanket of snow. White Christmases don't happen very often, but I didn't imagine I would have much time to enjoy this one. Catherine and I woke early, exchanged our gifts and attempted to be as festive as possible. In the back of my mind was the knowledge that I needed to be in the police station by 10 a.m. Looking out of the window at the snow scene emerging from the Christmas morning darkness, I was also worried about whether I would actually be able to drive to the police station. Before breakfast, I decided to call custody in Llandudno Police Station to find out how things were there.

'It's a bit dangerous on the roads – it's passable, but you'll have to take care, Mr Jones,' was the answer I got. 'If you want us to send a Land Rover or something for you, we'll try and arrange that.'

I said that I'd give it a try and if I had problems, I'd give them a call. I set out from home at about nine o'clock, promising to be back home for a late Christmas lunch. The roads were treacherous and for most of the journey I was driving slowly in snowy tracks. By the time I arrived in Llandudno, the sun was beginning to break through the clouds and it seemed a little warmer, and the snow had started thawing from the roads.

'Nice weather for it!' said DC Morris as I walked into the custody suite. They were waiting for me, though I'd arrived early. 'Keen to get going,' I thought to myself – possibly we were all keen to get home.

I spoke to the Custody Sergeant, seeking confirmation that everything was fine with Moore. He appeared to have had a comfortable night, had a good breakfast and was well and talkative. Everything seemed positive on Christmas morning.

When we got to the interview room and Moore was brought through, there was a surreal exchange of Christmas greetings and merriment from us all, as if we'd arrived at some weird Christmas party. I suppose none of us knew quite how to behave in such a situation: it was serious, it was macabre, but it was Christmas. Even Moore appeared to have an affable, even convivial, look in his eyes as he settled down for interview.

Morris explained that their intention was to conduct further interviews during the morning and then suspend them until the following day, unless there was something which required immediate attention. All in the room, including Moore, nodded and agreed with the approach and when the formalities were over, the interview commenced.

Moore clasped his thin hands on the desk in front of him again, sighing as if the whole process was becoming tedious and dreary. His eyes fixed on Morris, he was listening, but I was unsure whether everything was registering. I wondered if he was fully engaged or had become bored with the whole process. Maybe the excitement of being caught and those early days was wearing thin. I studied his body language. He had placed himself in the same position as in previous interviews: hands clasped, sitting forward in his chair, shoulders hunched, eyes staring at his inquisitor intently without flinching. His stubble was longer and greyer and he looked unkempt, untidy and less compelling than he had the day he was arrested. Despite the assertive persona that Moore was aiming to convey, it looked to me as if this was beginning to slide. He appeared to be losing control of the dominant man in black, the man who I imagined would force himself on other men and dominate them, subjecting them to violence of a brutal and sexual nature. Moore today appeared less frightening and less intimidating. On that day, the aura had gone and we sat in the interview room with what appeared to be a tired old man.

The morning's interviews proceeded as expected, with questions about Jason and the relationship between Moore and Jason – details were sought of where they had been what they had done. Moore's replies continued to be vague and unhelpful, and often he deflected questions by asking other questions.

'Why aren't you looking for Jason? Why aren't you looking at the evidence and linking it to him?'

His approach that morning was diversionary and it appeared that the veil of apparent truth with which he was seeking to shroud everything was becoming thin and fragile. It was clear that Moore had lied to both me and the police officers on numerous occasions, but now those lies were tired and exhausted. The police officers, myself and even Moore were becoming weary and worn out by the continual questions.

The morning proceeded slowly. At about 12.30 it became clear that Moore was unlikely to co-operate further and that the police were not going to succeed in eliciting valuable information with their questioning.

'Why don't we call it a day?' asked Morris.

'Yes, good idea,' said Moore, enthusiastically. 'You go home to your families and enjoy the rest of Christmas Day.' It was a thoughtful remark, but from someone in Moore's situation it also sounded farcical.

I called my wife from the police station, telling her that I was on my way home. The house was filling up with family and she was glad to hear the news. The snow was thawing and the snowy tracks on the roads were beginning to turn into a slushy mess. I stopped for a moment before getting into the car and took a deep breath of fresh wintry air. It was refreshing and cleared my head, hazy from the morning's questioning. I was glad to get out of the stifling atmosphere of the custody suite and away from the interviews, consultations and court hearings. I'd got into a pattern which was far from my normal daily life and though courts and police stations were a regular feature, in the last few days they had become my everything. The interview rooms, cells and custody suite had become claustrophobic, an airless confine spinning around in endless frustrating circles.

There was also a strange feeling of unpleasantness. It was a sensation of being in familiar but nonetheless unfamiliar territory, of knowing what to do and how to do it but of having encountered something so unfamiliar and unknown to me. I had met bad people before, I had been surprised and sometimes shocked by what people had said and done, but this case was very different. The whole experience stirred emotions in me which made me question whether I was doing the right thing in representing this man. I was questioning whether I should be wishing him a Merry Christmas and exchanging idle pleasantries with him over a cup of tea. I was beginning to feel that I had encountered what some would call a 'force of evil'. I had never been one to overdramatise a situation and neither did I believe it sensible to dissect a client's character and motives. I was, though, a product of my Methodist upbringing. I still had in my genes the feeling that heaven was up there somewhere and hell was down the other way. I had the uncomfortable sensation that Peter Moore had become the personification of what I believed to be evil, concealed among us as a rather unspectacular businessman.

These were outlandish and ridiculous thoughts. On reflection, they don't stand up to logical examination. Moore was a product of his time and his circumstances. He lived in a closeted community where he had little opportunity to express himself even during his adult years, and upon the death of his mother, something seemed to have been unleashed from within him which compelled him to act out his wildest and most evil fantasies without any thought for others and the destruction he was causing.

During his early-morning interview, it is very likely the reality of Moore's actions dawned upon him. Even for a brief few hours in the middle of the night, Moore had put into words what seemed to me to be the trigger for his behaviour.

'My mother died just over a year ago, and then two of my dogs passed away, and then a cat that we'd had for years died, and unbelievably my koi carp in the pond then died. Death literally seemed to be following me everywhere.'

'Did you miss your mother, Peter?' asked Morris during the interview. Moore looked heartbroken for a moment: it was a look of someone who in all honesty had nothing to live for.

'I missed her dreadfully,' was his reply, and then he added, chillingly: 'You see, killing someone was the only way for me to feel at peace.'

Murder was a route to gain 'peace' – it's a chilling statement and a reminder that this was not an ordinary case, that they were not ordinary murders and that Peter Moore was a psychopath.

Moore clearly exhibited psychopathic traits at the time of his arrest, and maybe still does to this day. Other than with his mother, he appeared from my knowledge of him to be lacking in meaningful and close personal relationships, and from his own admissions manifested behaviours which would be considered amoral and antisocial.

During the early-morning interview, Moore was asked whether he had derived sexual pleasure from the process of killing. It appeared to me that his behaviour had worsened over time due to him possibly having to behave in more extreme ways so as to derive sexual pleasure from the experience of dominating and torturing an individual. He admitted to attacking people over a number of years, and I wondered if it was possible that murder was the inevitable and logical end to this behaviour. Wherever the compulsion to kill came from, Moore had been willing to concede during his early-morning interview that it was a 'job well done'.

There appeared to be no feeling or regret expressed in that statement. It was detached from any human sentiment, expressed in a way that someone would reflect on a task or a burden. Moore considered what he had done a 'job', a function that he had to perform, and in his opinion, he had done it well. The window into his psyche which was opened during that interview showed Moore to be a man compelled to kill, and he was good at what he had chosen to do – he believed himself to be a successful and effective killer.

Driving home from the interviews on Christmas morning, I found my mind was full of thoughts and theories. Moore had confused me, as he had confused everyone. I knew that I was dealing with the most complex and manipulative of characters, I knew that he appeared to have committed some horrendous crimes which he was now denying. My job wasn't to challenge Moore's version of events. Moore was entitled to put forward that defence and to tell his story and be given the best possible opportunity to do so. I was his defence lawyer: my role was not to decide on how truthful he was; that was the responsibility of the jury in a Crown Court trial. Moore had a story and whether I liked that story or not, I was now responsible for telling it. My duty to Moore now was to ensure his instructions were carried out effectively and that I put forward the best defence possible on his behalf.

It was wonderful to get home that Christmas lunchtime, to escape from the madness of the previous few days. We ate lunch as a family, laughed about silly things, drank wine, pulled crackers and did all the crazy Christmas things that families do on Christmas Day. It was pure escapism, and for a few hours I forgot about Moore and about all the strange and wicked things I'd heard over the previous few days.

Catherine and I sat by the fire at the end of the evening and stared into the flames in silence. I recall being too tired to even talk, but being quiet was fine and Catherine was happy to allow me some time just to switch off completely.

'I can't ever remember being this exhausted before,' I finally said. 'It's not so much a physical tiredness, it's something else:

it's a deep feeling of exhaustion in the pit of my stomach. Maybe it's some kind of emotional thing?' We talked for a while about what the next few months could bring. I was worried about how I would run my business with all the work that involved and the Moore case on top. We agreed to take one day at a time, to talk to my business partner when he got back from holiday and to see if I could get some help over the next few months. It wasn't that I was afraid of work – far from it – but I was afraid of things getting out of control, and I knew that I would be facing the biggest and most challenging few months of my professional life. I was travelling into unknown territory and I needed to be prepared. Talking with Catherine helped. I always knew she would be on my side and though she was a very busy teacher herself, I knew that she would help and support me as much as she could.

Chapter 12

THE SNOW HAD more or less cleared by Boxing Day. Usually I'd be going out to meet friends in Denbigh but I was on my way back to the police station in Llandudno by mid-morning. When I arrived at the custody suite, things seemed a little lethargic. Neither of the detectives had arrived and the custody area seemed unusually quiet.

'Calm before the storm,' predicted the Custody Sergeant. 'It can usually be pretty wild here on Boxing Day – fights, domestics, drunkenness, you know: all the fun of the fair!' We both laughed and I took my place in the interview room as the Sergeant went to fetch Peter Moore.

Moore arrived looking tired and weary. He said he felt a bit exhausted and that he hadn't slept well. We talked about the previous interviews and what he should expect today. I then suggested that I believed it very likely that the police would consider charging him today.

'What do you think I'll be charged with?' Moore asked. I was unsure if it had been asked to test me out in some way, or whether he really didn't know what to expect.

'It's likely you'll be charged with four counts of murder and possibly they will consider assault charges as well. Alternatively, the police may investigate those offences and lay some further charges later on. It will certainly be the four murders.'

Moore nodded, but he didn't respond. It was as if he'd accepted his fate and any inclination he may have had to prolong things had gone.

'Where do you think I'll be taken?' he asked.

'Well, you'll be brought before the next available court, which I suspect will be tomorrow in Llandudno, so it's likely you'll remain here until then. Afterwards, due to the nature of these changes, you're going to be remanded in custody, which means you'll be taken to a prison somewhere – most likely Walton Prison in Liverpool – until your next hearing.'

Moore looked at me for a moment in silence, his thin lips tightly shut. He looked as if he was straining for something to say but just couldn't find the words. I sensed he was upset and maybe even about to cry. I averted my eyes from his: if he was about to cry, I would rather not be a witness to it – I was unsure how I'd react, and would rather not know.

We sat in the interview room with the door open, without saying a word. I suppose there was nothing else either of us could say. It had been a long and stressful few days, emotions had been running high and the journey we had taken individually and jointly was one that neither of us would ever forget.

'It's been a strange few days,' Moore finally said. I laughed in response.

'You can say that again,' I said. 'Not really the type of Christmas I was planning.'

'I'm sorry about that,' Moore said. We sat again in silence, immersed in our own thoughts. I wondered what he was thinking. Was he reflecting on what had been said during the past few days? I wondered if his emotions were tainted with a grain of remorse or regret, and if so, was the feeling of guilt about to overwhelm him? I couldn't tell, but I wasn't about to ask him either. I knew where my duties lay and I was sure that he wasn't about to gush out some emotional confession to me.

Sitting in a room with an alleged serial killer is an experience. But what he appears to be as he sits across the table from you is just a man, another human being. The way he talks or looks at you, or pushes his hair back from his forehead, the noises he makes as he clears his throat or the way he taps his fingers on the desk or the shuffling movements he makes in his chair as he becomes uneasy, are all just like anyone else: they are the similarities that we all display as humans.

It would be impossible for anyone to have known what was going through Moore's mind as we sat in silence in that room. The feelings, desires, experiences and appetites which drove Peter Moore. Those hidden failings which we all possess as humans but choose never to display to others. Those wants and cravings which occupy our private thoughts and feed our desires. We cannot see any of these things in someone else and will likely never really find out about them. They are, though, the fabric of every being and as such they are also the fundamentals of any serial killer. It's what makes them tick, it's the fuel that enables them to function and it's what compels them to think the way that they do, to behave the way they behave and ultimately to kill the way they kill.

Someone like Peter Moore is thankfully unusual. It needs a certain set of circumstances, personality, upbringing, experiences and opportunity for a serial killer to be shaped. Experts with far greater knowledge than myself will have identified the 'perfect storm' of circumstances and propensities necessary for someone to become such a killer. I can only testify from my own experience of observing Moore at close quarters that they don't seem outwardly to be monsters. It is very convenient for society to label people as 'evil', 'sinful' and 'depraved', and their behaviour and the deeds they have committed must be categorised as such. But when one sits in a room with a serial killer, wasting time, waiting for something to happen, drinking tea and passing the time of day – even laughing, on occasion – it's exactly the same as sharing time with a colleague at work or an acquaintance in a café. It seems that for those few moments, the acts they've committed have become divorced from the person sitting in the room with you. I suppose it's necessary for that detachment to happen, if you are to relate in any way to such a person. We lawyers must see them as people, because the relationship we build with them will enable us to do our job. It may seem strange to some, but this was the reasoning I adopted so that I could begin to cope with the horrors of this case.

The detectives finally arrived and I got the immediate impression that, as time before they would have to charge Moore was now becoming limited, the police had decided that they had got as much as they could get from interviewing him. DC Morris explained that there were a few things that they needed to clear up in interview, and following that they would be speaking to the Custody Sergeant with a view to deciding what to do next.

The interview was brief. The detectives had a short list of points about locations and evidence they were trying to substantiate, and also returned to Jason and whether Moore would be willing to volunteer any more information about him, but Moore seemed by now to have lost interest in the whole interview process. His answers were short and he simply repeated what had been said in previous interviews. It all felt as if we were just going through the motions and that there was nothing further that either the police could ask or Moore would add to the process. Maybe we were all punch-drunk, like staggering and exhausted boxers who had been at it for round after round and had little, if any, fight left.

Finally, the interview ended and the cassettes were removed from the tape recorder and sealed in their boxes. Both officers disappeared into the back office for a conversation with the Custody Sergeant while Moore and I remained in the interview room. The officers took their time, though we knew what to expect. After about ten minutes, we were called to the custody desk. The Custody Sergeant, computer screen in front of him and a bunch of papers in his hand, took over the proceedings, with DC Morris and DS Guthrie standing behind him keeping an eye on the process.

'Peter Howard Moore,' the Sergeant announced.

'Yes,' Moore replied. There was a crack in his voice as he spoke. He cleared his throat; the Sergeant waited, then continued.

'I have spoken with the officers at length and in light of what they have told me, I am satisfied that you can be charged at this stage with four counts of murder. What I will now do is go through the formal process of charging you, and then I will explain to you what's going to happen afterwards. Do you understand that, Mr Moore?'

The Sergeant then read out the police caution and asked Moore to again confirm his understanding of it.

'I do,' said Moore. The Sergeant then turned towards me, standing at Moore's side.

'Are you happy with that, Mr Jones?'

'Yes, I am,' I said.

'On a date in September 1995 at Caergeiliog, Anglesey, that you Peter Howard Moore, contrary to common law, did murder Henry John Roberts. Do you have anything to say?'

'No,' Moore said, shaking his head and staring at the floor. I made a note of his response.

The second charge, of the murder John Randles, was then read; and then the third, of the murder of Edward Carthy; and then finally the fourth, of the murder of Anthony Davies. Moore said 'No' when asked after each charge whether he wanted to comment.

Now it was real. Moore had been officially charged with all four murders and the process of moving towards a trial, whenever that was to be, had begun.

It was explained to Moore that he would go before the Llandudno Magistrates' Court the following morning and that matters would then proceed to the Crown Court. Moore and I chatted again for a few moments about the hearing the following day. We agreed to speak again in the morning, and he seemed resigned to his immediate future. I looked back at him as he was escorted to his cell by one of the police officers:

his shoulders were hunched and he seemed to shuffle slowly in his police-issue flip-flops. To me, at that time, he appeared a dejected, sad and lonely figure.

I was glad to get home that Boxing Day. I spent most of the day being lazy, though the Moore case was never far from my thoughts. I always found when working as a lawyer that I could never switch off completely. Even on days when I was not working or in the evening after work, certain cases would be in the back of my mind constantly. Sometimes something would remind me of a case, something that had been said, and it would stay in my mind for hours on end. Questions, problems, uncertainties and insecurities would come to fore, and I found it very difficult to put them to one side.

The following morning, I was in my dark court suit, fresh white shirt and appropriate-looking tie – no doubt selected by Catherine. She wished me luck and gave me a hug and a kiss as I left the house. I'd been awake for a few hours, going over the day's proceedings in my mind, considering the options, what could happen and what should be said in court. It was to be a very straightforward hearing; in theory it should last only a few moments. In a usual case I wouldn't have worried – it would have been a regular day in court. This case was different on so many levels: it was the first court hearing after Moore had been charged and it was likely to receive local and national attention. My words would be reported widely, questions would be asked by reporters and everything would be open to scrutiny.

I arrived at Llandudno Magistrates' Court, located at that time, like the Colwyn Bay one, next to the police station. The court was old fashioned and unsuitable even for the 1990s, but convenient as prisoners could be easily brought from the police station custody suite to the court building. Having arrived at the court and spoken to the Court Clerk to confirm my presence, I went over to the police station for a quick word with my client. Moore seemed jovial and in good spirits. He smiled at me as I arrived and we sat and chatted for a few moments. I wanted to make sure that he was fine – before speaking to Moore, the Custody Sergeant had confirmed to me that they had been checking on him on a regular basis all night.

'Just to make sure you know, Mr Jones, we put him on suicide watch. You never know, do you? When someone is charged with murder, none of us know how they'll react.' It was a fair point and highlighted again how seriously the police were taking their responsibilities in this case. I was pleased to see that Moore had reportedly slept well, had a shower and eaten a good breakfast. He appeared to be calmer than I was.

I returned to the court. By now the reporters were beginning to file into the public area. Some photographers and TV cameramen stood outside kicking their heels and looking on edge, worried that they could miss out on that valuable paying shot. I noticed a few familiar reporters in the court corridor, milling around and chatting to each other. As I appeared, their focus seemed to change – they all wanted to exchange pleasantries with me.

'Had a good Christmas?'

'What was Christmas dinner like in the cells?'

We all laughed. It was all a bit nerve-wracking and tense but it was good to share a joke. The prosecutor, Nita Dowell, arrived, with a large file of papers in hand and a jovial smile.

'Mr Jones,' she said acknowledging me. 'Are you OK after the past few days?' It was nice of her to ask me whether I was keeping well. As a fellow lawyer, she would have realised how the pressure and demands of such a case could affect a defence solicitor, and I appreciated her enquiry.

'Yes fine – no problems,' I replied. I suppose I wouldn't have said anything different even if I hadn't been feeling all that great. We chatted about the case and agreed a way forward. Clearly she and I both had a considerable amount of work ahead of us, but she was also a person I could always rely upon to be straight and honest, and that made a difficult process a little easier.

By the time Nita and I had finished chatting, some other lawyers and interested parties had appeared in the court. It was likely they had cases which were going to be called later that morning, but I got the feeling that they'd made sure they arrived early so as to see the Peter Moore case being called. There's nothing quite like a nosy lawyer snooping around to get the blood going. I got to know the ones who would ferret around other solicitors' cases, loudly expressing opinions and even coming over to your client for a chat and a joke. There are a few in every court – the ones who, though working as lawyers, would have been more suited to a career as a bookmaker or a confidence trickster. I used to try and avoid their gaze and their car-salesman patter and get on with my work.

The Moore case was the first to be called that morning. The Court Clerk wanted to get the case over and done with before dealing with anything else, everyone agreed. A phone call was made by the Court Clerk, asking the police to bring Peter Moore into court from the police cells. The court sat in silence but for some paper shuffling and the clearing of throats. Heavy metal doors could be heard opening and closing in the distance, and sets of keys rattled in locks. The banging got nearer and footsteps became discernible. Eventually the door beneath the court dock was heard opening, then a metal gate which allowed the prisoner and two accompanying police officers to walk up a set of stairs and directly into the court dock.

Moore emerged into the dock, all eyes on him. He looked around before being directed by one of the police officers to stand in front of a chair in the dock and face the Magistrates. I noticed that he seemed to be grinning slightly – I was unsure if it was nerves or a look of self-satisfaction. He looked down from the dock towards me and gave me a nod of acknowledgement. A murmur of conversation travelled in a wave through the courtroom, reporters were writing and a few busybody lawyers standing at the back and side of the court seemed deep in whispered conversations. The door at the front of the court opened and three Magistrates trooped into court and took their places on the bench. The Magistrates, two men and one woman, looked nervous and intimidated by the whole process. Self-consciously, they arranged their notepads and paperwork, everyone in the court watching them intently. The woman Magistrate seemed unwilling to look out at the courtroom, her mousy hair like a curtain over her eyes. She looked down at her notes and then across at the Chair of the bench. The Chair was a headmasterly middle-aged man who always appeared to be on the brink of giving a stern telling off to anyone who looked at him in the wrong way. Straight backed and with fountain pen poised, he peered across at the lawyers and then towards the dock and directly at Peter Moore. The third Magistrate, who always reminded me of a small grey mouse, seemed to be having problems with his papers and was constantly shuffling them around – I imagined he was trying to make a little nest for himself.

Eventually the Court Clerk took a dramatic intake of breath, then stood up and announced the case. Peter Moore was asked to confirm his name, date of birth and address. Once done, he was invited to sit down in the dock and Nita Dowell and I were formally introduced to the Magistrates as the prosecution and defence lawyers respectively. The Chair made diligent notes of everything that was said. The Court Clerk then continued by saying that matters would not be proceeding any further today but that there was the question of bail to be discussed. The Clerk reminded the court, as if they needed reminding, that 'the defendant, Mr Moore, has been charged with four offences of murder and that this will have to be considered when making a decision about bail.' Nita then made an application to the court that Peter Moore be remanded in custody until the next hearing due to the nature of the charges and the danger Moore would present to any witnesses and to the public in general. The Chair of the Magistrates looked in my direction.

'Mr Jones?' he said.

'I'm not opposing my friend's application for a remand in custody,' I said, getting to my feet as I spoke and looking in the direction of the Chair, who was by now writing again.

'Very well,' the Chair said. 'When is the next hearing to be?'

There was then a half-whispered discussion between Nita, the Court Clerk and me about when the next hearing should take place. In those days we didn't have the advantage of video connections with a prison and therefore it would be necessary to arrange for the prisoner to come to court even when the hearing was a purely administrative one. In Peter Moore's case, it would mean transporting him from the nearest prison – HM Prison Walton in Liverpool – to the Magistrates' Court on a regular basis. It was necessary in those days even in cases like Moore's for the prisoner to be remanded in custody by the Magistrates' Court and then formally committed ('sent', in plain English) to the Crown Court for the trial on a future occasion. In my opinion, things have become a little more efficient in the court system now, though I'm uncertain if all criminal lawyers would agree.

The Magistrates decided that Moore would be remanded in custody for three weeks and then be returned to court, at which point it was hoped that some progress could be made.

'Mr Moore?' the Chair of the bench declared loudly across the courtroom. He had arrived at his big moment and wanted to make sure that everyone heard what he was about to say.

'Stand up, Mr Moore.' Moore got to his feet, as did the two police officers, who stood behind him.

'Peter Howard Moore, we are unable to progress your case today. You've heard what the lawyers have said, and we have decided that you are to be remanded in custody for three weeks until the next hearing of this matter, and that hopefully we will be able to make some further progress on that occasion.'

There was a moment of silence as if no one knew what should be done next. Moore stood in the dock looking pleased with himself, the hint of a grin remaining. He stood with his arms behind his back – from my angle, his chin looked even longer and more protruding. The Court Clerk looked round towards the Chair, who seemed to have frozen with a stern look fixed on his face. I thought maybe he was attempting to prolong his time in the limelight just a little longer, and then he got to his *pièce de résistance* – the moment I imagined he'd been rehearsing in his mind, over and over, the night before while in bed. In a loud, booming, severe tone he said, 'Officers, take him down.' I had a little chuckle and I suspected that Nita in the seat next to me was also stifling a laugh. I thought maybe he'd seen someone say that in a movie sometime, and this was his opportunity and he was damn well going to say it.

Moore was escorted down the stairs of the dock and back towards the police cell. The atmosphere in the court toned down a few notches and conversations could be heard escalating in volume. Even the Magistrates on the bench seemed to have relaxed, and began to chatter among themselves excitedly. I got up and collected my papers.

'I'll be in touch,' I said to Nita.

'I bet you will,' she responded. We both smiled nervously.

It seemed that everyone present during the short hearing had decided to leave at the same time, and the courtroom exit was full of departing reporters and lawyers, gossiping with each other as they left.

'You're going have some fun with that one,' one lawyer said, in an attempt at humour.

'Bloody better watch your back,' said another. As I turned into the court waiting area, one of the local reporters tapped me on the shoulder.

'Dylan, got a moment?'

'Sure, how can I help?'

'Well, it's like this.' The reporter seemed to want to move me away from others so that our conversation was private. I found myself with my back to the wall facing the reporter, who had now begun what I assumed was a rehearsed speech.

'You know we're a local paper and so on, so I thought you would maybe want to talk to us first about the case and any developments and what was going to happen next, sort of thing?' He gave a friendly and slightly expectant smile, as if I was about to give him some great exclusive story on all the goings-on in the case. I admired his brass neck in approaching me as soon as he could and setting out his position as clearly as possible. I'm sure he would return to his office and tell his Editor how forward-thinking he had been, but he wasn't about to get anything from me that morning. I think he actually knew that, but I suppose it was worth a try. I let him down gently.

'Look, it's an early stage and it wouldn't be right for me to speak to anyone about the case at the moment. There are still so many uncertainties – the last few days have been a complete whirlwind. Let's allow things to settle down.' The reporter seemed to understand and moved away with a last-ditch attempt.

'Well, you know where I am when you want to talk, Dylan,'

'Sure,' I said with a laugh. 'Of course I do.'

I'd never been so popular within the court community – everyone seemed to want to have a word or share an anecdote, and it took me a while to leave the court building and get back round to the police station entrance. I was greeted by a group of photographers and news cameramen who had now decided to move from the court entrance to the custody entrance in the hope of getting a shot of Moore as he left in the police van for prison in Liverpool.

'Do you know when he'll be leaving, Mr Jones?' asked one.

'Not too sure – it could be a while yet.' My response was greeted with a few groans from those who may have been ready for a cup of coffee rather than standing outside a police station in the December cold, waiting for a glimpse of a serial killer.

When I arrived in the custody suite, Moore was already in the process of being checked out of the police station and handed over to the authorities to transport him over to HM

Prison Walton in Liverpool. I stood to one side by the custody desk as the paperwork was being completed. Moore was calm and co-operative as the formalities were being done. He glanced over and smiled and I decided to have a quick word with him before he was escorted into the van. I explained that I would write to him in the next few days with an update, and that I would also hope to come over to Walton Prison in the next couple of weeks for a discussion before the next hearing. Moore seemed content with the arrangements and thanked me for everything I'd done so far for him. The police seemed keen to get moving so after snatching those few words, the door at the rear of the police station was opened and Moore was escorted to a waiting van, its doors open to accept its cargo, who was quickly becoming notorious. As I surveyed the scene from the door of the police station, I thought I saw Moore pause for a moment before entering the police van. It was as if he'd stopped and looked over towards the cameramen, who were positioned to his right and over a fence, about 20 m or so away. It appeared to me as if he'd stopped and posed for the cameras, just for a brief second. Maybe it was my imagination, given that the whole scene appeared a little surreal and strange, but as I stood by the police station doors looking at Moore leaving, I wondered if he was actually enjoying the attention he was now receiving.

The police van departed and the press photographers and cameramen slowly moved away. Things on the street outside the police station got back to normal as the throng of interested parties and busybodies evaporated. I walked to my car, parked up the road from the court. It was a relief to leave the court, police station, questioning eyes and back-chatting gossipmongers. It was the day after Boxing Day but it felt as if I'd been in the middle of a whirlwind for months. I could have gone home – the firm was still officially shut for the Christmas break – but I decided that I'd call into work on my way to get my head and all my notes in order.

The peace and silence of my office was comforting. There were no phones ringing or staff members with messages making demands and asking questions. I sat by my desk and looked at the bundle of messages: things to do, phone calls to make, people to chase. I put the bundle to one side – they would have to wait until after the Christmas holiday. I gathered all the notes I had complied over the previous few days and briefly skimmed through them. They were notes of conversations with the police officers and Peter Moore himself, and then notes of everything that had been said during the countless interviews. In the margins, I'd noted some brief observations with my impressions of a situation or my views on Moore himself, his manner and behaviour. I thought these notes would be useful in the future, if only for me to recall the full context of everything that took place during those few days in the police station.

I sat in my office for an hour or so getting my notes in order, reading what I'd written and making sure that everything I needed was available for future reference. I then made a brief note of what I thought I would need to do before the next hearing and before I saw Peter Moore again.

I decided that I needed to get an expert on board to work with me on this case. Even though I'd handled everything that happened in the police station alone, I knew that this case would require more than one set of hands. I suspected that help was unlikely to come from my colleagues at my firm: they either had no knowledge of criminal law or had been out of regular contact with criminal cases for some time and were now practising in other fields of the law. My business partner was still on his holiday and though he had in the past been a criminal practitioner, he'd never dealt with anything as big as this case. I felt that I needed someone outside my firm who could give me the necessary support and guidance, someone who had been involved in similar cases and with people like Peter Moore. I was confident that I'd earned Moore's trust during those few days in the police station, and I needed someone to work with on the case who would continue to build on that.

Developing a relationship of trust and understanding with a client in any case is crucial, and that understanding must work both ways. The client must trust the advice and guidance the lawyer gives to him or her, and in turn the lawyer must be confident that the client is being as open and honest as he or she can. Of course, that doesn't always happen: there are times when clients decide to lie to their lawyer and to everyone else, and that is their choice, though sometimes the consequences can be dire. That lawyer/client relationship is key to the success or otherwise of the case. I wanted to make sure that the team I put together for this case was suitable for a client like Peter Moore and for a murder case such as this one. I needed to consider my options and thought I should speak with a few lawyers that I trusted for some advice and guidance. There was a lot to think about and some big decisions to be made.

HM Prison Walton, Liverpool
(Wikimedia Commons)

Chapter 13

PREPARING ANY BIG criminal case is difficult. Once the client has been charged, and in serious cases remanded in custody, then the lawyer will need to work to regular deadlines to get the case ready for trial. It may be easy to forget that in reality a lawyer may have twenty, thirty, even up to fifty other ongoing cases at the same time, and rather than focusing all their energy on only one case, they will very often have to juggle cases, clients, witnesses and paperwork from many different cases all at the same time. This takes great skill but is a necessity of our business and is what our senior partners demand, though it can be very difficult. One of my weaknesses as a lawyer was that when I became involved in a case I found interesting and intellectually stimulating, it would then take over my working hours and regularly also all my free time. Often my wife would catch me on a day off, lost in my own world, and say, 'You're thinking about that case again, aren't you?'

I suppose that this was my strength as a lawyer, but also eventually my downfall.

'You do realise that this Peter Moore case is going to be all-consuming for a while?' I asked Catherine on one occasion. 'You know that this is going to be full-on for the next twelve months or so?'

'When you say full-on, does that mean it will be more or less the only thing you think and talk about for a year?' she asked, half in jest and with a smile. I smiled back at her.

'I think maybe you're right.'

Having an obsessive nature is not a bad thing for a lawyer; it means not being able to give up on a case. Ideas and thoughts about cases occur in the strangest places and not always at convenient times. It's a blessing but also sometimes a curse, especially in the early hours. And it means that you never switch off – you're always thinking, always planning.

When the Magistrates' Court case had finished that morning, on 27 December 1995, and the crowds of journalists had left, the other lawyers had gone back home or to their offices and had forgotten about the case until the next hearing or the next article they read in the newspaper, I was left with a mountain to climb, and at that time I believed that I was climbing it alone.

My greatest concern was engaging a suitable experienced junior barrister to work with me on the case. I was firmly of the opinion that as I had never been involved in a case like this before, I needed a barrister who had been there and done it all before. Having spoken to a few colleagues and friends, the name of Dewi Williams, from a chambers in Liverpool, was suggested. I knew he was experienced and knowledgeable, he was Welsh and lived somewhere near Ruthin, and he'd dealt with all sorts of criminal cases in the past both as a solicitor and then as a barrister. He seemed to me to be the ideal barrister for this case and I decided to call his chambers and have a word with him.

When I called the barristers' chambers in Liverpool, Dewi Williams was in a meeting. 'Let me take a message and he'll get back to you sometime today,' said the receptionist. I explained that I was the solicitor representing Peter Howard Moore, who had been charged over the Christmas break with four murders in north Wales, and I was looking to speak to someone for some advice and guidance and believed that Mr Williams could assist. The receptionist seemed to be rather unresponsive and I began to wonder whether she was listening or had fallen asleep.

'OK, that's fine, thank you,' she said and put down the receiver. She may have thought it was a prank call – 'A serial killer in north Wales?'

I decided to give her the benefit of the doubt and allow her half an hour or so to convey her message before I called the chambers back. My doubts about the receptionist were greatly misplaced – within about two minutes of my call, my phone rang.

'Dylan, Mr David Williams, barrister from Liverpool on the line,' said our receptionist. I'd forgotten that though he was actually called Dewi, for work purposes he was called David, my theory being that long ago a decision had been made that the criminal fraternity of Liverpool were better equipped to cope with 'David' rather than the Welsh 'Dewi'.

'Dylan, *sut dach chi* [how are you]?' Dewi could speak Welsh, but had a habit of moving from one language to another seamlessly. English appeared for him to be the language of business and the law.

'I'm very good, thanks. Have you heard about this Peter Howard Moore case?'

'*Iesu Mawr* [Jesus], have I heard of it? It's been all over the *Daily Post* like a rash. You've been in the middle of it, I gather.' He had an excited, quick-fire voice.

'Well, I thought you could possibly help me with this one. It's a pretty substantial case.'

'Most certainly, Dylan; I would be more than happy to help – thanks for thinking of me. From what I've heard, it sounds extremely interesting.'

I described in detail the events of the past few days: the allegations made against Moore, the evidence against him, the admissions made by Moore during the early-morning interview and his conduct afterwards. Dewi listened intently, making the odd sound of agreement as I spoke.

'I think we should meet very soon to discuss this case. How about you come over to my house in Ruthin on Saturday morning? We can have a chat and go over everything.' The suggestion sounded good to me; I had confidence in Dewi and believed he would be an asset to the case. I would need Peter

Moore's agreement for him to be formally instructed, but I didn't foresee that being a problem.

I found my way to Dewi Williams' house near Ruthin. It was a quaint rural cottage which felt homely and far away from the bustle of crime in Liverpool and the North West, where Dewi had most of his criminal clients. We sat, drank coffee and spoke about the case and Peter Moore. We thought about tactics and how we could construct a defence after the defendant had made so many admissions and then backtracked.

Dewi believed we needed to go and see Moore at Walton Prison in Liverpool as soon as possible. We needed to find out if he'd reflected on the Jason story. We also thought it wise to get an impression of Moore's mental state and decide whether we needed to get a psychiatric assessment – we needed to be sure he was of sound mind.

These were complex issues to consider. We had to know how reliable Moore was going to be and how likely it was that he would change his story again as we got closer to a trial. I agreed to go to see Moore the following week and report back to Dewi with my impressions of Moore. I left his home confident in Dewi as a barrister and satisfied that we had a strategy that would allow us to move forward. A lot would now depend on Moore, how reacted to me engaging Dewi on the case and whether he was beginning to have second thoughts about his story.

The following Monday morning I contacted HM Prison Walton. I explained that I needed to see my client, Peter Howard Moore, and through a rather complex booking system, I was able to arrange a one-hour appointment on the Thursday at 11 a.m.

I had seen many clients at Walton Prison before. The system for lawyers booking appointments with their client was different from the regular family appointments, the main difference being the element of privacy given to the meetings, as opposed to family meetings which took place in a large open-plan area with tables and chairs and a coffee machine in the corner.

On Thursday morning, having called in at the office, I was then off to Liverpool as soon as I could. Usually the journey to the prison would take just over an hour from Abergele, but I gave myself plenty of time. Walton in Liverpool is mostly known in north Wales for the renowned hospital in the same area as the prison – for many patients suffering head and brain injuries, this is the closest hospital for specialised treatment. Criminal lawyers, though, will also be familiar with HM Prison Walton.

I would usually drive to Walton through the Wirral and then cross under the Mersey via the Kingsway Tunnel. Liverpool is a very different city now to the place I was driving to in the 1990s. Liverpool had suffered greatly from years of neglect and lack of investment: there were boarded-up shops and decaying streets, houses looked unkept, with faded paint peeling off in swathes, roads were badly maintained and it seemed that this was a forgotten place full of forgotten people. It was to the side of one housing estate that the grey walls of HM Prison Walton would appear. They were thick, intimidating walls, running along one side of the street towards a car park at the end. I was always fascinated by the curved tops to the walls, and imagined how someone would even try to plan to get out of such a place. At the end of the street, the car park was generally full and it was necessary to find somewhere to park on the roadway. Whenever I had visited Walton Prison, it appeared I would arrive at the same time as family visiting hours. I would line up with a mixture of families, some with children running around and their mothers attempting to keep them under control. I always thought it was a strange and confusing scene, children lining up to see their fathers in prison – 'What memories will the children have of this?' I wondered.

Having queued for a good fifteen minutes, I finally reached the head of the line.

'Yes, sir?'

'I'm here to see my client, Peter Howard Moore.'

'Name, business address, sign here.' Then I was off through the security checks, searches of bags and of my person. After all the checks, I was led by a prison officer into a small waiting room, decorated with posters and notices warning visitors of lengthy prison sentences for passing prohibited items to prisoners. There were four others in the room, who I assumed were solicitors, sitting quietly, staring at the cream walls and notices opposite.

'Morning,' I said. There was little response: clearly it was not a room full of conversationalists. They looked a dejected lot. Maybe they were regular visitors, seeing one client after another in this impersonal sterilised atmosphere. There were two young – I suspected newly qualified – solicitors, both wearing what looked to be newly bought grey suits. I noticed one was wearing white socks. They held a couple of files each and ragged notebooks, one of which had doodles and pictures on its cover in blue biro. I thought that maybe they worked for the same firm, but suspected they weren't friends. The other man was older, maybe in his fifties, and maybe wasn't a solicitor but rather an ex-police officer who now worked as an assistant for a criminal law firm in Liverpool, doing their court and prison work. He had close-cropped hair and wore a dark blue blazer and black trousers. I imagined that he had made a mistake when getting dressed and put on his blue rather than black jacket by mistake. By the time he'd got to work, it was too late. The fourth was a woman in her thirties. She had shoulder-length mousy hair and wore a black jacket-and-skirt suit with a white, high-collared blouse and very sensible black court shoes. She stared at the opposite wall as if she was worried about catching anyone's eye and having to engage them in conversation. We all sat hesitantly for five minutes or so, as if waiting for a dentist to appear and call us to receive some serious root-canal work. Finally, we were released from this self-conscious hell and were led into the prison. Thick metal doors were unlocked and then locked again; we were led by two prison officers, who chatted superficially as we carried on through the prison. Occasionally an inmate would pass by and one of the officers would shout a comment or a joke to them. We approached a red-brick building with bars on the windows and one of the officers unlocked the door. We were greeted by another officer holding a clipboard; we gave our names and the name of the prisoner we were visiting and then took a seat. They were plastic chairs, secured to the floor and the walls along one side of a corridor. We joined another group of three visitors and sat in a line, not speaking a word, waiting to be led to our clients. Finally, another officer appeared from a room at the end of the corridor and began calling out names and room numbers.

'Mr Jones, for Peter Howard Moore? That will be Room 3, Mr Jones.' I got up and made my way towards the room at the end of the corridor. As I got to the door, I was directed towards a cubicle which was rather grandiosely called 'Room 3.' If I had brought a cat with me, which I don't think I would have been allowed to do, then I think it unlikely that I would have been able to swing it.

There in a chair which was chained to the floor, by a small desk which had also been chained to the floor, sat Peter Moore.

When I walked into the cubicle, he looked up.

'Mr Jones – how are you?' He looked grey and exhausted. Though he was clean-shaven, his skin appeared ashen and his hair also looked as if it had got slightly whiter. Maybe it was the harsh fluorescent lighting in the room. I sat down across the desk from Moore and the door was closed behind me by a prison officer. The cubicles were made of toughened glass so that the guards could see everything that was happening in the room, making it also possible for the occupants of each cubicle to view every other inmate and solicitor in their consultations as well. We looked like strange exhibits in a museum.

Moore was dressed in the standard prison clothing of the time: grey jean-type trousers and a shirt with light blue stripes. He looked neat and tidy.

'It's good to see you again, Mr Moore. How have you been?'

'I've been fine, thank you. Not bad at all.'

'I know it's difficult, but have you settled in here?'

'Oh yes, I've settled in – no problems.' Moore sounded assured, in fact he appeared rather content with himself. I wasn't necessarily expecting him to be depressed, but to hear that he had settled into prison life was interesting, and maybe told me something of the man I was dealing with. He seemed happy with the routine and security that the prison offered him. I thought that possibly this was something he had missed since his mother had died, and now that he was back to a regular routine, having to follow rules set out for him by others suited him.

I began to explain the work I'd been doing since I'd seen him last. I went through the meeting with Dewi Williams, and Moore seemed impressed and satisfied with my choice. I explained that it was likely that Dewi Williams would accompany me on my next visit. Moore was happy with this suggestion. I'd gleaned early on that Moore liked the knowledge that people were talking about him and wanted to speak with him – it gave him a sense of importance. There was a narcissistic element in Moore that needed feeding: he was now the centre of attention, which he liked. I thought back to when he had left the Magistrates' Court in Llandudno and stopped for that moment to lookd over at the cameras. It wasn't because he was fearful or concerned about his situation, it was because he enjoyed the attention of the cameramen and reporters. He'd never experienced such attention before, and now – possibly like a film star on the silver screen – he was getting it.

'How are things in prison?' I asked Moore. I wanted to know that he wasn't being pestered, or worse.

'It's fine, actually. I'm being left alone and everyone is very nice.' I knew that a prisoner like Moore wouldn't be placed into the general prison population: he was on remand and hadn't been found guilty by a court of anything, so would receive certain privileges. He would have been allowed to wear his own clothes rather than prison-issue ones if he'd had any, but Moore had nobody other than myself to visit him and so had no clothes from home. Even at this early stage of his prison life, Moore would have had a certain notoriety among the prison population – he was the man who was on trial for killing four people. In prison, that carries some kudos.

He would also have been carefully observed by the prison guards and put on suicide watch. The authorities would have been concerned that as the reality of prison life dawned on Moore, he might decide to end his life. Behind the toughened glass of the interview cubicles, the guards were watching his every move even now. They walked slowly from one window to another, peering in as we spoke inside our little glass boxes.

The hour in the glass cubicle flew by, prison guards appeared more regularly at the door and eventually the one with the clipboard gave a knock on the door.

'It's time, gentlemen.'

I got up and said my goodbyes and assured Moore that I would see him at the next court hearing and then we would meet with Dewi Williams. Moore appeared content. The hour had flown by and though not a great deal of actual progress had been made in preparing a coherent defence, we had spoken and he seemed content with his situation. As I left the cubicle, I turned round and looked back at Moore as he remained sitting by the desk, gave him a nod and he nodded back. He seemed a lonely, isolated figure. No one had contacted him since he'd arrived in prison, he was just there by himself. Maybe that's the way he liked it – possibly that's the way he'd always been.

I headed back to my car. I couldn't get out of my mind the sense that I was feeling sorry for Peter Moore. Why I would feel like that about a person that I hardly knew? He'd been accused of the most horrific crimes, of frenzied attacks and killing people 'for fun', and I was walking to my car feeling sorry for him. I shut the car door, put the file on the passenger seat and took a deep breath. This whole thing was beginning to get me very confused. I'd spent days in Moore's company at the police station and a couple of weeks thinking about the case and the task ahead. I'd met Moore again and knew that his defence was weak at best, but I felt sorry for this forlorn, grey man. I was struggling to explain why I would feel this way. It wasn't that I had no sympathy for the victims, or their families. Those four murdered men had clearly all gone through hell before they died – they knew they were about to be murdered, and if we are to believe Moore, some pleaded for their lives. But at that moment I had the sense that Moore was also in some way a victim and that due to his upbringing and circumstances there was somehow an inevitability to what had happened.

We are all a product of our past, our upbringing, our parents, our circumstances. Inevitably we are who we are because of a cocktail of chemistry, biology, sociology and maybe a myriad of other complex factors. Criminologists over the years have attempted to define the elements which make the criminal what he or she is. Inevitably we have little choice in some aspects of what makes us the individuals we are, but throughout life we face choices: various paths are open for us to choose and it's the way we address those choices that makes us who we now are, in the present.

Maybe I felt sorry for Moore because of the choices he'd made, because he'd become a slave to his own dark desires and fantasies, which had grown and festered until he was unable to resist the desire to kill any longer.

I had another worry, and that was Jason. Despite the instructions I'd received from Moore and what had been said by him during the interviews, nothing had convinced me of Jason's existence. He'd been mentioned as an afterthought, brought into the picture after Moore had had his moment of weakness in the early-hours interview.

As I sat in the car outside the prison, I made a link – something that, unknown to me at the time, others had made as well. Moore was a cinema proprietor and not only that, he was a film enthusiast: he knew a lot about the cinema and films. I'd once asked him (in one of the meetings about his mother's estate) what type of films he liked and he told me he loved all kinds, from the old classics to Hitchcock films, and more recent films in the horror genre. That had meant nothing to me at the time, just that maybe he knew his stuff.

In the 1980s and early 1990s, one of the most famous of horror film franchises of the time was the *Friday the 13th* series. It began as far back as 1980 with the original *Friday the 13th* film, and there then followed a lengthy series of sequels which, as far as I could gather, followed very similar themes. By 1995 there had been nine films in the franchise – I'll be honest and say that I'd only seen the first, but it could be assumed that Peter Moore had seen all of them. It was therefore also the case that he was aware of the theme running through all of the films. The main focus of the franchise is the main character, a man called Jason Voorhees, who drowned in a lake as a boy while he was staying in a nearby camp. It's suggested that Jason's death was due to the camp owners' negligence. People suspect that the lake may have become cursed due to Jason's untimely death, and the films focus on the curse and Jason's return from the dead to wreak havoc in a series of mass murders. It's possible that the franchise may have left an impression on Peter Moore.

We could theorise for too long about the effect of these films on Moore. They may not have had any effect at all, though their possible influence is something which Alex Carlile QC chose to point out in his opening remarks during Peter Moore's trial in November 1996. Moore himself didn't at any time mention the film franchise, but once the connection had been made, it was difficult not to imagine the influence it may have had on him. The title to the most recent of those films at the time, the 1993 *Jason goes to Hell: The Final Friday*, seemed to encapsulate not only the killing spree which Moore may have undertaken, but also the inevitable consequences of his actions.

During my initial discussions with the barrister Dewi Williams at his home in Ruthin, I had considered with him the horror of the murders committed. We needed to work on the basis that it was either Moore or Jason who had committed them. I asked one question which had been bothering me – maybe something born out of my Methodist upbringing, which needed to be addressed at some stage. I'd also sat for hours in countless interviews with Peter Moore, listening to graphic descriptions of murder, stabbings and sexual misconduct, and it had begun to unnerve me.

'Is this man "evil"? Is that even a term we should even be using as lawyers?' I asked Dewi.

'I don't use that term very often, but I have used it in the past – only for a few of my clients,' was his answer. Dewi then recalled his involvement in the Jamie Bulger case in Liverpool. It was a case which attracted both national and international attention in 1993 when a 2-year-old child from Kirkby in Liverpool was abducted, then tortured and subsequently murdered by two 10-year-old boys called Robert Thompson and Jon Venables. That case was still very fresh in all our minds in 1995, due to the horrific circumstances of the murder and the shock that two such young boys could have been capable of behaving in the way that they had. The authorities and the community as a whole were unable to come to terms with why and how these boys had become motivated to commit such heinous acts of torture and murder. Dewi Williams described that case as the only occasion when he had encountered real 'evil' in a person; where, in his opinion, he couldn't find any redeeming feature, any reason or influence or even excuse for an act or a crime but that of 'evil' itself.

'Does "evil" therefore exist?' I wondered.

'We're both former Sunday School boys, Dylan,' Dewi responded with a smile. 'I think we have to accept that it does, and maybe we are now encountering it in Peter Moore.'

This term 'evil' is bandied about everywhere. It's used loosely and without much consideration, with the danger that it somehow becomes meaningless. I suppose it's only when something truly horrific occurs and we encounter it ourselves that we can testify that we've confronted what we would interpret as 'evil'. Driving home from Walton Prison that day, I contemplated my conversation with Dewi Williams and how complex and difficult he believed this case was to become. I reflected upon the difficulties we faced, both personally and professionally, and the challenges we needed to overcome. I also thought about Peter Moore as a person and as a client. I'd already concluded that representing this man was going to be difficult: he liked using and manipulating people and wouldn't think twice about manipulating his lawyers, given half an opportunity. I thought about the local news items I'd seen of him months before the murders, talking about his cinemas and the hope he had that they would be serving communities across north Wales. He wanted his cinemas to be a hub for towns which had no other community activities, offering something for children to do on Saturday mornings. Parents would leave their children in his care to watch these Saturday-morning films while they went off to do some shopping. It takes some time to adjust to the clear contrast between the 'jolly uncle-like figure' in the cinema and the murdering psychopath killing 'for fun'. I was beginning to wonder if both personalities inhabited my client, not because he may have been suffering from schizophrenia but rather by his own choice.

Chapter 14

LOOKING BACK AT those first months of 1996, it's difficult to recall how I had the time to get everything that required my attention done. Work proceeded as usual with other cases, many clients and the day-to-day pressures of running a busy office. I'd decided that I was going to take sole responsibility for the Peter Moore case, and as it happened, it was a wise decision as none of the other solicitors in the firm volunteered to help much. I'd realised at the beginning of 1996 that it was going to be very busy year and I'd face unprecedented pressures. I promised myself that I'd face everything head-on, without complaining or placing undue strain on others. I was working as many hours as I could physically achieve, including many weekends.

My business partner still had his demands, and billing time (as a lawyer, every second you work is billed to someone) was a regular subject of discussion. The main problem I had was that I was spending far more hours on the Peter Moore case – out of necessity – than could ever be claimed in costs from the Legal Aid Board. Billing hours are everything in a legal firm but the criminal legal aid practitioner is never the big earner. Despite the impressions given to the contrary, you don't become a criminal lawyer with an expectation of also becoming a millionaire. It was my responsibility to make sure the office was running efficiently, everyone was doing what they were supposed to do and that money was coming in and bills were being paid. It remained a constant pressure.

There were regular court hearings regarding the Peter Moore case which were initially scheduled for the Magistrates'

Court. Due to the problem of transporting Moore regularly from Liverpool to the north Wales court, these were heard in his absence. Nowadays such hearings would be heard via video conferencing, with the prisoner appearing on a screen in the court directly from the prison. We didn't have that luxury back in 1996.

A few months had passed and one morning I received a call from Nita Dowell at the Crown Prosecution Service office.

'The committal documents and all the unused material are ready if you want to collect them, Dylan,' she said. These were the documents, statements and all the evidence the prosecution were going to rely on in court, and also the papers and statements which were not going to be used by them but were available to us, the defence, to read and use if we wanted. They were usually sent to the defence lawyers in a neat bundle in the post. But not on this occasion. Nita asked, 'What kind of car have you got, Dylan?'

'It's an estate – a BMW, why?'

'Well, can you put the seats down in it? Because you've got a hell of a lot of papers to collect.'

'How much do you have?' I asked, in a panic.

'Come and see – it's a lot,' she responded with a laugh. That afternoon I travelled to the CPS offices in Colwyn Bay, rather unsure of what to expect. Nita was correct: when I got to the offices, I was unsure if I'd be able to transport all the papers piled up in one of the CPS's offices in one journey. It looked like a massive pyramid of white boxes all full of papers, notes, statements, photographs and other evidence. I piled everything into the car, with my back seat folded down and filling up the footwells and the front passenger seat, and just managed to squeeze everything in. There was just about enough room for me to get into the driving seat so I could take everything back to my office in Abergele.

'Happy reading!' said Nita as I left. I think I may have looked in a state of complete shock as I squeezed into my car.

When I arrived at my office, the main problem was where to put all the papers. My office wasn't particularly large, so the only option initially was to pile everything in my room and see whether I could sort things out over time. The reality of the situation was that I had four separate murder cases to deal with, plus a series of assaults including sexual assaults going back a long time. The reading work alone was enormous and initially I was daunted by the volume.

Then there was all the unused material: the statements and documents that the prosecution didn't intend using in their case but which might be useful to the defence case. In order to find out whether those statements were of any use, I'd have to read every one of them and then refer them to Dewi Williams and whoever we would be instructing as our senior defence barrister – the QC – for their consideration as well. This is the donkey work that every solicitor is required to do as part of a big criminal case. There's no avoiding it: it has to be done and no diligent defence lawyer would approach their case without undertaking this lonely, sometimes mind-numbingly boring, hard graft.

Then there were the photographs. Most evidential bundles in criminal cases will be accompanied by photographs, video evidence of the crime scenes, sometimes CCTV evidence, maybe pictures of identity parades and other such evidence. What the Peter Moore case had in abundance were photographs. Mostly these were photos from the crime scenes and there were a substantial number of photographs taken at every scene. Additionally, there were photos of Peter Moore's home, possessions, car and other items considered relevant, such as the knife, truncheon, police clothing and Nazi items recovered from his house. Many of the photographs were explicit and thoroughly unpleasant. I had never before seen photographs like these in any criminal case. They were as graphic as photographs could be: bodies lay in pools of blood, stab wounds gaped open like torn clothes with innards spewing out of ripped skin. Faces stared out of photos in blank vacant looks of death, betraying nothing of their last thoughts. Bodily injuries were photographed in macro detail – every stab wound and every scratch were like blemishes on pieces of meat on the butchers' block. One body – the one in the forest – had been torn to pieces by wild animals and gnawed body parts left across a wide area in decaying mounds. Everything was photographed, and every photograph catalogued, numbered and filed away. They were shocking, disturbing and unforgettable. I recall sitting in my office one evening alone, looking at them one by one, thinking of the people involved. Every photograph left an abiding imprint on my mind, the contorted body shapes and the look on the victim's face, eyes wide open, in their moment of death. These photographs were crucial items of evidence in the case, but as I looked at them, it felt as if I was intruding upon very private moments. I began to realise fully that these victims were people – not bodies, not crime numbers or indictments on a charge sheet; that behind each tragic scene was a wife, a partner, parents, a family. Everyone had a story, a history; every one of these lifeless bodies had people who had loved them and now grieved for them. I thought about what Moore had conceivably done, and imagined the terror in those now lifeless eyes. Strangely, I began to experience a feeling of guilt which until now I'd avoided. I realised that it was only now, months after Moore's arrest, that I was properly reflecting on these appalling acts of murder and their effects and consequences on others.

I wondered if I'd got carried away with the thrill and excitement of dealing with a murder case and forgotten its crude reality: that people had been slaughtered in appalling circumstances. Now, as I looked at the photographs, I was able to see their faces and imagine the horror of their final dying moments.

Thinking about the true reality of these murders and their consequences began to make me feel dirty and tainted, possibly even guilty. Guilty of what, I couldn't be sure, but as I looked at those photographs that evening, it was as if I'd become an accomplice to the terror and murder.

Those photographs and those murder scenes are with me, sometimes every day. They run through my mind like celluloid prints running through a projector in one of Moore's cinemas. They're constantly clicking over from one picture to another. Sometimes they'll fade into the background and I won't take any notice of them for weeks, sometimes even months. Then I'll be reminded of them: some news story or programme on television will prompt a recollection and I'll see those pictures again, still clicking over, one by one, from body to body, from one horrific scene to another. I suppose they'll always be there, reminding me of this case and all its destruction.

I wanted to make sure was that nobody else in my office stumbled across those photographs by accident. They were placed in a locked cabinet and all my staff were told to avoid them at all costs. I'd been in the habit of taking work home with me, but I vowed that those photos would stay in the office and only be removed from the cabinet when necessary. The fewer people who saw those photographs, the better.

Many years later, having suffered a nervous breakdown, I discussed with a counsellor the ever-present flashback images of these photographs. I knew that I could never unsee them, so indelibly were they imprinted on my mind, and during some very dark days they appeared on a regular basis to haunt me.

'It's a type of Post-Traumatic Stress Disorder,' said my counsellor. 'You've seen horrific things, things which you may not have been prepared to see, images which you can't forget or unsee. It's not surprising that these have had a long-term effect on you.'

'But why have they affected me in this way? Some people seemed to cope with it without any effect at all.'

'How do you know that, Dylan?' the counsellor responded. 'How do you know who's been affected and who hasn't? They don't know the effect this case and those photos have had on you, do they? So how would you know who and how others involved were affected by it? You don't.'

He was, of course, correct. I could only focus on what it had done to me, what the consequences of those days were on me and how I would subsequently recover from them.

It took a long time for me to read through all the papers released by the CPS to me. During this time I was in regular contact with the barrister, Dewi Williams. We got to the stage at which another visit to see Moore would be beneficial, and this time Dewi Williams agreed to visit him with me. Moore had by then been moved from Walton Prison to HM Prison Wakefield, which was and still is a Category A secure prison. Wakefield Prison holds some of the most dangerous criminals in the country, and we knew that visiting Moore there would involve making a lot of arrangements beforehand.

When the day of the visit arrived, I met Dewi Williams in the prison car park and we both ventured through the imposing visitors' entrance to the prison. There were the expected security checks of bags, coats and clothing and then lockers were offered for most belongings to be deposited. By the time we were on our way to the interview rooms, we each had a notepad and a pen and that was about it. The prison bristled with security, from cameras to checks at each door or gate – it was clear that Wakefield was a high-security establishment. We finally arrived at the interview area, with large toughened-glass cubicles where prisoners sitting at tables awaited us. We were both checked in by a prison officer and led to the cubicle where Moore sat expecting us. I introduced Dewi to Moore and vice versa, and we made some jolly small talk for a few minutes about the prison, its security and how Moore had settled into his new environment.

Moore looked pleased to see us. He appeared to have lost some weight and his hair had become thinner on top, but he looked surprisingly well. As we chatted, I looked around the interview area. There were about ten cubicles in total, located each side of a large room where prison guards walked constantly from one door to another, glancing into the cubicle as they passed. I glanced into the next-door cubicle and noticed a solicitor I knew, giving him a slight nod as I caught his eye. He was interviewing another notorious criminal from north Wales who was on remand awaiting trial: the tall, gangly, slightly oversized figure of Howard Hughes, who had been charged with the abduction and murder of little Sophie Hook. Both Hughes and Moore had caused a great deal of trouble and heartache to the population and police in north Wales during the previous year, and here they now were, both in the same prison, awaiting their fate.

We discussed many of the intricacies of Moore's case with him, and the meeting allowed Dewi to get to know Moore a little and then decide on how best to move things forward towards the trial. Moore was sticking to the Jason story rigidly and we again emphasised the need for us to therefore identify Jason in more detail, as he was to be the cornerstone of our defence.

Dewi and I chatted upon leaving the prison. Dewi seemed struck by the complexity of Peter Moore's character: the polite, well-spoken man who could discuss the case in a clear and logical way, juxtaposed with the horrendous allegations made against him and the charges he faced. Dewi was finding it as difficult as I had to reconcile these two apparent totally opposed aspects of Peter Moore and to bring them together into the man who had just sat facing us.

'We've got our work cut out with him, Dylan,' Dewi said. 'He's certainly a fascinating character.'

We agreed to move on with the preparation of the case and arranged to speak soon regarding the pre-trial hearing, which was listed in a few weeks' time, and the engagement of a senior barrister – a Queen's Counsel – to represent Moore at trial. We'd considered the engagement of a QC during our previous chat, and Dewi had suggested a QC called Eric Somerset-Jones as someone suitable.

'He's very experienced and has the right temperament. I've worked with him before as his junior and I think he would suit Moore,' said Dewi. We agreed that Dewi would give him a call and get then back to me.

The next few weeks flew by and I discovered that the pre-trial hearing was to be held in the Royal Courts of Justice in London rather than in north Wales, as the Judge who was listed to hear the case at trial – a Mr Justice Maurice Kay – wished to conduct it himself rather than leaving anything to another Judge. As Mr Justice Maurice Kay was a senior High Court Judge as well as the most senior Judge on the Chester and North Wales Circuit, there was no arguing. If he was down in London on another case and wished to hold the pre-trial hearing there, then that's how it was going to be.

I met Dewi Williams on the morning of the pre-trial hearing in the imposing Royal Courts of Justice. We were both going through security at the entrance of the building and exchanged a few words before joining up again in the grand, palatial meeting area. I'd been to the Royal Courts of Justice on a couple of previous occasions, firstly as a sixth former when we went on a Politics class trip to Parliament and then the courts, and the place had made a real impression on me then. My second visit was a few years before the Peter Moore case, when I was involved in another high-profile case and the final hearing took place in one of the Royal Courts' many oak-panelled courtrooms. One can't fail to be impressed by the building and the surroundings of the Royal Courts of Justice. They convey status, confidence and solidity in the law, which is why they were built in that way in the first place. The main reception area is an enormous echoing grey granite space with a churchlike atmosphere – everyone there seems compelled to speak in hushed tones. There are small crowds of lawyers and clients gathering in various corners, balancing papers and law books and takeaway coffee cups as they speak. Cloaked and bewigged barristers rush across the hallways like bats swooping from one courtroom to another. Noisily victorious and celebrating clients and their supporters spill out of courtrooms in a babble of excitement, leaving the red-eyed and tear-dabbing defeated to leave dejectedly by the back door.

In the middle of the large churchlike Great Central Hall (to give its official title) is a wooden board where the cases of the day are listed, together with where those cases are to be heard. By the time we got to the board, we found that Nita Dowell from the CPS and her barrister were already there, trying to come to terms with the complicated listing system.

'I think we're in Court 15,' said Nita. 'All we now need to do is find the place.'

There were corridors leading every which way and courtrooms and meeting rooms for a variety of purposes signposted in all directions. After some false starts, we finally found Court 15.

The courtrooms themselves are surprisingly small. They have a claustrophobic feel, doubtless assisted by the heavy dark-oak panelling on every wall. I felt as if I'd walked into a large box – in all honesty, I thought it felt like a dark coffin. There were a few lawyers milling around in the courtroom; we went to the front set of benches and took our places, setting out our paperwork as we made small talk. The Court Clerk, who sat at the front, facing us, smiled at us sympathetically. I suspected she was thinking to herself, 'Here they are, the country bumpkins, having their day out in the big city.'

Moore had been 'excused' from this hearing: the expense and logistics of getting him down to London for what was due to be a short hearing couldn't be justified. I'd promised to let him know the outcome as soon as I returned to the office – in particular, the date of his trial, which was to be agreed today.

Mr Justice Maurice Kay entered the courtroom on time at 10.30 a.m. I knew him to be a very experienced and knowledgeable Judge and as he sat down, he wasted no time in proceeding with the main issues of the case. During hearings of this kind, the Judge will discuss the practicalities of the forthcoming trial and the main issues. In Moore's case, he wanted to know the nature of the defence. Dewi mentioned 'identity' as the main issue, i.e. that Moore was claiming it was not him who committed the murders.

We all knew what the Judge would be asking next – it was like waiting for a small firecracker to explode, bracing ourselves for detonation. The Judge expertly kept us all in suspense for a few seconds as he shuffled the papers and made a few notes.

'Yes, Mr Williams. I believe we are talking about this "Jason" gentleman?' It was subtle, but not that subtle.

'Yes, My Lord, you are quite correct.' Anticipating the Judge's next question, Dewi added, 'We don't have much additional information about this individual at the moment, but we are working on that.' Judge Kay looked directly at Dewi over the small wire-rimmed spectacles balancing on the end of his nose. It was a look of grave scepticism, if not suspicion.

'Mr Williams, with respect: your case is based on this "Jason"?' It seemed to be half statement, half question, with an element of incredulity.

'Yes, My Lord, together with issues of evidence and including identification as well,' Dewi replied, cleverly trying to deflect the Judge's pointed question. The Judge continued to look at him over his spectacles, fountain pen in hand. For a moment or so he appeared frozen – whether he was frozen in thought or in a state of disbelief, I couldn't be certain. Eventually he cleared his throat and rather loudly continued.

'Yes! Well, we will have to see, won't we?' He'd made his point: as far as he was concerned, 'Jason"s inclusion in this case wasn't impressing him. It wasn't unexpected of course. Experienced Judges such as Judge Kay will have seen hundreds, if not thousands, of cases over their years in the courts; their expertise was to identify the strengths and weaknesses of a case. He had done so here, and made it clear that he wasn't impressed.

We then proceeded to identify the number of witnesses and the anticipated length of the trial, and to fix a date for that trial. There was the usual performance of all involved, Judge included, checking their diaries and making sure of their availability for the trial at some distant date in the future. Finally, after a lengthy process of discussion and haggling, we arrived at the date of Monday 11 November 1996, at Mold Crown Court, Flintshire, north Wales. It was a date about five months away, and for a big trial seemed quite close.

We left the Royal Courts of Justice that morning with a clear idea of a date and knowing also that the Judge had grave doubts about the defence that Peter Moore was proposing. I agreed with Dewi to speak to Moore as soon as possible, and that we would also arrange to see him at the prison and take with us the Queen's Counsel we had appointed to represent him at trial, Eric Somerset-Jones QC.

In the meantime, we needed to visit each of the murder scenes. It was one thing to look at plans and maps drawn by the police, showing the location of the bodies and other items of evidence discovered at each of the scenes, but both Dewi and I needed to see the places for ourselves. I knew about the beach in Pensarn and I was aware of the locations on Anglesey, but it was important to get a real first-hand sense of the places and an idea of what Moore saw and what his alleged victims experienced.

I arranged with Dewi to have one day when we would travel to each of the murder scenes, take photographs and get a feeling for each of the places in question. I needed to notify the police, even though the crime scenes were no longer in their hands. The one location which was potentially a problem was the site of the murder in Clocaenog Forest, where Edward Carthy had been killed. The map drawn by Moore on the night of his confession had been good enough to lead the police to the body, but I knew that the Forestry roads in that area were complex and that we could easily get lost. Having spoken to the police, I arranged to meet an officer by the entrance to the forest near Ruthin, so we could then be led to the crime scene and back out of the forest afterwards.

Dewi and I met at my office in Abergele and then took my car on our macabre and slightly weird tour of north Wales. Dewi was an interesting and talkative person and though he was about twenty years or so older than me, we got on very well. He was always smartly dressed in a black pinstripe suit and an eye-catching colourful tie. He was tall, with a full head of greying hair, and had a barrister's confident swagger. Polite and well-spoken, he had the air of someone who had done it all. When he was reading, he would perch his barristers'-issue half-rimmed spectacles on his nose. We went for a bite to eat at a local pub before beginning our trip, so as to get clear what we were looking out for at every scene. We sat at a pub table planning and talking, as a young waitress that Dewi had charmed with his debonair patter fussed about us.

After lunch we went to Pensarn beach. Even though it was towards the end of May, the beach was still quiet. I parked in the part of the car park where, it was suggested by the police, Moore had parked that night in December 1995.

'I'm sure it's dark here at night – look, there are no street lights here,' Dewi said.

'That's why people meet here at night, I suppose,' I said. We got out of the car and walked onto the beach – it was difficult to walk on the pebbles in our smart shoes. We stopped for a moment to look at a plan drawn by the police of the crime scene, to work out exactly where Anthony Roberts' body was lying when discovered. It took a little time to make out the location as the pebbles made the whole beach look the same, but by measuring from the carpark to about halfway down the beach in a straight line, we could make a good guess at where Roberts was murdered.

'I'm sure it's a desolate place on a cold dark night in December,' commented Dewi.

'I can't understand what would make someone want to be out here late at night in the dark and the cold. It must have been about midnight or one o'clock in the morning when the murder took place.'

'Human nature, young man,' was Dewi's answer. 'Ours is not to question why.' We both laughed and made our way back to my car.

The next scene was on Anglesey, a fifty-minute journey or so from Abergele. The A55 Expressway took us all the way to Anglesey and then across the island. We drove to the scene of the first murder, that of John Henry Roberts.

The village of Caergeiliog where Roberts lived was only a few miles away from Holyhead. Now the village is bypassed by a new part of the A55 but at the time, if driving to Holyhead, you had to drive through the village and pass Henry Roberts' house, which was located on the right-hand side as you left the village. Though we had a map and the house was clearly marked, it was initially difficult to find as roadside shrubs and hedges had become overgrown and hid most of the house from the road. After passing by a couple of times and having to turn back, we discovered the driveway to the house and were able to park a few yards beyond it, allowing us a short walk back along the roadside to the house itself.

With a plan in hand, we got to a rusty metal gate which needed to be lifted up before it would open. I managed to open the gate a couple of feet, to the accompaniment of a rusty creak, allowing Dewi and myself to push through. We found ourselves in a small yard in front of a ramshackle grey cottage. The cottage may have been white in colour at some time in the past but by now the paint had either faded or peeled off and even the grey stone underneath had become discoloured. The yard would have been big enough to house a couple of vehicles if it hadn't been full of every kind of junk under the sun. A rusty washing machine stood in one corner, a couple of chest freezers in another and it was as if every inch possible had been filled with rusty metal and broken pieces of decaying wood. There were old buckets and piles of litter all over the place and it was a challenge to negotiate the yard to get to the front door. There appeared to be a couple of holes in the door, which had either rotted away over time or had received a few hefty kicks. The door had also at some time housed a couple of panes of frosted glass; one and a half of them had disappeared leaving just the jagged edges of one piece hanging precariously. I'd been given a key by the police, but to my surprise, one push of the door and it swung open – until it came to an abrupt stop against something that was blocking its path. We were then hit by a horrendous smell coming from inside the cottage.

'Good God!' said Dewi as we both backed into the yard again. 'What the hell is that smell?'

'It looks pretty bad in there,' I said, moving forwards towards the door again and peering into the darkness of what looked like a kitchen. There seemed to be litter, discarded food wrappers, newspapers and all kinds of rubbish strewn across the floor everywhere. As I ventured a few steps into the building with Dewi gingerly following me, the smell became overpowering and I needed to hold my nose closed just to be able to breathe.

We both ventured into the kitchen. Discarded tins and half-open packets of food with families of flies congregating around them could be seen on more or less every surface. Mouldy food, maybe cheese of some kind, had been left on the draining board and had now become green and furry. The tap was constantly dripping and water splashed onto discarded dirty and mouldy plates and bowls in the sink and then ricocheted out onto the floor, causing an enormous soggy pool of water on a filthy dirt-encrusted carpet. I noticed a couple of large buckets in the corner of the room which seemed to be full of something or other, though I couldn't be sure what. It wasn't until I got closer that I discovered the buckets were both full to the brim with dried-up human excrement.

'*Iesu Mawr* [Jesus]!' I jumped back in shock and revulsion. 'There are buckets of human shit here.'

'*Iesu Grist* [Jesus Christ], we don't have to stay here, Dylan – this is a complete shithole,' said Dewi, making his way to the door, with me following him at close quarters. It was only when we were back in the yard that we both began to breathe again and we stood there for a few minutes, gasping for air and fighting off the desire to vomit at the same time.

'Imagine living like that,' Dewi said when we'd both come back to our senses.

'That was like a hellhole! I've never seen anything like it.'

There had been some evidence from the police that Henry Roberts' house was chaotic but from reading the statements, I hadn't realised that it was as bad as we had witnessed. We both stood for a few moments in the front yard of the cottage, gathering our thoughts. By using the plan we had, we could identify where Roberts' body lay after he was killed.

'It was a strange murder, this one, don't you think?' said Dewi. 'I mean, clearly he'd planned it. He may have thought about it for some time before deciding to go ahead, and as far as we know it was the first murder. By why remove his trousers and stab him in the backside?'

'There wasn't any explanation of that given during the early-morning interview,' I said. 'He admitted then that he had stabbed him in the buttocks but gave no reason why.'

We both agreed it was strange behaviour and that it must have some homosexual and possibly psycho-sexual link. It was a sinister and unpleasant scene.

'How could someone live like this?' I thought. 'And then die in this squalor on the ground in this dirty yard.' The scene seemed to have been void of any dignity or respect. It was a disgusting and vile deed, a horrific and nasty execution of a lonely man who lived in his own filth. Why had Roberts been chosen? What benefit or pleasure could possibly have been derived by the killer from such a revolting act? It was difficult to imagine.

Both Dewi and I were shaken by what we'd witnessed at the Roberts house in Caergeiliog. I turned the car round and got back on the A55 in the direction of Llangefni and the scene of Keith Randles' murder.

Randles again didn't fit into any pattern. He was certainly not gay: he was a family man and worked as a security nightwatchman in a compound where plant and other machinery was being kept during substantial roadworks on the A55. The compound was just off the A55/A5 junction with the A5114, which led to Llangefni. The location of the compound was clearly shown on the map drawn by the police, though by the time of my visit with Dewi, it was just an empty field. The opening to the field was where you would have accessed the compound a year or so earlier, but the work on the junction had finished and the plant and machinery gone. Tracks and deep indentations of tyres and machinery could be seen in various places across the field but other than that, there was little evidence of what had been there.

There was no evidence either that the small field had been the scene of a brutal murder, where a few months prior to our visit a middle-aged man had apparently pleaded for his life before being stabbed to death. Possibly, I thought, it was better that no reminder of that incident existed and that the only echoes of that murder are on paper in police statements, and in the memories of those affected by it.

We decided we ought to drive on to the final scene in the Clocaenog Forest near Ruthin. Arriving at the agreed time, a police car was waiting for us at the main turning to the forest off the Cerrigydrudion to Ruthin road. Though we'd begun our trip across north Wales in pleasant enough weather, by the time we arrived in Clocaenog, dark grey clouds had congregated and rain seemed likely.

'We'd better get this one over and done with as soon as possible, Dylan,' said Dewi, looking up at the threatening clouds. The police officer got out of his car as we arrived and I rolled my window down to speak to him.

'Mr Jones, Mr Williams? Follow me, it's a couple of miles or so.' He returned to his car and we began our journey along the Forestry roads of Clocaenog. There were a number of turns at junctions, left and right, and then turnings into narrower roads with steep, uneven corners.

'We would never have found this place in a million years,' I said, after a while.

'I'm wondering how Moore found it,' Dewi said. 'I mean, if he found his way in, how the hell did he find his way out?'

'Good place to dump a body,' I replied. 'No chance of anyone finding it in here.'

It was a good two miles before I noticed the police car ahead of me indicating that he was pulling over to the left verge. I stopped behind him and Dewi and I got out of the car and walked towards the officer, who was holding a map and studying it carefully.

'I think, if I'm right, that the body was found down the bank on the other side of the road, beneath the trees. Bear in mind, gents, that by the time it was discovered, the animals had got to it. The head was found about 50 m into the woods in that direction,' the officer pointed straight ahead, 'and then other bits were discovered over a wide area to our right from here.' It was difficult to come to terms with what the police officer was actually saying. I was aware from the crime scene photographs and my earlier conversations with the police that Carthy's body had been interfered with by animals, but I hadn't realised how much. It must have been a horrific sight to those confronted by it in December 1995, and a tough job for any Scene-of-Crime or Forensic Officer involved the day the body was recovered. Difficult as well for the victim's family to be told that this was the way their loved one had met his end.

Dewi and I crossed the Forestry road and approached the verge. I noticed that from the road, the verge sloped downwards for a few feet before it reached the edge of the trees. The trees were thickly planted pines, established over many years and now 30 ft tall at least. We moved down the bank from the road and to the edge of the forest. The police officer had walked over to the edge of the road and was looking down at us.

'It's a few metres into the forest from where you're standing, Mr Jones,' he shouted to me. Initially my eyes found it difficult to adjust to the darkness – only a small amount of light could penetrate through the thick dark green foliage. I took a couple of steps further. Underfoot was a thick carpet of brown pine-needles, and I could feel my feet sinking a few centimetres into the forest floor as I moved forward.

'There – it's there, Mr Jones.' I stopped immediately and looked around, then crouched down to see closer.

'You can see where the body was lying there, Mr Jones.' Initially I wasn't sure what I should be looking for: was there a mark or a police cordon or some sign to show where Carthy's body had been discovered? As my eyes got accustomed to the semi-darkness, things became clearer. A foot or so ahead of me I could make out the shape of a body, clearly coming into view on the forest floor. It was as if someone had drawn the silhouette of a body and left it lying there. I remember seeing something very similar on a TV documentary about the detonation of the atomic bomb in Hiroshima. When the bomb detonated, some people had been vaporised – the only trace left of their existence being their silhouette, etched on the wall near where they had been standing. It was as if the same thing had happened on the forest floor; there, as clear as day, lay the silhouette of Edward Carthy.

We both scrambled back up the bank to the road to join the police officer. I was shocked at what I'd seen. I hadn't expected to be able to see exactly where Carthy had been lying under the trees – maybe even where he'd died.

'You could see the shape of a body,' I said, to nobody in particular.

'Yes, I know,' said the police officer. 'I think it must have been lying there for some time before being disturbed. And with the forest floor being so sheltered and dry underfoot, you know, the body made a mark in the ground.'

We left the crime scene, following the police car again until we got back to the main road, and then heading back towards Abergele over the Denbigh Moors. We didn't speak much on the way back; it had been a long and emotional day, and there had been some unexpected reminders of how brutal and unpleasant the whole Peter Moore case was in reality. As we drove over the bleak moors, I was reminded of Moore's admission during the early-morning interview, when he'd talked about driving Carthy back from Liverpool. How Carthy had tried to get out of the van as Moore was driving, because he seemed terrified. I can't imagine what terror he experienced as he was being driven across these moors at night, not knowing where he was going, frightened and maybe even believing he was about to be killed.

Dewi and I parted that day in a solemn mood. We arranged to meet again soon to visit Moore in prison, but on this occasion in the company of Eric Somerset-Jones QC, our lead counsel.

That day has stayed with me – the locations, the sights and the smells. The silhouette of the body on the ground under the trees will haunt me forever: it's a still-life photo etched into my memory which sometimes, even to this day, I'll see in my mind's eye. It's a reminder that murder isn't some gruesome game or a gripping series on TV. It's grim reality in its cruellest form; it's bloody and shocking and a dirty business of the vilest kind. Behind every murder, somewhere on the ground, on a floor, a wall or ingrained into someone's memory, is a silhouette of a person, lying there dead or dying.

The road leading into Clocaenog Forest

Location near to which the body of Edward Carthy was found

Chapter 15

PREPARING FOR ANY murder case is complicated but, as with every other case, there are times when little progress is being made and then there are times of frantic work. We knew that the trial was to begin on 11 November and by the beginning of October, preparations were in hand. I had spoken to Dewi and Eric Somerset-Jones numerous times on the phone and we had arranged to meet for a full pre-trial conference with Peter Moore at Wakefield Prison. We agreed that we might then need two or three further meetings before the trial date, so seeing Moore at the beginning of October allowed us some time to fit in other meetings if necessary.

On the day of our conference with Moore, Dewi, Somerset-Jones and I met up outside the prison as arranged. I hadn't met Eric before. He turned out to be exactly how I'd imagined him from our phone conversations. He had the look of my favourite fictional barrister, Rumpole of the Bailey. He wore a dark pinstripe barrister's suit and matching waistcoat, covering a slight paunch, and was in his late fifties or early sixties, I suppose. What hair he had was combed back from his forehead and seemed quite dark in colour ('Maybe he colours it?' I thought). He had a jolly, chatty disposition and nothing of the aloof air that some senior barristers adopt. He made a couple of jokes as we walked into the reception area and I thought immediately that Dewi had made the correct choice. From the beginning, I liked him and knew that we'd get on well. More importantly, I believed Moore would get on with him.

We got through all the security checks and were led by an officer over to the consultation rooms. As in my previous visit,

Peter Moore was waiting in the cubicle already. As we entered the little room, Moore got up and greeted the three of us, as if we were entering his lounge at home.

'Hello, gentlemen, how lovely to see you. Come in and take a seat.' There was a juggling of chairs and seating positions, and then we got comfortable. Eric sat at the small table facing Moore, his notepad and bundle of papers tied up in pink ribbon by his side. To the side of Eric sat Dewi, balancing his papers and notes on his knee, and then I took a chair and sat behind them both. On the other side of the table was Moore, facing us as if he was about to be interrogated. Moore looked worried, his brow furrowed and his eyes slightly reddened. His hands were clasped, as usual, on the table in front of him. I could sense that he felt that this was a big moment. Meeting the senior barrister who will be presenting the case is important.

Eric took charge of proceedings and began by going through a chronology of events. He would ask a question, get a reply from Moore, make a note in his notepad and then without comment move on to the next issue. Within a short time, we'd covered a lot of ground and it was clear that Eric was on top of his brief and knew the case from back to front. As he paused for a moment to consult his notes, Moore spoke.

'I've met you before, Mr Somerset-Jones.'

All three of us looked up from our notes and papers, more or less at the same time.

'Have we met before?' Eric asked.

'Oh yes, don't you remember?' Moore seemed slightly offended that Eric couldn't recall their meeting.

'You live on the Wirral, don't you?' Eric looked slightly uncomfortable and began moving around in his chair and clearing his throat.

'Well, yes, I do, Peter – and how do you know that?'

'Oh yes, we met a few years ago now; I can't exactly recall when it was. I was driving to Liverpool and I began to have mechanical problems with the van. I decided to pull over and I parked on the side of the road in a driveway and called the AA. I'd been waiting for a while in this driveway when a lady came out of the house at the end of the drive and asked me how long I was planning to be there. She asked me to move a bit so her husband could drive in, so I did that. It was a big house with a flagpole in the front.'

'Well, yes – it is,' Eric responded with a slight chuckle, possibly nerves.

'A few moments later I saw you drive in. You were driving a Jag. I saw you quite clearly.' For a few seconds, there was silence. I'm certain that none of the three of us was sure what to say. I'm also sure that Eric, for those few seconds, was in a state of complete shock. It seemed that Moore *had* met him before, however briefly, and the detail given by Moore clearly convinced Eric that it was true. I couldn't believe such a coincidence would have been possible, and for Moore to remember the incident in such detail – the house, the flagpole, even the car – was astounding. Maybe even unnerving and frightening.

After the silence had hung in the room for what felt like minutes, Eric cleared his throat again.

'Yes, so Peter, moving on...' he finally said, and started to shuffle his papers at the same time. The rest of the interview passed without incident. Eric wanted to know more about Jason, but there wasn't much forthcoming from Moore – this was clearly going to prove very difficult. Eric was of the opinion that the more information we could get about Jason, the better it would be. Though we all doubted Jason's existence, it was the sum total of Moore's defence and so anything that could substantiate that someone who could possibly have been Jason actually existed would have been helpful at trial.

We left Moore after about an hour and a half. Eric said he wasn't sure if he required another meeting, but would let Moore know if he did. While walking out of the visitors' centre and back to our cars, there was only one subject of discussion and that was the revelation that Moore had met Eric in the past. Eric was clearly shocked, not only that it had happened but also that Moore recalled the incident in such detail and could describe his car and house.

'I think that says something about our client,' said Eric. 'I think the boundaries between the different lives he's led in the past seem very narrow and permeable. He seems to remember lots of things in detail. In that middle-of-the-night interview he remembered the murders in detail. We need to be careful with this man – he seems a very dangerous character to me.'

'And he knows where you live, Eric,' said Dewi, with a grim laugh.

'He bloody does,' Eric responded, with a chuckle but also a serious look of concern at the same time. 'Wait till I tell my wife that story.'

We didn't need another meeting with Moore. Eric seemed to have got a clear picture of the case, what Moore was saying and what the defence was going to look like when we finally got to trial. The following month involved a great deal of preparation. Documents were copied, witness statements were agreed with the prosecution – that is, if we didn't require a witness' presence at court – and a phone meeting took place between the three of us in the defence team in preparation for the day of the trial. We had agreed with the Judge that the trial would take two to three weeks, though Eric believed that the way the preparation for this case was going, it was likely to be finished in two weeks. It was still going to be a long and possibly harrowing two weeks, and I needed to prepare a strategy at my office to make sure that things kept ticking over while I attended the trial every day.

My business partner believed that I could hand over the case to someone else now the trial was upon us; that I should ask a junior member of staff to sit in court and make notes of what was said. It showed a failure to understand the demands of a case of this magnitude. My view was that doing what he suggested would disrespect the client and my colleagues defending him. I'd invested so much time and energy getting things ready that I knew every detail, and it would have been impossible to hand the case over to someone else at that stage. I needed to be present and, more to the point, both Eric and Dewi felt that my intimate knowledge of the case required me to be there for the duration.

I'd also developed a good working relationship with Peter Moore over the past months. I believed that he trusted me and knew that I'd do my best for him, as was my duty and responsibility. This case had brought out many emotions. My job wasn't to be Peter Moore's friend or even to like him, but I needed to work with him so as to ensure he was given the best possible representation in court.

I decided to give the case everything I had over the next few weeks. Because of the lack of assistance from colleagues at the office, I was planning to arrive at work at about 6 a.m., do two or three hours of paperwork and then go to the trial at Mold Crown Court. I would then return to my office at the end of the court day to catch up with phone calls and office work. I knew this schedule was going to be tough, but it was my choice. I needed to be in control of everything and as there was no one to help me, this was my strategy – as exhausting as it appeared. I was young and fit and I decided that I would relax and sleep after the trial finished.

'After this is all done, I'm going to book a treat so we can go away somewhere for a couple of days,' Catherine said one day when I was worrying about my demanding schedule. I was holding her to that promise, and as I was working 16 hours a day by the time of the trial, I knew I would need a break.

Chapter 16

THE WEEKS LEADING up to 11 November flew by. The paperwork was in place, the lawyers were ready and I'd prepared thoroughly for the weeks ahead at the Crown Court. The court was in Mold, a town in north-east Wales which was the administrative centre for the county of Clwyd when it existed, and then more recently the county of Flintshire. There are two Crown Court centres in north Wales: one in Mold and the other at Caernarfon. The murders had occurred across north Wales but because, at the time, Mold Crown Court was a larger court building, it was considered more appropriate for this trial.

I was up early on the 11th and had decided to get everything prepared at home that morning rather than going to the office, so I could get to court early. Catherine fussed around, making sure I was in a suitable-looking suit, shirt and tie. I collected my papers and files together and after a bit of breakfast, I was ready to leave home. I nervously gave Catherine a kiss and a hug and she gave me some last-minute words of encouragement.

'You're going to do brilliantly. You've worked so hard on this case – now go and show them what you can do.' It was fighting talk, as if I was about to go out on a rugby field to play for Wales, but it was the positivity I needed before such a big case. However much you prepare, there's always that element of doubt that something's been missed or that some piece of evidence you've somehow overlooked becomes a crucial part of the prosecution case. As a criminal lawyer, you're always expecting the unexpected. Your best-laid plans can be thrown into chaos by something said by one of the witnesses, or even by your own client, and the whole case is turned on its head. The most unexpected things can happen during the first morning of a case and suddenly all that preparation is wasted and a different approach is required. That's the nature of being a criminal practitioner: rarely are things what they seem.

It was a nervous drive to Mold Crown Court. By the time I arrived and parked, I could see a few reporters already milling around the entrance and a couple of cameramen setting up their equipment. Mold Crown Court was built in the late 1960s or early 1970s and has the look of a building of its time, constructed in grey brick and with a large glass frontage which makes anyone sitting in the reception area feel like they're in a huge greenhouse. Leading up to the front entrance was an imposing flight of stairs, the type seen in films of the 1930s, where a man in a top hat and tails and a troupe of girls will be dancing down them together. Occasionally I was tempted to do a bit of a Fred Astaire routine as I left the court building, but I never did.

I avoided the attention of the reporters on the way into court carrying two boxes of papers, and then returned to my car for more files. I may have looked like a removal man – though in a suit, of course. I took the boxes into a side room on a corridor adjacent to one of the courtrooms and then went to find one of the Listing Officers, who are responsible for the practical and administrative arrangements at court, to find out which courtroom was going to be used for the trial.

'You'll be using Court No. 2, Dylan, so you might as well get comfortable there,' she said. Courts No. 1 and 2 in Mold are identical courtrooms. They're both large, high-ceilinged rooms built in the early 1970s, with sturdy light wooden benches and a public gallery high at the back of the courtroom. They didn't possess the stern gothic authority of courtrooms built in an earlier era, but some would argue that this was a good thing. Personally, I liked the drama of the courtrooms at the Crown Court in Chester, with their dark wood and eerie appearance, where the Judge sits high up on a bench looking down at proceedings, like God.

I fetched as many papers as I could and took them into Court No. 2 and left them on the second bench along – the first bench is always reserved for the barristers. The Court Clerk was already busy organising her paperwork and gave me a cheery 'Morning!' as I entered the courtroom.

'All ready to go, then?' she asked.

'I certainly hope so,' was my reply. There was a nervous energy in the air: everyone busied themselves checking and rechecking. I noticed the Court Usher filling water jugs and ensuring the cards with the oaths written on them were placed in the witness box and near to where the jury were to sit. Everything in the courtroom seemed to be in its place and ready to go. Like a frustrated actor pacing in the wings, I felt like it was the final moments before the opening of a show. The excitement and tension of opening night; the apprehension and the edginess – it was all in the air that morning.

I decided to go to the barristers' robing room to check if Eric and Dewi had arrived. The robing room is where the barristers get ready and usually engage in jovial chatter. It's like going to some inner sanctum. I liked going there, though I always suspected that many solicitors would avoid it completely. There may have been the odd barrister about who would frown and consider a humble solicitor gaining entrance into 'their robing room' a bit of a transgression, but I never took any notice of them. I liked the chatter and the banter and usually the camaraderie as the barristers got prepared for their day in court. They would arrive with their papers tied up in pink ribbon, their red velvet tie bags containing robes and their wig boxes. It looked glamorous and exciting and I regretted not becoming a barrister myself every time I went there.

When I arrived in the robing room, both Eric and Dewi were there getting ready and were deep in conversation with the barristers on the opposing side in the Peter Moore case. I was introduced to them by Dewi, though I'd met them both before. The senior barrister for the prosecution was Alex Carlile QC. He was an experienced barrister and was the first lawyer I'd ever seen in action in court. When I was a sixth-form student, our Politics teacher took our class to Mold Crown Court for a day's outing, for the class to see the law and the Crown Court in action. The experience was an eye-opener for me. I remember being impressed by one barrister in particular who seemed assured, confident and articulate, and when he spoke, it appeared everyone in the court listened. I assume he was a very young barrister at the time, but he made an immediate impression. He was Alex Carlile. If only I could stand up in court with his confidence, I thought at the time. I've never had the opportunity to tell him, but it was his performance that day in Mold Crown Court during my sixth-form years which drove me to become a lawyer. To see Carlile in the robing room that morning at the Peter Moore trial brought some extra excitement and nerves. This was going to be a difficult few weeks: as a defence team, we were up against some tough opposition. Carlile's junior was a barrister called Steven Everett. I'd met Steven on a few previous occasions and always found him to be thorough, intelligent and very good company, with a great sense of humour, which in our line of work is important. He was fairly young at the time, but it was clear then that he was destined for a successful future career in the law. Steven is by now a very respected Judge.

We all chatted for a while about Peter Moore and the strange particularities of both him and the case. Jason's name also popped up in our discussion. The prosecutors laughed and suggested that if we found Jason before the end of the trial and brought him before the court, then they would both believe in miracles.

'Well you never know, miracles do happen!' said Dewi. Eric then went to the window and pretended to commentate on Jason's arrival outside the court in a taxi. It was all harmless banter and seemed to cut the tension at the beginning of such an important and serious trial.

'Well,' said Eric, 'we'd better go and visit the man himself.' I'd made sure earlier that the prison van had arrived with its precious cargo of Peter Howard Moore, and it seemed an opportune moment to check on the well-being of our client and give him some last-minute advice and guidance. Both Eric and Dewi collected their papers and decided to take them and leave them in Court No. 2 before we made our way down to the cells to see Moore.

In court, Eric asked the Usher if we could access the cells via the dock of the court, and the Court Clerk called the officer in the cells to ask for the doors of the dock to be opened to allow the three of us through. By this time, both Eric and Dewi were in their barrister's regalia, apart from their wigs, which had been left on the bench in the courtroom.

The cells seemed busy, with a number of prison officers and security personnel milling around. We asked to see Peter Moore and were told that the only place we could see him without any disturbances would be in his cell. The three of us were led to the cell and the door was opened by the guard.

'Peter, some people for you,' he said as we marched into the small cell. Moore was sitting on a metal bench, covered with a blue plastic mattress of some kind, at one end of the cell. He wore the prison-issue grey tracksuit bottoms and what looked like a grey T-shirt and then a patterned crew-neck jumper. He'd had a shave and a haircut and seemed relaxed as we arrived to see him.

'Everything fine with you this morning, Mr Moore?' asked Eric, politely.

'Yes, I'm fine, thank you,' said Moore, with what appeared to be a smile.

Eric then explained the procedure in the court, in particular the process of jury selection. He emphasised that if Moore knew any one of the potential jury members, he should let us as his lawyers know as soon as possible. Moore seemed happy to go along with the instructions given to him and in control of his emotions, considering he was facing a trial on four murder charges. It was as if he didn't care much about what was going on: he was there and following the instructions given to him, but there was a disengagement from the situation which was a little worrying. I concluded that maybe he didn't much care about his fate, that he had already come to terms with what his future was likely to be.

We left the cell and returned to the courtroom.

'Everything is OK, I think?' said Dewi in my general direction as I began to arrange my paperwork on the bench. At the other end of the bench, Nita Dowell from the CPS was doing the same and soon Alex Carlile and Steven Everett arrived and took their places on the bench in front of her. The actors were finally all in their positions and limbering up for the long-awaited performance. Members of the press took their places and even the court artist arrived to take her seat in one of the benches at the side of the court, so she could see all the cast, including Moore himself, and draw sketches for that day's news programmes and the following day's newspapers.

As more people entered the court, the tension grew and as I looked round, I noticed that only a few seats were still empty in the public gallery. I guessed that most of those present were family members and friends of the victims – it was unlikely that anyone was there for Peter Moore. It's often the case that those close to the victims wish to be present when the suspected perpetrator faces trial. I can understand why they'd wish to see justice being done and the murderer of their family member being sentenced and punished. Sometimes, though, I've wondered if it's wise. I'm not convinced I'd be able to sit through the graphic details of how one of my loved ones was murdered, or face the accused without resorting to some sort of violent outburst. You never expect to face circumstances such as these – it's the unthinkable, and most of us go through life never having to consider it even being a possibility. I've thought many times that sitting in the public gallery listening to details of the last moments of a relative's or close friend's life, or to the horrific detail of a rape or the abuse of a child, must be such an excruciatingly painful experience as to be unimaginable. But people put themselves through these experiences: they wish to be there to see the wheels of justice turning and the truth being revealed, however painful it may be.

The Court Clerk hurried into the court and reported that the Judge, Mr Justice Maurice Kay, would be a few minutes late as he had been required to deal with some other urgent matters. Usually that is Clerk code for an urgent bail application or some other similar business. We continued to wait, making small talk and pacing up and down. Eventually we got going: the Judge appeared in all his High Court regalia and got matters under way by asking for the prisoner to be brought into the dock. The Clerk phoned down to the cells and within minutes, the clanking of keys and pacing of feet on the stone floor could be heard. Peter Howard Moore was led into the dock by two police officers, who removed his handcuffs and then led him to stand by a seat allocated for him at the front of the dock. Whispers could be hear circulating around the court, reporters began writing and the pencil of the courtroom artist began to move across her sketch paper. Some of the occupants of the public gallery who were unable to properly see the dock leant over the barrier in front of them so as to get a better look at the defendant, Peter Moore. There were whispered conversations and mumbling amongst the members of the public, and the Judge looked up at them with a firm look and cleared his throat loudly to attract their attention. The lawyers at the front of the court all turned round as one to see Moore standing there looking through the toughened glass at the front of the dock, staring at the Judge, Mr Justice Kay. The stage was set, but this wasn't a play: this was real life at its most intense. The Court Clerk spoke first.

'Peter Howard Moore, you have been charged with four counts of murder under common law. The indictments read as follows.' The Clerk then proceeded to read out the four charges against Moore, setting out the dates and the individuals Moore was accused of murdering: John Henry Roberts, Keith Randles, Edward Carthy and Anthony Davies. Moore was asked to confirm his plea after each charge was read. A confident response of 'Not guilty' was heard from Moore after each charge. Following the fourth charge, there seemed to be a lull and a realisation that what we had been preparing for for nearly a year was about to begin.

'Mr Moore, you may sit down,' the Judge said as he looked over his spectacles at Moore. It seemed a lingering look as he watched Moore move to one side and into his chair at the front of the dock. It was a look of someone studying their quarry, measuring up each movement and gesture, searching for any available clue as to what this man, Peter Moore, was about.

I turned in my seat to lookd at Moore. He gave me a quick nod and a smile of acknowledgement and mouthed, 'Are you OK?' I found it amusing that he was asking me if I was OK. I mouthed back, 'Yes, what about you?' He nodded back, but there was a nervous, hesitant look in his eyes. It was the look of someone who was facing the unknown, and though he could put on a confident bold bravado when necessary, I sensed that maybe the tentative look in his eyes at that moment betrayed the fact that a frightened, timid man existed within the hardened outer shell of this accused serial killer.

The process of selecting and then swearing in the jury always takes some time, and there are always nervous jurors who have trouble reading the oath and seem totally embarrassed at being present at court. In most cases the twelve men and women good and true look as if they'd rather be anywhere else rather than exercising their civic duty. This case, though, may well have been different. Most, if not all, would have known about the case; they would have seen it in the newspapers and watched the news reports on TV. They would have seen photographs and TV footage of Moore and they might have drawn their own conclusions already as to the type of man he was and what he'd done. Jurors would probably have already made up their minds as to whether Moore 'looked like a murderer' or even if he 'looked guilty', possibly weeks before knowing they were to be a jury member at his trial. Lawyers and Judges are aware that the morning of the trial is not necessarily the beginning of the trial: they are aware of the preconceptions and assumptions – even, some would suggest, the prejudices – of a jury. They will be prepared to face and overcome these challenges during the trial process.

The Judge made his usual speech to the jury after they had been sworn in. As usual he thanked them for serving on the jury and then reminded them of the importance of keeping an open mind, of not taking account of anything they had previously heard about the case and of making their decision only after they had heard all the evidence in the case. The jury, which consisted of eight men and four women, listened intently. They were warned that they were facing a harrowing few weeks of evidence, but that they must set aside any preconceived ideas that they may have had, and listen to the evidence.

I always find those first few moments of a trial fascinating. Before any evidence is presented to the court, I look at the faces of those jurors and imagine what they're thinking, how daunted they may feel by the responsibility of the task ahead of them and how frightened they may be. Some listen to the Judge intently, looking directly at him or her without averting their gaze. Others are fixated by the defendant; they can't seem to stop looking at him or her. It's like sitting in a doctor's waiting room and someone walking in with a tumour or birthmark on their face. You're telling yourself not to look at that person, but you can't help but stare. Many jurors kept taking brief repeated glances at Moore – back and forth they went, as if they were staring at a monster in the corner of a room.

Then there are the 'rabbit in the headlight' jurors, totally daunted by the whole court setting, the barristers in their wigs and the Judge in his regalia. The whole thing is so far from their past experience that it takes some time for them to get used to it all; they gawk and stare wide-eyed at everything and seem to not listen to anything that's being said.

Lawyers have to deal with these difficult beginnings to trials. They must draw the attention of the jurors, as confused and baffled as they may appear, to the matter in hand. That's why on such occasions the inner actor or performer in every barrister worth his or her salt comes to the fore. They need to hold the jurors' attention and focus their minds on the decisions they need to make as a jury and how they are going to make them. Jurors need to understand what charges the accused is facing and how they're going to weigh up the evidence presented to them so as to make a fair decision.

Alex Carlile QC rose to his feet. All eyes were on him and he knew how to use those moments to his advantage. With a lengthy and dramatic pause, he organised his papers on a small lectern on the bench in front of him.

'My Lord.' He began by addressing the Judge and then the jury, moving his gaze from one to another throughout his opening address to the court. Carlile described the accusations against Moore in detail, going from one murder to the next and explaining to the jury the intentions of the prosecution to call evidence to substantiate each and every allegation made against Moore. Carlile also described what he perceived to be the real character of Peter Moore, the darkness that surrounded him, his interest and participation in sexually deviant behaviour and the perverted and twisted life he had conducted in the shadows and away from the image he had built of himself as a legitimate businessman and cinema owner.

'Peter Moore was a sadistic and predatory homosexual who became a serial killer, killing for fun. He stabbed four men in a killing spree which left him "at peace".'

It was a dramatic and forceful opening speech, Carlile had the jury hooked from the beginning but it was the flourish at the end which I most admired. Carlile had spoken about the darkness surrounding Moore and had then mentioned his propensity to wear black clothes. The reason Moore had given was that it was necessary for him to wear black clothes for his work as a cinema projectionist. Alex Carlile's interpretation of this was different.

'Peter Moore was the man in black, with black thoughts and the blackest of deeds.'

Alex Carlile's words left the court in no doubt about the way he viewed Moore. I suspect he was quietly proud of the closing sentence of his opening speech. It certainly had an effect on me and I'm sure also on Peter Moore, who was sitting behind me in the dock. It was clearly going to be the headline-grabbing sound bite used by the TV news bulletins and the following day's newspaper headlines. I suspected that Carlile, in that short but dramatic sentence, had sought to encapsulate the whole case and also Peter Moore's character, and by doing so had drawn the attention of the media and the public to this unusual case.

The case for the prosecution had begun and Alex Carlile QC, with Steven Everett supporting him, started their case by calling the prosecution evidence. One of the many difficult aspects of the case was that there were no direct witnesses to any of the murders. There was no one alleged to have been present at the murders other than the victim and the accused, neither were there any eyewitnesses testifying to have seen Peter Moore in the vicinity of any of the murders, other than that one sighting of a van like his near the beach in Pensarn. There was no evidence of Moore having been in contact with any of the victims before the murders or having been at the locations of the murders at some other date or time. Nobody had seen Peter Moore wielding a knife and stabbing his victims, and therefore it was necessary for the prosecution to rely on other evidence which would allow the jury to slowly piece together the story from the complex criminal jigsaw.

The prosecution had to present forensic and other more circumstantial evidence which would allow them to place Moore at the murder scene at the time of each of the four murders. Crucially, the blood spatter on the beach in Persarn, the scene of the Anthony Davies murder, had been positively identified as being Peter Moore's. The hand injury suffered by Moore was confirmed to have been inflicted by the hunting knife found in his house. The knife also had on it blood from not only Anthony Davies, but also the other three victims.

The prosecution had another trump card, and that was the early-morning interview in which Moore had confessed to the murders. That interview was of course pivotal, and from the details provided by Moore at that time it was possible to identify elements of each murder that only the killer would have known. Clearly the prosecution also knew that Jason would appear as a key part of the defence case, and that it would be necessary for them to make a link between whatever evidence they presented to the court and Moore directly. The prosecution were aware that when it came to defending Moore, we would be trying to throw that connection into doubt by the introduction of Jason as a possible alternative murderer. It was the prosecution's task to prove their case against Moore 'beyond all reasonable doubt': our tactic as the defence team was to cast doubt on as much of their case as we could. If we could demonstrate the possibility that Jason existed and had taken part in or was responsible for the murders, then we would set the jury a difficult problem to resolve. They would need to decide whether the prosecution had proved their case 'beyond all reasonable doubt'.

Some consider this all a bit of a game. Why do defence lawyers approach cases in this way? I suppose the easiest answer is that the prosecution always know that no trial will be easy. They will always have the responsibility of proving their case with convincing and clear evidence, so that the jury has no doubt of the accused's guilt. Our legal system places that responsibility on the prosecution and grants the defence opportunity to challenge every part of their case. We in the defence must ask the questions which make the jury consider the strength of the prosecution evidence. It's the right of the defendant to have the evidence tested, challenged and examined in detail. This is what happens during every criminal trial, be it big or small, long and detailed or simple and clear. The responsibility of the lawyer is to ensure that it is done properly, so as to protect the rights of all involved. Whether we are prosecuting or defending, in essence, we are always on the same side: the side of the law, making sure it works properly.

The prosecution case was to be heard over the first week or so. Some of the evidence was thoroughly unpleasant and involved details of each victim from the Home Office Forensic Pathologist Professor Bernard Knight: their stab wounds, the blows that killed them and the horrendous injuries each victim of them suffered. Each murder scene was described in detail by forensic and scene-of-crime officers, then they described their findings in Moore's home, garden and van. Police officers gave evidence about items discovered at Moore's home – the knife, truncheon and police uniform, the Nazi paraphernalia and also the victims' possessions – then they highlighted small spatters of blood, from an unknown source, discovered on the walls of some of the rooms in Darlington House. It was as dark as it gets.

Then DC Dave Morris and DS Mike Guthrie gave evidence. They both gave details of the lengthy series of interviews conducted during December 1995 after Moore's arrest. The interviews were read out in court and, as expected, particular attention was given to the early-morning interview where Moore confessed. The jury listened intently throughout, making notes and – when directed – looking through the large book of photographic evidence.

During those long days in court, I sat and made notes of all that was said in evidence. I would look back at Peter Moore occasionally, checking that all was well and whether he had any comment about the witness evidence. Moore seemed for the most part disconnected from what was going on around him, as if he'd lost all interest in the case. When evidence about the murders was given by the Home Office Forensic Pathologist, Moore appeared aloof, as if he was there in body but somewhere else entirely in his mind. He continued to acknowledge me and chat with his defence team when necessary, but there remained, during those many days when the prosecution evidence was heard in court, a separation from reality that I found concerning.

Maybe it was his way of coping and he'd convinced himself that this was all Jason's business and that he was a mere bystander, a dispassionate onlooker, to all the drama happening in front of him in court. It was clear that he enjoyed the attention given to him by the press: from the beginning of the trial, rather than hiding away when arriving at court each morning and being escorted into the court building from the prison van, Moore would hold his head up high and look towards the photographers. There were countless pictures of him on the front of newspapers looking directly at the camera with what seemed to be a slight smile, or maybe a smirk. I got the feeling that he rather enjoyed the notoriety and the description given of him as 'The Man in Black'. Maybe he believed he was starring in a film playing in one of his cinemas, a sinister man from the edge of darkness now thrust into the limelight.

At the beginning of the second week of the trial, after seeing his face grinning back at me from the front pages of the *Daily Post* on more than one occasion over the preceding week, I decided to have a word with him at the beginning of the day. I was down in the cells as he arrived from prison. He was checked in as usual and we were placed in one of the cells to have a chat.

He seemed fine and in quite a buoyant mood considering the extensive and convincing amount of evidence presented by the prosecution the previous week. I explained that it was going to be an important week for the trial and that towards the end of the week, I expected us in the defence to begin presenting his case. It was therefore likely that he'd be called to give evidence sometime during the week and should be preparing himself for that experience. Moore nodded in agreement.

'And Mr Moore, I have one other area of concern that I thought should be mentioned. I think it would be better if you try and hide from the cameras a little as you arrive and leave here every day. I realise there are cameramen trying to get a shot of you from every angle and it's not easy to avoid them. I just thought it would be a good idea to keep your profile as low as possible during this crucial week?' Moore again agreed with my suggestion, which I'd put to him as subtly as I possibly could. My advice made little difference: Moore continued to leave court every day with a smile on his face and to stare directly at the eager photographers. I decided not to mention my concerns to him again.

The week began as the previous one had ended, with a continuation of the prosecution case. Evidence was presented by the senior detectives in the case, describing the multiple investigations involved and how they had come together into one large investigation focusing on Peter Moore. Clearly the investigation and everything relating to the case had been complex and sometimes confusing. The prosecution succeeded in emphasising the horror and chilling nature of the murders, and the effect of this could be clearly seen in the faces of the jurors. They appeared astonished by the evidence they'd heard, the horror appeared etched in their faces and their disgust was evident in the brief conversations I heard them share between listening to the witnesses.

Eventually by midweek, it was time for the defence to begin presenting our case to the jury. I was confident in both Eric and Dewi and reassured by their obvious spirit and tenacity as lawyers. I'd enjoyed their company over the previous week and admired their knowledge, experience and jocular wit. By that second week of the trial, both we in the defence team and the two prosecution barristers had begun to get to know each other pretty well. We would sit in the barristers' robing room each lunchtime, putting aside the complications and horrors of the case for about 45 minutes every day, and share stories and anecdotes over sandwiches, crisps and a cup of coffee. Occasionally one of the circuit Judges from the other Crown Court would also join us for lunch, catching up with the gossip of the Peter Moore case and generally chatting about the legal world and its personalities. I was intrigued by their conversations and, though I contributed little myself, listening to these lawyers talking was fascinating and totally absorbing.

Eric Somerset-Jones QC stood up on the Wednesday afternoon to begin presenting the case for the defence. There was an air of experience and gravitas to him. He was a man who appeared to have the respect of all, including Mr Justice Kay. His slightly rotund figure made his waistcoat stick out a little in front of him and it would catch the podium occasionally. His wig was set on his head at a jaunty angle, not straight on top like the other barristers. The jury may have considered this barrister to be slightly different and captivating, and he was able to hold their interest from the beginning of his opening speech. But this was no comedy routine: Eric had to set the record straight right from the very beginning about Peter Howard Moore.

'I hold no brief for Moore's way of life. By his own admission, he is a bad man. I am not here to excuse his behaviour or the way he has conducted his personal life and neither is he on trial for that behaviour, as unsavoury as it may appear to many of us.' Eric was aware that the jury had been bombarded by the prosecution with evidence of Moore's sexual preoccupations and deviance. They had been told at length about his behaviour, going back over twenty years: of the sexually motivated violent attacks on men, mostly in the Conwy Valley area, and of Moore's interest in regularly visiting clubs and other gatherings where sexual violence and extreme sexual excesses were the norm. But Somerset-Jones emphasised that this was not what Moore was being tried for in the Crown Court. He was on trial for the murder of four men, and as such it was the responsibility of the prosecution to present to the jury convincing and overwhelming evidence of these murders having been committed by Moore, 'beyond all reasonable doubt'.

Eric's opening speech was both logical and reasoned. It was his clear intention to throw doubt, as much as he possibly could, on the prosecution's assertions. The greater the doubt raised in the minds of the jury, the more likely it was that our defence would succeed, despite the substantial odds stacked against us in this case.

At the end of his speech, Eric called Peter Moore to the witness stand to give evidence. Having considered our options carefully, we in the defence team had realised that this was our only option. Some may have believed this to be a case of throwing Daniel into the lions' den, but from a defence point of view, it was our only real option – the alternative being not to call any evidence at all. We wanted Peter Moore to explain why he had made a confession during the early-morning interview, and also to convince the jury that Jason actually existed. We were, though, aware that adopting this approach would leave Peter Moore open to being cross-examined and challenged in court by Alex Carlile. With all the skill and verbal dexterity in Carlile's armoury, I favoured him to be the odds-on favourite in any such confrontation, but it was a risk that we had no choice but to take.

Moore entered the witness stand warily. He knew, as we did, that his future would be affected by his appearance on the stand. He read the oath from card presented to him by the Court Usher, his voice hesitant and gentle. All eyes were on him: the jury, the Judge and the lawyers, and the usual coughing and stirring in the public gallery had all but disappeared. Moore's thin lips looked dry and he pressed them together tightly, which made his chin stick out further than normal. He clenched his hands, and placed them on the small stand in front of him in the box. He looked a bit ungainly so the Judge invited him to sit down – he thanked the Judge quietly and politely, then took a seat. It seemed that everything he did, every move that he made, was being scrutinised by everyone in the courtroom. There was complete silence, the only sound being the air-conditioning system humming steadily in the background.

'Mr Moore,' began Eric in a loud and dramatic voice. Moore turned to look down to his right, where Eric was standing, and fixed his gaze on him. Eric then began to go through some of Moore's background and family history, setting the scene on how he was brought up in Kinmel Bay near Rhyl, the dominant nature of his father and the death of his mother in 1994. The replies Moore gave were short, accurate and to the point. Eric then moved on to his sexual interests and proclivities and his liking for violence within what Moore considered to be a consensual situation. By the end of the day, a considerable amount of ground had been covered and though there were many issues still to be addressed, on leaving the witness stand, Moore looked relatively comfortable. I spoke to him briefly and he confirmed that he was fine and there were no problems.

The following day, Moore was back in the witness box and Eric resumed by asking him about Jason. Eric was prepared to press Moore as much as he could for details about Jason. We knew getting additional information from Moore was going to be difficult, but I assume Eric felt there was no harm in trying his hardest as such information was crucial to our defence. The testimony from Moore regarding Jason was brief, thin and added nothing to what he had said in interview. I asked myself whether any of this testimony was believable, whether it was at all possible to plant the seed of doubt in the minds of any of the jury that there was at least a possibility that Moore wasn't guilty – after all that was our job. It was proving even more difficult than I had envisaged.

Eric pressed on and began to ask about the early-morning interview and the confession made by Moore. It was clearly a hurdle we needed to overcome as much as we possibly could so as to sow doubt into the minds of the jury. Moore stuck to what he'd said at the following interview: he was protecting his friend, and had only related to us information given to him by Jason about the murders and his victims. He was adamant, though I felt not persuasive, that Jason was a real person. He said he cared for him and was in a relationship with him, and had no wish to betray him.

Eric finally sat down. I was satisfied that he'd done as much as he could. I leant back in my seat and prepared to watch Moore being mauled by Alex Carlile QC.

As it turned out, it wasn't the drubbing that I expected – for the simple reason that Carlile had sensed that such drastic action wasn't needed. It was clear to him, as it was to the rest of us in court, that Moore's testimony was weak and not believable. We in the defence had done the best we could with it, but it was far from enough. At this point, a sacrificial tearing to pieces of Moore's evidence seemed unnecessary, and frankly not worth the effort. Carlile asked the questions that needed to be asked, looked at Moore with the disdain I would have expected, and backed him into an evidential corner from which there was no escape. Carlile didn't raise his voice or become irritated or cross, and, for Moore, I suspected that it was all rather anticlimactic. Carlile was prepared, detailed and surgical in his cross-examination. By the time he left the stand, Moore looked deflated, tired and disorientated. I sensed that he knew that though his story had been told, it was far from being enough to exonerate him for these four murders.

The following morning, Eric closed the case for the defence with a speech which was consistent with all that had been heard and presented by the defence in court. Despite these valiant efforts, it was clear that Moore couldn't call any witnesses to his defence who would be willing to corroborate his story. Eric pointed out the positive elements to Moore's defence – his attempts to protect his friend Jason – and then asked whether the jury believed the prosecution had adequately managed to prove their case *beyond all reasonable doubt*. Eric was a barrister of the highest calibre, but pulling this one out of the bag was beyond even his capabilities.

The Judge, Mr Justice Maurice Kay, delivered a brutal summing-up of the case. He dissected every part of the defence case, highlighting the questions that the jury needed to ask themselves in the process of deciding their verdict. He emphasised the weaknesses in what Peter Moore had said in evidence, and compared it with the strength of evidence presented by the prosecution. It's not the responsibility of the Judge to tell the jury what decision they should make in any trial, but there could be no doubt about the Judge's view of Moore's defence. Mr Justice Kay told the jury to take as much time as they needed to decide their verdicts, and instructions were then given to the Court Usher to help the jury get ready to deliberate.

Just before lunchtime, the jury were discharged to make their decision. Peter Moore was returned to the cells beneath the courts and the lawyers went for an early lunch in the barristers' robing room. This stage of a criminal trial is strange: there's nothing more the lawyers can do to influence the jury – it's all now in the hands of those twelve people. The jury hold the ultimate power in any criminal trial. For us lawyers, it's a matter of waiting. It may take two hours, two days or even longer. Most of us get used to the lethargic hanging around and the endless coffee-drinking – it becomes part of the job. We call the office or our chambers, we try and get some paperwork done, we gossip about other lawyers and discuss other cases. Every time the phone rings or the Court Usher appears, there's a moment of gasping anticipation. There are always those among us who believe they can guess the length of time the jury will be out.

'Give them an hour; they'll have sorted this one out.'

'Well, we've certainly given the jury something to think about. They're going to be days on this one.'

Invariably, all the predictions are wrong. When you believe it's a done deal, the jury will deliberate for days and come back to the Judge with questions and enquiries which cast doubt on their comprehension of the whole case. On other occasions when we're expecting hours, if not days, of hanging around, they're out of the jury room in an hour and ready to go home.

By early afternoon, we'd eaten our sandwiches, drunk our coffee and made all our predictions. We were settling down to an afternoon of catching up with paperwork. Then the phone in the robing room rang and Steven Everett answered it. We all looked at him, like pilots in a Second World War film, ready to scramble. Within seconds his face lit up. He didn't need to say anything: by the time he'd put the receiver down and said, 'The jury are coming back', we were collecting our papers and getting ready to return to the courtroom. It had been two and a half hours since the jury had retired.

There's an atmosphere of excitement in a court every time the jury returns with a verdict, as if a charge of electricity has been fired into the room. There's a feeling of heightened sensitivity, expectation and drama buzzing through everyone in the court. Even when you believe you know what's about to happen, there is always that possibility of the unexpected.

The whole scene plays out as if we are characters in a film. It seems unreal and theatrical and though I've experienced the return of the jury on many occasions, this time it's different and I feel as if I'm watching it all from afar, playing before me on a big silver screen.

We all file into court and take our places. The Court Clerk gives an indication that the Jury are returning with a verdict.

We all stand as Mr Justice Kay comes in and then the jury file into court and take their seats. The door to the dock is opened and we hear the footsteps of Peter Moore and his two guards coming up the stone steps. I turn around and see Moore, and give him a smile. He smiles back as he takes his place, standing in the dock facing the Judge. The Clerk asks the jury foreperson to stand and to confirm that they have reached a verdict on all four of the charges.

'Yes, we have,' replies the foreperson nervously. As he speaks, his voice cracks and the Court Usher begins fussing around, getting him a glass of water. The whole process becomes unnecessarily elongated, and we wait impatiently for the juror to take a drink and gather his composure.

'On count one...' the Court Clerk begins, asking the foreperson for the jury's verdict.

'Guilty,' is his response.

'On count two...'

'Guilty.'

'On count three...'

'Guilty.'

'On count four...'

'Guilty.' The foreperson's voice expires in a croak as he announces the final verdict.

There is a collective sigh from the packed public gallery, a few celebratory gasps can be heard from others and voices are raised in brief congratulatory conversations. Moore is unmoved in the dock. I look at him for any sign of emotion, but there's nothing there. He stands still, facing the Judge, his hands behind his back, his lips pursed, his eyes vacant and impassive. I wonder if the verdict has even registered with him or whether he's switched off and become totally detached, unmoved in any way by the moment. There's a brief lull in proceedings as the foreperson sits down and the court and its participants come back to the business in hand.

Mr Justice Maurice Kay then speaks, thanking the jury for their hard work and dismissing them from the court. They file out, some looking exhausted, others emotional. A few take a last glance at the court or over at Moore as they leave. Their part in this surreal scene is over.

Now it's over to Mr Justice Kay. He adjusts his notebooks and gathers his thoughts for a moment, then focuses his attention on Peter Moore in the dock, and looks over his spectacles as he addresses him directly. I notice Moore is still standing in the same position, staring directly at the Judge. It's as if they're facing off in some strange staring competition: neither give way, neither willing to cede to the other.

'Peter Howard Moore,' says the Judge. 'You have been found guilty of four sadistic murders over a period of three months in 1995. These were innocent people that you didn't even know. None of those victims had done you the slightest bit of harm. I can't find that at any stage you have shown the slightest bit of remorse or regret for these killings, nor for the twenty years of terror and violence that preceded them.' He looks up from his notes again, and fixes Moore with a glare as full of contempt and distaste as any Judge could possibly direct at a defendant.

'I consider you to be as dangerous a man as it is possible to find.' It's a sobering statement, and to me as a lawyer, it brings home the true reality of the man I've been representing for the last year or so.

'I have to report to the Secretary of State,' Mr Justice Kay continues, 'advising him of my view as to the earliest date that you should be considered for release. I don't want you or anybody else to be in the slightest doubt as to what I shall say. In a word: never.'

The word echoes through the courtroom. There's no reaction to it for a few moments – the word hangs in the air, and the silence that follows gives it greater resonance.

'Take him down,' says Mr Justice Kay to the officers standing each side of Moore in the dock. They handcuff him and lead him down the stairs of the dock. We hear a bunch of keys rattle and a metal door open as they reach the bottom of the stairs, and then the metal door bangs shut and an echoing thud fills the courtroom. And Peter Moore is gone. The silver screen goes blank and the unattached spool of film unravels and begins rhythmically clicking round and round. The film is finished.

We all sat in court for a moment or so as the Judge took some time to thank us all for our hard work on the case. He then retired from the court and the tension broke and everyone seemed to relax. There were a few laughs and some congratulatory shaking of hands on the prosecution side. It was difficult to believe that the case had finished. As I collected my things together, Alex Carlile approached me and thanked me for my work representing Moore.

'You dealt with this case in an exemplary fashion, Dylan, I just had to let you know. Thank you for all your hard work,' Carlile said. I think it's safe to say that it was my proudest moment as a lawyer: to be approached by someone of his calibre and complimented in such a way; it was an affirmation that my efforts had been well directed and those countless hours of toil were recognised and appreciated.

On leaving the courtroom, I was told by one of the Court Ushers that there were reporters and cameramen gathering on the steps leading up to the Crown Court, requiring some comments or a statement by me on Peter Moore's behalf. I wasn't too sure what to say and so had a word with Dewi for some suggestions.

'Let's go down to see Moore and explain that we're being asked for a statement and see what he says,' he suggested.

The three of us went off to the cells to speak to Moore. We found him back in the holding cell. He'd been given some tea in a plastic cup and was sipping it slowly. He was sitting down as we entered the cell and started to get up as we arrived.

'No, no, Mr Moore – you take a seat and drink your tea,' said Eric. 'Look, we are very sorry for the way the case went.

You'll understand that things were against us right from the very beginning, and it all proved to be very difficult,' he added, very diplomatically. Moore agreed and apologised to us.

'I'm just sorry to you all for having such a difficult case.'

'Well, that's the way things go sometimes in the law,' replied Eric. 'Now, Dylan's been asked by some reporters for a statement, so I suggest that you speak together and then he can go out to the baying press and give them what they want.' The four of us laughed, as if we all needed to break the tension, and I got out my notepad to prepare a brief statement. We agreed on something which was as succinct as possible, and I left Peter Moore in the cell after agreeing to be in touch with him soon to discuss any future matters that required my attention. Moore seemed calm and resigned to his fate; he wasn't cross or bitter and he remained polite and well-spoken throughout. I wished him well as I left the cell, and he thanked me again as he shook my hand.

'Good luck with the press,' he said as I was at the cell door. We both laughed.

I arrived at the main reception area of the court and looked out towards the multitude of press and cameras waiting for me at the bottom of the stairs. I checked my statement: it was short and to the point and I considered it appropriate for the circumstances. A security officer was by the door as I looked out at the awaiting throng.

'Are they all for you, Mr Jones?' he asked.

'I suspect they are,' I replied.

'Well, you'd better not keep them waiting, then,' he said, with a chuckle. He opened the main door of the court for me, and I ventured out and began walking down the stairs. As soon as I was visible, reporters with microphones and notepads, cameramen and soundmen with large furry mics on poles all moved towards me up the stairs. We met halfway and they gathered around me in a constantly moving and jostling scrum of clicking cameras and a sea of questioning faces.

'I have a statement from Mr Peter Moore which I have been asked to read out on his behalf.' I cleared my throat and looked out at the crowd. I'd seen these statements being made on countless occasions on the evening news – I'd never imagined delivering one myself in such a surreal situation. 'I'm actually doing this,' I thought to myself, and for brief moment I felt as if I was floating above the horde, looking down at myself delivering Moore's statement.

'It is with regret and disappointment I face my conviction for four murders today. I will continue to assert my innocence to these charges and it is my intention to seek advice as to the possibility of lodging an appeal against my conviction as soon as is possible.' Questions began firing towards me from every direction and so I replied that I was unwilling to add anything further to the statement and turned on my heels, retreating back up the stairs to the court building and leaving the disappointed throng.

I returned to the robing room and conveyed my thanks and appreciation to Eric and Dewi, and told them of the statement I'd made to the press.

'Good luck with the appeal!' said Eric with a hearty laugh, as he left with his red velvet bag in one hand and his briefcase in the other. I promised to get in touch with him for some written advice on an appeal, which we all agreed was unlikely to succeed.

After saying my goodbyes, I walked to my car. I deposited my papers and files on the back seat and stood for a few moments looking out from the car park across the town of Mold and towards the Clwydian Hills beyond. It was a pleasant, sunny afternoon; despite it being November, there was a warm breeze and the hills were green with the odd tinge of autumn brown and gold. I can't be sure if I felt relief at the trial having ended or exhaustion from the mental, physical and emotional stresses of the past months. For those few moments, looking out on those green hills, I felt a freedom that I hadn't felt in a long time. I could have jumped in my car and driven for miles, hundreds of miles, without thinking about anything at all. I felt as if a burden had been lifted from my shoulders and that I was at the end of an arduous journey. What I didn't realise as I admired the view that afternoon was that as one journey ended, an even more difficult, painful and harrowing journey was about to begin.

Peter Moore, around the time of his arrest in 1995

(Wikimedia Commons)

Chapter 17

THE TRIAL RECEIVED a considerable amount of attention in the press and on the radio and television. I did a number of interviews about the case and received some attention and prominence as a result. It may also have benefited my firm, as some clients chose us to represent them because of our links to this high-profile case. I hoped that things would calm down before Christmas 1996 and a few weeks before the Christmas holidays Catherine, true to her word, surprised me by telling me she'd booked us a weekend away in London. I was still feeling totally exhausted and was beginning to realise how much the past year had actually taken out of me.

I'd promised Peter Moore on the final day of his trial that Eric Somerset-Jones and I would look into the possibility of an appeal against either the conviction or the sentence he'd received. I'd written to both Eric and Dewi for their opinion and awaited their response, in the knowledge that both believed that an appeal was unlikely to be viable or successful. It was, though, important to consider the options available to Moore and review the verdicts reached by the jury and the sentences imposed by the Judge. The full-life tariff recommended by the Judge under the then system was to be reviewed and approved by the Home Secretary, and as Peter Moore's defence team we were duty-bound to look into whether there was anything we could do to influence the Home Secretary's decision.

I'd been informed that following his trial, Moore had been taken to HM Prison Frankland near Durham, which is quite a distance from north Wales. I wrote to Moore, informing him that once I'd received our barristers' advice, I would then arrange to go and see him at Frankland. I didn't expect to have news of an appeal for him to digest and consider, but I believed that having a discussion face to face about the matter was better and more respectful of him as my client than sending him a brief letter dismissing the appeal out of hand.

In the meantime, despite my continued feelings of exhaustion, we went on our trip to London. To avoid me having to drive, Catherine had organised a flight from Manchester to Heathrow and a taxi into London. She'd booked a lovely hotel and a table at a nice restaurant; it was extravagant but delightful and I appreciated it so much. The following evening, we had tickets for the theatre, to see the play *Death of a Salesman* by Arthur Miller – not necessarily a fun night out but, as a theatre buff, it was just up my street. The lights went down and the play began. I was excited to see it, especially as Alun Armstrong was taking the lead role of Willy Loman. Unfortunately, I didn't see much of Alun Armstrong's performance that evening: as the play got started, my exhaustion took over and I fell asleep. I am reliably informed by Catherine that Armstrong was excellent as Loman and that I didn't interrupt his performance by snoring.

Throughout this time, I tried to continue as normal, and as far as my wife and my work colleagues were concerned, I was just the same as I'd ever been. On reflection, this was far from the truth. My health was gradually deteriorating: I was suffering from regular migraines and was generally unwell, though I couldn't actually get to the bottom of why I was feeling so bad. It was as if a malaise had gradually come over me without warning. Every morning I sensed a gloomy feeling of grey clouds forever hanging above me, never parting to allow even a glimpse of the sun. Life was a daily monotonous grind. I started to feel that I was without purpose or direction, in a darkening place which seemed to become more overwhelming with each passing day. I carried on with my work, attempting to brush off my feelings of unease. At home and at the office, I functioned the best I could, pretending that everything was fine. I didn't want to trouble anyone and hoped that in time things would just get better and these feelings of sadness and despair would pass.

I received the written advice on the appeal from Eric, which – as expected – didn't hold out much hope of success. I decided early in 1997 that a journey to see Peter Moore at HM Prison Frankland near Durham was now necessary. Moore was a Category A prisoner and because of this, making arrangements to see him – even as his lawyer – was not easy. I travelled to HM Prison Frankland in early March. It was a long but pleasant journey, but a feeling of apprehension came over me as I drove. I thought about the past year and the continued strain that I had felt following the case, and wondered how Peter Moore would have changed since I'd seen him last and how prison might have affected him.

Frankland is a high-security prison with countless checks and procedures before you're allowed into the visitors' area. After some delay, I arrived in the visitors' room. Peter Moore was already waiting for me at one of the tables. He looked surprisingly peaceful and serene, as if he was on holiday, and he began to smile as he noticed me crossing the visitors' room towards his table. Apart from Moore, the large room was empty but for two guards, who stood together by a door which I assumed was the exit into the main prison.

Moore chatted enthusiastically and confirmed that he was comfortable and had settled in at Frankland Prison. It was very modern compared to the prisons he'd been in before then, and he liked that. He asked how I'd been since the trial had ended, and enquired about my family. I wondered if he'd heard from anyone since the trial – he told me that he hadn't, but didn't sound disappointed. A week or so before our meeting, I'd sent him a copy of Eric's advice, which wasn't particularly positive, to say the least. We discussed its contents for some time and considered the options that were now available to Moore, which in reality were relatively few. It was strange to see him again. He looked far less stressed and troubled than at the time of the trial, as if he'd accepted his fate and relaxed into his current situation. I supposed that he'd begun to adjust to the fact that in all probability his whole future would be behind bars.

I left Frankland and Peter Moore, having agreed to stay in touch and that if there were further developments in his case or his circumstances, we would arrange to meet again. As things turned out, it was the last time I saw Peter Moore. We exchanged a few letters after that, but we never met again and after a few years of receiving the odd letter from him now and then, there was silence. Life went on, other cases took over, there were other priorities and big cases – though nothing became as all-encompassing as the Peter Moore case.

In reality, Peter Moore and the effect of his case on me did not fade into the background. I would have argued at the time that it was all done and forgotten about, but that wasn't true. I was asked for stories about the case regularly by friends and colleagues for years after the trial had finished. I enjoyed telling the tales of this and other cases I'd encountered; they seemed to be entertaining after-dinner or evening-in-the-pub stories. I knew, though, throughout this time, that there remained a darker fallout to my involvement in the case. My health continued to deteriorate. I would suffer flashbacks and thoughts about the case at the strangest of times. Something would remind me of an incident, photograph or conversation from the case and the emotions, stresses and angst would begin to flood back in a torrent of anguish which I was unable to explain or control. There were times when I'd visualise the crime-scene photos as clearly as if they were in front of me – I'd be at home or going for a walk and suddenly in the corner of my eye I'd glimpse a body lying on the ground or a headless corpse lying amongst the trees. It would happen at the most unexpected of moments and take me straight back to the case and the horrific scenes associated with it. It made me feel scarred, uneasy and angry. I couldn't understand what was happening to me – I was beginning to believe I was going mad. I was under constant stress because of other cases and business worries, and somehow these would worsen my flashbacks and my general state of unease. I felt trapped in a vicious whirlpool of anxiety and torment from which I couldn't find an escape. I spoke to no one about this – not even my wife or my best friends. I kept my feelings hidden from my work colleagues and decided that the way to get over these experiences was to battle on, carry on working as normal and try to forget about it. It was only years later that I learnt that many men believe this is the best way to address their mental health problems.

It took years for me to accept that I was suffering the after-effects of the Peter Moore case. Sometimes when alone, I'd begun to relive the experience I'd had just after Moore's arrest, the terrifying sensation that someone was running up behind me, knife held high in readiness to plunge it down into my back. It would terrify me, and it would happen without warning, as if there was something in my mind testing me out, trying my patience and reminding me of my own weaknesses. I would get angry at the slightest thing; silly arguments with Catherine would result in me going into an uncontrollable rage of shouting and throwing things. I even threw a vase at a wall so hard that it left a gaping hole in the middle of it. When the rage died down, I'd be unable to understand what had made me behave in such a way. Catherine was so patient with me during this time. She clearly knew that there was something wrong, and would implore me to go and see the doctor. But I couldn't see it: I couldn't accept that there was anything wrong with me. I'd become convinced that this was the way I was destined to behave at home and at work – I'd turned into a different person, unreasonable, self-centred and stressed beyond all imagination, but still I refused to go and see a doctor and just carried on.

Things got difficult with my business when I split with my business partner in 2005. He was twenty years older than me and his priorities – to retire and plan for the future – were very different from mine. I wanted to invest and build the business, whereas he wanted to cash in and plan for retirement, which on reflection was fair enough. At the time we didn't agree. Business separations can be worse than divorces: we parted on bad terms and to this day that's a regret of mine. But it did nothing for the stress levels and things got worse: my rages became more frequent and my behaviour, reasoning and decision-making went out of the window. I was functioning, but not as a sensible businessman nor as a prudent and logical lawyer most of the time. I would have constant migraines, would wake up in the middle of the night suffering from flashbacks and then I began to suffer panic attacks. Still, despite my wife's encouragement, I refused to go and see a doctor.

'I'm fine, it'll pass – it's just one of those things. It's the stress of business getting me down.' How many people have used those lines and tried to hide how they feel under a pile of useless excuses? I was certainly one of them.

Then the economic disaster of 2008 happened and as with many businesses, mine began to seriously suffer. Work took a downturn and I would be panicking every month about how I would pay my staff. I didn't care much about myself, but I wanted to make sure they were fine. Some of them were supportive of me and my difficulties; others were trying to save their own skins and their loyalty to me as their employer had gone. Maybe that was understandable: it's human nature to look after number one when there's a crisis. I was like a headless chicken – the stress levels were sky-high, I'd wake up at all hours of the night and cry myself to sleep, trying to hide my distress from Catherine. I was still having flashbacks and recurrent nightmares. I would dream of finding myself in a field of dead bodies – it was like a scene from the film *The Killing Fields*, dead and decaying corpses everywhere and

I seemed to be running for my life through them. On other occasions I'd be driving a car on a motorway and would see a large truck directly in front of me. I'd put my foot on the accelerator and drive as fast as I could into the back of the lorry. Upon impact, I'd wake up, more or less jumping out of bed in a state of complete panic and sweating profusely.

Things worsened even further. At work, my business and career were falling apart and I'd lost all interest and control over what was happening. My moods would swing from anger to complete despair: I wanted to cry one moment, the next I wanted to punch someone really hard in the face. I decided that there was only one option left for me. My mental anguish was causing me physical pain; my flashbacks and nightmares were a regular occurrence; I couldn't sleep; I couldn't think properly. I decided to kill myself. I had a plan: I'd chosen the place where it was to happen, and even had a rope I could use. I decided I'd write a letter to my wife and family to tell them that I loved them, and another to my office staff thanking them for tolerating me for so long. Then I was planning, as the frustrated amateur actor that I was, to take a gracious bow and leave 'this mortal coil' to others.

Clearly things didn't happen that way. I had a complete mental breakdown which left me hardly able to function in any way. Catherine and my best friend Eilir took me to hospital one day in June 2009, and I was admitted to a psychiatric department. Thankfully, I remember little of the whole experience. The following days and weeks are a hazy mishmash of brief and cloudy recollections to which I would rather not pay a second visit. I was diagnosed with depression, anxiety and some type of PTSD. My recovery was long and difficult – I suspect that I'm still recovering to this day.

I survived the biggest battle of my life by the skin of my teeth. Days and weeks became months and years, and gradually I was able to ease myself gently into being a husband, father and human being with some feelings of self-worth and confidence.

I received the help and support of family, good friends and some equally good doctors and counsellors. I have, over those subsequent years, faced many of the demons which had haunted and mocked me and driven me to despair, leading ultimately to my breakdown. The Peter Moore case, though, remained a 'no go' area for me for a very long time. I realised the effect the case had had on me at the time in the mid 1990s, and was also acutely aware of the deep and unhealed scars that remained somewhere in my psyche. My main problem was that for many years, I was unable to confront these issues. I would still sometimes suffer flashbacks, and nightmares would occasionally revisit me, and I concluded that maybe they would for the rest of my life. I hadn't realised that tackling this problem would inevitably become necessary at some stage in my life.

During the summer of 2019 I decided that the time had arrived for me to face my darkest feelings and experiences by finally telling my story. Clearly the Peter Moore case has had an extraordinary effect on my life since the day I was called to see him at the police station following his arrest in December 1995. I believed that I couldn't possibly tell my story fully without including elements of Peter Moore's story too. Those months in 1995 and 1996 brought both our lives into parallel: for a time, my life was entirely focused on his story and his case, and I felt that to an extent his future depended on me. In 2019, quarter of a century after the murders took place, I decided that it was finally time to unburden myself of this case, to discover answers to some unanswered questions, and if possible to do so with the co-operation of Peter Moore himself. I am under no illusions that some will applaud me and others will criticise me for this. I know that some may think writing about the case may be my way of just trying to make a fast buck. Nothing could be further from the truth.

While I was gathering my thoughts and planning this book, I decided to write to Peter Moore at HM Prison Wakefield, where I knew he'd been transferred at some point since our last communication. I was uncertain if he was still an inmate there and even more unsure if I'd receive a reply from him. I explained in the letter that I was planning a book about my involvement in his case and was hoping he might be able to assist me with a few things. I also expressed the wish to meet him sometime in the near future so we could talk about the case and discuss both our feelings about it, 25 years after the event. It also appeared to me to be a clear opportunity to give closure to feelings and anxieties which had troubled me over the years.

To my surprise, I received a letter from Moore, dated 23 August 2019. I was nervous on opening the envelope, unsure what his response might be after so many years. The letter from Moore was friendly and courteous. He told me a little about his recent health problems and that he would be willing to meet me anytime that could be arranged to discuss the book I was writing, with which he was happy to co-operate. He then asked me an unexpected question.

'Have you heard of Clocaenog Forest Man? There's another body found in exactly the same place as Edward Carthy, no matter what the police say. In spite of enquiries, they don't have a name for him. Fortunately, the victim's clothing was manufactured by Pringle and Marks and Spencer after I came to prison, so that ruled me out.'

I found this to be an intriguing comment, particularly as it was totally unsolicited. I was aware of another body having been discovered in the forest and I was also certain from what I'd heard and read that the police had investigated the possibility of connections with Moore. What I found difficult to understand was why Moore wanted to raise this issue with me in his first letter after so many years. Did he wish to tell me something? Alternatively, did he think I was investigating this as part of his story? It was a matter I'd want to pursue if and when I had the opportunity to meet him again.

In his first letter from prison, Moore continued by saying that, while doing the research for my book, I may have some 'trouble' from the North Wales Police as: 'they are under notice together with the crematorium at Colwyn Bay regarding necrophilia at the crematorium...' He then went on to suggest that he was being blamed for this. It was a thoroughly unpleasant and shocking suggestion, which made me immediately uncomfortable. I have no idea whether any of what was stated by Moore was true or not, but it gave a clear indication to me of the world in which Moore continued to exist and into which I was choosing to reimmerse myself for the purposes of this book.

I replied to Moore, thanking him for his letter and checking that he was willing to co-operate with me in my research for the book. He sent a further letter to me on 17 September 2019, in which he said that he'd also been working with someone else who was writing a book, and that he would co-operate with me as he had done with this other author. He also seemed keen to meet me to discuss his case, as I'd mentioned that I was trying to make arrangements for such a meeting to take place in the near future.

Making arrangements to visit a Category A prisoner at a high-security prison is far from simple, and I had to make a formal application with the prison authorities at HM Prison Wakefield to become an approved Category A visitor before I was even considered as being suitable to visit Peter Moore. To complicate things even further, it was necessary for Peter Moore to submit an initial application for me to become his approved visitor before the authorities would start the approval process. Peter Moore went ahead and made his application for me to become his Category A visitor, and then the grinding wheels of officialdom started turning. This entailed me receiving a visit from two local police officers at my house so that they could verify my identity on behalf of the prison authorities, and also complete a lengthy form.

In the meantime, I continued to correspond with Moore. It appeared that he appreciated the contact and promised in one letter to prepare for me a '...resumé of the details of my life and friends, etc.'

It appeared that Moore believed that such details would help me in understanding his story and that I would find this background information useful and interesting. I thanked him and agreed that it would be useful for my book, and that I'd appreciate such information. At the end of October 2019, I received the promised 'resumé', which was in the form of a lengthy four-page letter. The letter began in this way:

> 'Dear Dylan,
> I have been thinking about your task of putting my case and life down on paper. There's a lot of changes since I left north Wales so I have prepared the following to assist you.
>
> I would like an acknowledgement in the preface of your book stating that I apologise to the people of north Wales for my actions, but I don't admit being responsible for the four murders. Are you willing to include this?'

The beginning of Moore's letter took my breath away for a few moments. What exactly was he asking me to do? Clearly I couldn't make any such promises – and didn't do so – but the main question I was left asking myself was, what was Moore apologising for? It seemed he was apologising for his conduct and saying sorry for the murders but also absolving himself of any responsibility at the same time. Was this an attempt, weak and ridiculous though it seemed, to relieve himself of the feeling of guilt? By now Moore was in his mid-seventies: it wouldn't be unreasonable for him to try to get some kind of absolution for his past deeds. In reality, it was only half an apology, regarding something or other which remained deliberately ambiguous: it leaves you unsure about what exactly he was referring to. Did giving that qualified apology give him the feeling of purging some of his guilt, but without admitting to anything in particular? Understandably this declaration by Moore bothered me and was something else I would want to clarify if we were to meet.

The rest of his letter gave details of other people who had expressed an interest in writing a book about him and also said that he'd written his own story, which was apparently being kept by a friend of his. Reading this rekindled the feeling that Moore liked the attention: he seemed to thrive on those who were interested in him because of his infamy. I was aware that I was playing to that part of his personality myself by taking an interest in him and writing this book. I thought back to the apparent enjoyment he had had from 'posing' for the photographers when arriving or leaving the court. Moore's letter then included a number of pages detailing his life from his early days in St Helens, Lancashire and the family's move to Kinmel Bay when Moore was six. He described being picked on by other schoolchildren on first arriving in Kinmel Bay but then found his feet when attending secondary school in Abergele, where he passed with distinction before leaving to work in his father's shop in Kinmel Bay. He recalled his father Ernest's liking for alcohol, though he said that he'd never seen him drunk. Then he described his father's death in 1979, the initial success and then decline of the family business, and then beginning his cinema business. He talked about his concern about his mother Edith's health and her subsequent death in 1994. Moore then commented:

'There's nobody left in my family now, just me.'

His comment in the letter echoed to me the statement Moore had made during the police interviews – that everyone and everything had died and that it seemed that death was 'following him around'.

He then added, 'Of course, there's a lot more... that we can also discuss on the visit. Perhaps you will make a list.'

I continued to exchange letters with Moore through November and December 2019. Mostly those letters involved the arrangements being made regarding my Category A visitor's approval and my proposed visit. Over Christmas 2019 I received a Christmas card from him addressed to myself and my family. We continued to correspond in January and at the end of the month finally received confirmation of the date for my visit to HM Prison Wakefield to see Peter Moore: it was set for 10 February 2020.

I was nervous, though eager, for the visit to HM Prison Wakefield. The meeting and the book had been a long time in the preparation stage, but now Moore and I would meet and I believed that we were both enthusiastic for the visit. I received a letter from Moore dated 17 January confirming that he was looking forward to my visit. I began to prepare the questions I wished to ask and the subjects I wanted to cover with him. I was keen to see how he'd changed visibly after his time in prison, but also to discover the changes in his thoughts and psyche. The impression I'd received from his correspondence was that Moore had changed little since 1995: there remained a darkness and a disturbing macabre sense of evil in many of the comments made in his letters. I was concerned that he was still playing games, still operating from his prison cell in a dominant way – still trying to influence and affect people's lives and emotions. I was worried that Moore would attempt to influence my book and that this was his intention in meeting me. My intention was to tell my own story during the time of the case, not necessarily to paint a portrait of Moore – people knew a lot of his story, but mine was new and different. I believed that Moore might wish to change the direction of the book – he was, after all, trying to influence the contents of the preface with his half-apology.

A few days before my scheduled visit to HM Prison Wakefield, I received a brief letter from Peter Moore, dated 26 January 2020. It read as follows:

Christmas card received from Peter Moore, Christmas 2019

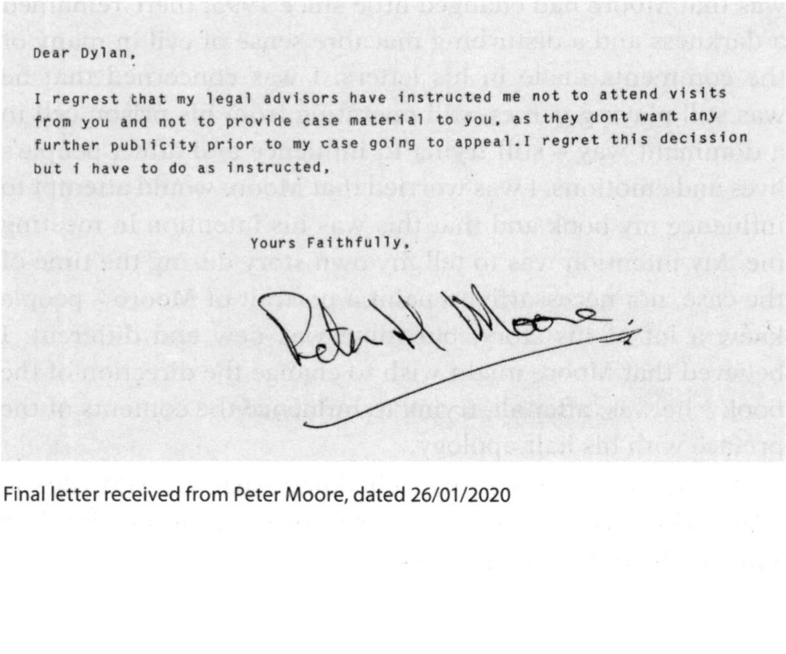

Dear Dylan,

I regrest that my legal advisors have instructed me not to attend visits from you and not to provide case material to you, as they dont want any further publicity prior to my case going to appeal.I regret this decission but i have to do as instructed,

Yours Faithfully,

Peter H Moore

Final letter received from Peter Moore, dated 26/01/2020

Dear Dylan,
I regret that my legal advisors have instructed me not to attend visits from you and not to provide case material to you, as they don't want any further publicity to my case going to appeal. I regret this decision but I have to do as instructed.
Yours faithfully,
Peter H Moore

I've heard nothing from Peter Moore since that letter, and haven't received any correspondence from anyone representing him, legal advisor or otherwise. I have no knowledge as to whether Moore really intends to lodge an appeal against either his conviction or his sentence. I understand that some years ago, he and other 'full-life' prisoners lodged an appeal with the European Court of Human Rights on the basis that a full-life sentence without any possibility of an appeal was illegal and contrary to a prisoner's human rights. To date Moore continues, as far as I'm aware, to be an inmate at HM Prison Wakefield, where he's serving four full-life sentences for the murders of Henry Roberts, Keith Randles, Anthony Davies and Edward Carthy.

I was disappointed to receive that letter from Peter Moore. I'd hoped to take full circle the path I've been travelling from my first day with Moore in the police station in December 1995 to the prison in Wakefield some 25 years or so later. The journeys that Peter Moore and I have taken have been different both before and after the time our paths crossed, but during those months in 1995 and 1996 they were intrinsically linked. That meeting in the police station after his arrest, its consequences and effects have resulted in my life since then being changed so fundamentally that in many ways I'm a different person. Closing that circle with Moore would have brought a suitable ending to this book and to my journey, but it was not to be. I suppose his life, as it is, remains on a very different trajectory to mine – possibly it was always destined that our paths would never cross again. On reflection, maybe that's for the best.

April 2020

Life has taken a strange turn, with the Covid-19 lockdown affecting us all and the virus now at its peak. I take my dog Twm for our one allocated walk of the day. Down through the deserted town of Abergele we venture, turning down Sea Road then past Pentre Mawr park and crossing the bridge towards the beach at Pensarn. Today the beach is deserted: there are no cars parked in the car park, the café is shut and the dog walkers have stayed away. As we get closer, I notice a sign informing me that for the foreseeable future the beach is closed because of the Covid-19 virus. I walk over to the beach wall. Twm is pulling on the lead eagerly, expecting to begin chasing seagulls again. The beach is empty – not a soul to be seen. There are birds congregating out on the sand a few hundred metres away, scavenging for rich pickings, and a few black crows stand on the verges, up to no good as usual.

'It's better like this,' I think to myself, 'better that the beach is so quiet and peaceful, as it is today.'

The tide comes in and sweeps the place clean of dirt, filth and the footprints of people and animals, and allows the beach a new beginning. The past and sometimes the present can bring pain, worry and heartache, but as the tide at Pensarn beach encourages fresh starts, there are always opportunities for them in our own lives as well. I turn away, leaving the beach to its own devices, and go home.

Pensarn Beach, Abergele

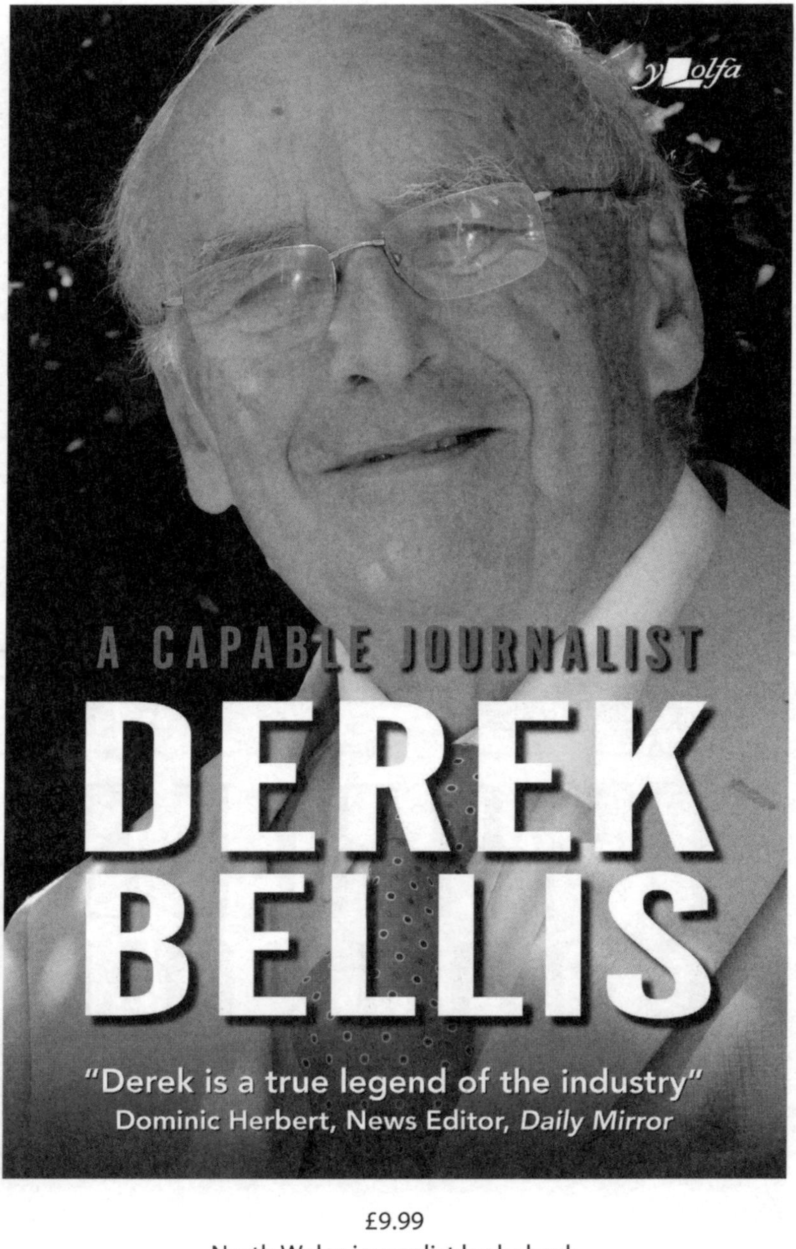

£9.99

North Wales journalist looks back on his most unusual stories

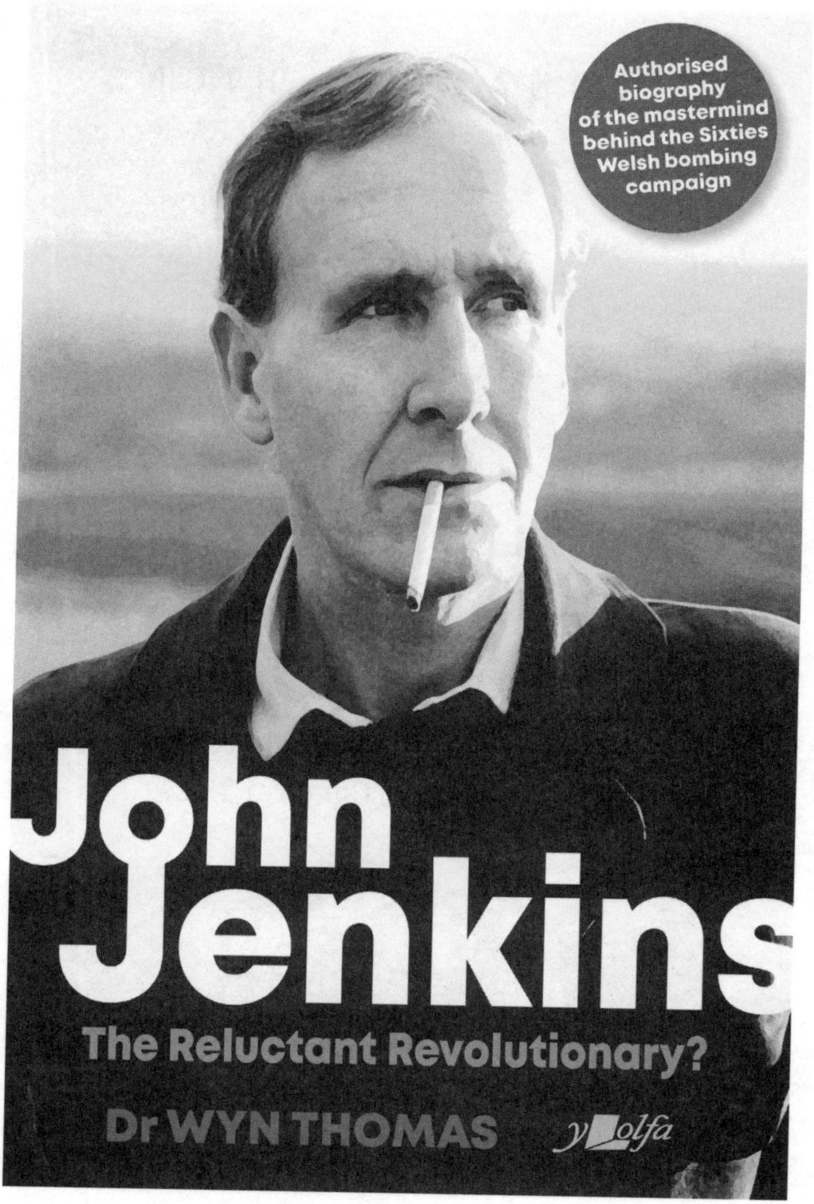

£12.99 (paperback)/£19.99 (hardback)

Warts-and-all biography of the mastermind behind the 1960s Welsh bombing campaign

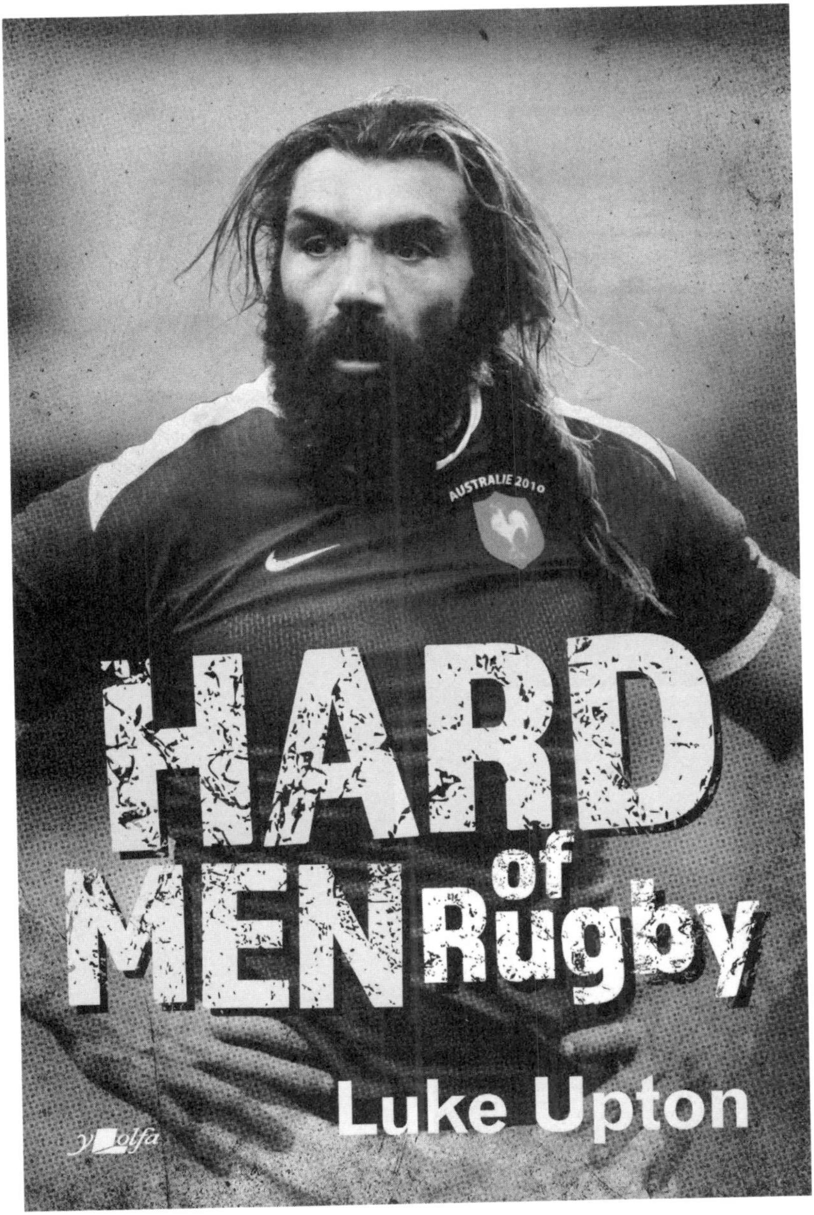

£9.99

The gruesome stories of the hardest,
most ruthless rugby players of all time

£8.95

£8.95

£8.99

Ultra-violent thriller trilogy, centring on
the Witness Protection programme

y lolfa

TALYBONT CEREDIGION CYMRU SY24 5HE
e-mail ylolfa@ylolfa.com
website www.ylolfa.com
phone (01970) 832 304
fax 832 782